The Day Comes

Clifford Hill is both a sociologist and a theologian. He is an ordained minister in the Congregational Church and was National President 1976/7. He has held two London pastorates and has preached and lectured extensively both in Britain and in the USA.

Dr Hill is known internationally for his writing and broadcast work in race relations. He is used as a consultant by the Home Office, the Police and the Prison Service on the issues of race, culture and violence in society and the problems of the inner city. He has had personal experience of living and working in a multi-racial community in the East End of London, where he founded the Newham Community Renewal Programme. He was also a co-founder of the Martin Luther King Foundation. He has been a senior lecturer in Sociology in the University of London, specializing in the Sociology of Religion, and a part-time lecturer at Spurgeon's Theological College, as well as an examiner in Divinity of the University of London Institute of Education.

Dr Hill is widely regarded as a modern-day prophet and is at present exercising an international ministry.

D0767717

By the same author

TOWARDS THE DAWN
What's Going to Happen to Britain?

CLIFFORD HILL

The Day Comes

A Prophetic View of the
Contemporary World

*

THE NIGHT IS FAR SPENT, THE DAY IS
AT HAND: LET US THEREFORE CAST OFF
THE WORKS OF DARKNESS, AND LET US
PUT ON THE ARMOUR OF LIGHT.
ROMANS 13:12

Collins
FOUNT PAPERBACKS

First published in 1982 by Fount Paperbacks, London

© Clifford Hill 1982

Made and printed in Great Britain by
William Collins Sons & Co. Ltd, Glasgow

BIBLE REFERENCES

Except where otherwise noted, all Bible references are
taken from the Revised Standard Version of the Bible,
copyrighted 1946, 1952 and © 1971, 1973 by the
Division of Christian Education of the National
Council of the Churches of Christ in the USA, and are
used by permission

CONDITIONS OF SALE
This book is sold subject to the condition
that it shall not, by way of trade or otherwise,
be lent, re-sold, hired out or otherwise circulated
without the publisher's prior consent in any form of
binding or cover other than that in which it is
published and without a similar condition
including this condition being imposed
on the subsequent purchaser

Contents

Preface

The Day Comes, like *Towards the Dawn,* began with a personal encounter with God that I do not at present have any liberty to speak about. But the experience led me to the passage in Isaiah sometimes known as the 'Isaiah Apocalypse'. I began to study it in depth with a new expectancy and an urgent waiting upon God in prayer. At the time I believed strongly that I was being given a message of the utmost importance and of world-wide significance.

Yet it seemed such a pretentious and wholly preposterous thing that God would actually communicate such a message to any individual and especially to me. My whole rational being revolted against it. I was being torn apart – faith on the one hand was asserting the validity of a vivid spiritual experience, while my academic background on the other hand demanded logical proof. What was for me a personal crisis resulted in the writing of this book.

As a sociologist I found myself almost unconsciously setting about testing the message that had sprung out of two or three verses in Isaiah 24, and testing them in much the same way as I would have set up a research project to examine a social science hypothesis. This led me to undertake fact-finding in some unfamiliar fields. The research took a year to complete and involved reading in widely divergent subjects that I found fascinating and challenging.

The result was to convince me not only of the validity of the personal encounter that began the quest, but that God is urgently communicating with his people in days of mounting world crisis. For those who have ears to hear, eyes to see and a heart open to God – the message is clear.

I should like to acknowledge a deep debt of gratitude to

Professor F. F. Bruce for help with the Biblical exegesis and general comment on the manuscript. Also, to the Rev. Julian Ward for his keen interest, practical help and concern that the message should be written. On particular sections of the book, I consulted a number of friends with specialist expertise. Amongst those who read the whole manuscript I am particularly grateful to the late Denis Clark, Andrew Shearman and Val Grieve. My wife, Monica, gave invaluable help throughout the research and writing.

A number of institutions gave valuable assistance in supplying data, and I should like to acknowledge the help given by the Nationwide Festival of Light, Society for the Protection of the Unborn Child, LIFE, International Institute for Strategic Studies, Institute for the Study of Conflict, the British War Museum, Friends of the Earth and the World Development Movement.

I should also like to thank Miss Marjorie Larcombe for typing the manuscript, William Collins and Company for speedy and efficient publication, and in particular their editor Lesley Walmsley for her keen personal help and interest.

Finally I should like to thank all those who have prayed for this book. As news of what I was working on spread I was very conscious of a growing body of prayer support. I am humbly grateful to God and I pray most earnestly that I have been faithful to him in what has been written.

Clifford Hill, *January 1982*

Foreword

There are few passages in the Old Testament which present so many problems to the interpreter as Isaiah 24–27, the four chapters commonly referred to as the 'Isaiah Apocalypse'. The date, authorship and structure of these chapters, their relation to the chapters which precede and follow them in the book of Isaiah, their historical setting – all these questions continue to receive a wide variety of answers. They contain some impressive pictures, giving vivid portrayal to majestic themes, recurrent throughout Holy Scripture, such as the desolation of the earth under the divine judgement, the downfall of the oppressor and the vindication of the righteous, the city of God and the resurrection of his people. Here the preacher may find magnificent texts setting forth the ways of God to man, even if there is no certainty about the meaning of their context.

Perhaps just because of the difficulty of pinpointing the primary situation which the prophet had in view, these chapters proclaim a direct word from God to fresh situations which reproduce the moral features depicted in this 'Apocalypse'. Dr Hill sees those features reproduced with startling clarity in the world situation of our own day, and applies the prophet's message of judgement and hope to ourselves.

The contemporary relevance of the message, as Dr Hill expounds it, is difficult to deny. There are many today, especially in the Western world, who live under an oppressive sense of impending doom. Is there any word from the Lord for them? Yes indeed; here it is!

F. F. Bruce
Manchester,
December 1981

CHAPTER ONE

Prophecy: The Neglected Gift

Is There Any Word from the Lord?

'Is there any word from the Lord?' pleaded King Zedekiah at one of the most momentous times in the history of Israel. The national life was in turmoil. The northern kingdom of Israel had already disappeared under the heel of foreign invaders. Now it was the turn of Nebuchadrezzar, King of Babylon, to launch the attack from the east. His Chaldean armies were sweeping across Palestine, conquering one kingdom after another and establishing for themselves a reputation for monstrous cruelty and merciless barbarity. Jerusalem was holding out in the hope that Egypt would come to its aid.

Time and again God warned them, through the prophet Jeremiah, of the futility of international pacts and treaties. Their only hope lay in putting their trust completely in the Lord, seeking his way and repenting of the evil in the moral and spiritual life of the nation and its rulers, and their lack of faith. Full repentance meant not just additional attention to the detail of religious observance but a total change in the national way of life, a real seeking of the Lord in humility and putting their trust in him. He would then cover them with his protection. If they did not, there was no possibility of their surviving and of the city being saved. Even if the Chaldean army was reduced to a handful of wounded men, they would still rise up and burn and sack the city because God was against his own people.

> For even if you should defeat the whole army of Chaldeans who are fighting against you and there remained only wounded men, every man in his tent, they would rise up and burn this city with fire.
>
> (Jeremiah 37:10)

11

Far from protecting the city because it was 'the holy city', God would allow it to be destroyed as a vindication of his own holiness and righteousness. This was the message Jeremiah was bringing to the king, the rulers and the people of the troubled city. They refused to hear and Jeremiah was accused of being unpatriotic and of deserting to the enemy (see Jeremiah 37:11–15). He was thrown into prison. But Zedekiah, the weak puppet king, afraid of his own shadow, unable to stand against the nobles of his own court, was uneasy at what the princes had done to Jeremiah. In all his hesitancy and uncertainty he longed to hear the authentic voice of God. Secretly, he had Jeremiah fetched out of the dungeon and brought to him for a private interview. As soon as they faced each other, the trembling monarch and the dishevelled prophet, straight from the filthy dungeon, the words poured out – 'Is there any word from the Lord?' (Jeremiah 37:17).

Jeremiah told him there was, but it was not a word that he would like to hear. Nothing was changed. The Word of God was still the same. Jerusalem would fall and he, Zedekiah, would be handed over to the enemy. The king was afraid to act, the rulers and the people refused to hear the Word of the Lord and scorned his warnings. Within ten years the prophecy was fulfilled in the most terrifying manner, Jerusalem falling after a two-year siege.

During the period leading up to the fall of Jerusalem and the exile, God raised up three of the greatest prophets of all time to speak to his people, Isaiah, Jeremiah and Ezekiel. The signs of the times were perfectly plain if men had the eyes to see and a heart after God to discern his mind. The warnings were clear, the message was unequivocal, the Word of the Lord was communicated with unquavering clarity by his prophets, but the people were blind and deaf. They refused to hear or to heed. The consequences were terrible.

God Speaks to Man

There is considerable evidence that in the closing years of the twentieth century we also live in momentous times. There are many signs confirming this in the community around us and in the world of international affairs. But there are also many signs that God is speaking to his people. This presents a difficulty for some Christians who frankly do not believe that God speaks directly to man. There is a spirit of unbelief abroad that questions every revelation of God to man and rationalizes it as some kind of psychological aberration. Biblical prophecies, like the miracles of Jesus, are dismissed as the unreliable evidence of an unscientific generation. On the other hand, there are many Christians who do believe the evidence of Scripture and who accept the Bible as the Word of God but who nevertheless do not believe that God speaks to his people today.

Why is this? Has God changed? Does not God wish to communicate with his people today? If we can believe that God spoke to his people in former days through the prophets, and then perfectly through his Son and that he continued to speak through the prophets in New Testament times, why can we not believe that God still wishes to speak to his people today? Could it be that we have had a surfeit of false prophets and the misuse of the gift of prophecy so that we have shut our ears as a defence against being misled? Or could it be that we are simply not listening and not expecting? There is nothing easy and automatic about listening to God and hearing him speak to us. We have to fulfil certain conditions.

'Operator! Information! Get me Jesus on the line! I want to talk to a friend of mine.' So said a pop song of the seventies, expressing in modern teenage culture the wistful longing of mankind for the authentic voice of God. But listening to God is not a problem that can be solved by technology, however good our communications system. We have to be a people open and ready to receive from him; we have to be a people expecting to hear from him; and we have to be a people with the humility to heed him, the faith to obey him, and the confidence to trust him.

The Bible shows God as a God who communicates. He loves to speak with his people. He reveals his nature, he unfolds his will, he makes known his good purposes and he communicates his love. From cover to cover, on every page of the Bible, God is shown as speaking to his people. There are many times in the history of Israel when they don't hear, when they are stubborn and hardhearted and rebellious. But God still speaks to them. Even though they stoned the prophets, imprisoned them and even murdered them, God still so loved the world that he sent his only begotten Son. Then they took him and murdered him. But through him, God began to raise up a new people to whom he could speak and through whom he could communicate his Word to the world. Thus, in both Old Testament times and in New Testament times, God spoke to his people.

Prophecy: Old and New Testaments

There is a difference between prophecy in the Old Testament and prophecy in the New Testament. In the Old Testament, God spoke to his people through the prophets. He spoke directly to such men as Moses and Joshua at critical points in the nation's history. He spoke to Samuel, Nathan, Elijah, Elisha, Micaiah, as well as to the great writing prophets such as Amos, Hosea, Isaiah, Jeremiah and Ezekiel. In each generation God raised up a man through whom he could speak to the nation, for it was the nation, Israel, which was in a covenant relationship with him. He was their God and they were his people. But in the New Testament there is a change.

As a nation Israel rejected the Messiah but to all those who accepted Jesus as Lord and Saviour, both Jew and Gentile, to them the Father gave a promise. That promise was to pour out his Spirit upon them, that the presence of Jesus and the power of the Holy Spirit should be with them for ever. Peter declared that the prophecy of Joel was fulfilled at Pentecost. God had said, 'I will pour out my Spirit upon all flesh, and your sons and your daughters shall prophesy and your young men shall see visions and your old men shall dream dreams. Yea, and on my menservants and on my maidservants in those days I will pour out my Spirit and they shall prophesy' (Acts 2:17–18).

In the New Testament, it is the whole community of Christians who become a prophetic people. God speaks through all his people of the new covenant. The gift of the Holy Spirit to the Church meant that God no longer spoke only through individual prophets but to all his people – all who had ears to hear and a heart open to God. This does not mean that prophets disappeared from the scene with the ending of the old covenant and the beginning of the new.

There are numerous references to prophets in the New Testament who appear to be a normal part of the Church's life, e.g. Acts 13:1. One outstanding man appears to have been Agabus who went from Jerusalem with a number of other prophets to Antioch, and there he foretold a great famine that was to come upon the Roman Empire. As a result of this, relief was organized amongst the churches for the Christians in Judea (Acts 11:27–30). Agabus was also responsible for warning Paul that he would be arrested if he went up to Jerusalem. He took Paul's girdle and bound his hands and feet, saying, 'Thus saith the Holy Spirit, so shall the Jews at Jerusalem bind the man who owns this girdle and deliver him into the hands of the Gentiles' (Acts 21:11). The only account of Agabus' prophetic ministry recorded in Acts is of his foretelling the future. Perhaps the reason for this is that it was this feature of his ministry that most deeply impressed the early Christian community. The foretelling of the future was always the most spectacular feature of the prophets' ministry. But this should not blind us to the fact that it was not the primary function of the prophet in biblical tradition.

The Gifts of the Spirit

In the New Testament prophecy is closely associated with the coming of the Holy Spirit and the gifts of the Spirit to the Church. There is no systematic teaching concerning the gifts of the Holy Spirit in the New Testament, but there is considerable evidence concerning the beliefs and practices of the early Church.

Paul appears to distinguish between the gifts of the Spirit that are major gifts of ministry, and the outworkings or expression of the Spirit that are generally found amongst the believers. A careful study of 1 Corinthians, chapters 12–14 gives considerable insight into Paul's teaching. He uses two different words in the Greek when speaking about the ministry gifts and the expression of the Holy Spirit, the significance of which is lost in the English translation. These are the words *charismata* and *pneumatika*. Charismata is the term normally used either for the gift of the Holy Spirit himself to the Church or the particular gifts of the Spirit to individuals, as for example, in Romans 12:6; and 1 Corinthians 1:7; 12:4,9,28,30,31.[1] Paul uses the term 'pneumatika' when he's referring to the expression or outworking of the Holy Spirit in the lives of individual believers. He speaks of pneumatika as though it should be a part of the normal spiritual experience of all believers. Just as it is open to all believers to speak in a tongue, so it is open to all believers to prophesy (1 Corinthians 14:5).

The distinction we are noting in Paul's teaching between charismata and pneumatika is further strengthened if we look carefully at two verses that occur either side of 1 Corinthians 13, and that apparently contradict the general teaching of Paul both in regard to the possession of spiritual gifts and status within the Church. Most English translations render these verses 'earnestly desire the higher gifts' or 'earnestly desire the spiritual gifts', as in the RSV.

---

[1] The same term is also used in a similar context in 1 Peter 4:10.

Paul's teaching on the gifts is that they are the gift of God, the free gift, and that he chooses to give them to whomsoever he will (1 Corinthians 12:11). The gifts are not possessions to be striven after as carnal men strive after material possessions or worldly status. God gives one gift to one person and another gift to someone else, but they are his to give as he chooses (1 Corinthians 12:4–11 and 28–30). For example, in 1 Corinthians 12:7 it is God who inspires, and in 12:29 it is God who has appointed.

This teaching on the gifts harmonizes with Paul's general teaching upon the status of the Christian both within the Church and within wider society. Christians are not to strive after status but be content with the position in which they find themselves, and serve God with the natural talents and the spiritual gifts that he has given them. In 1 Corinthians 7 Paul deals with the status of a Christian in a pagan society. It is summarized in verse 17: 'Each one should retain the place in life that the Lord has assigned to him and to which God has called him. This is the rule I lay down in all the churches.' Paul teaches that the reason God gives the gifts is for the building up of the Body of Christ. The gifts are the equipment, the essential equipment, of a Christian that enable him to serve within the Body.

Clearly, certain gifts do give status to the individual within the Christian community. The gifts carry with them a responsibility that has to be rightly exercised. Christians have to be subject to one another and while the gifts themselves do carry authority, they must be exercised under authority and within the authority of the Body. Certain gifts are to be especially subject to being exercised within the discipline of the Body, particularly tongues and prophecy.

Spiritual gifts, then, are not personal attributes after which Christians should strive. We are stewards of God's gifts, not owners. The Christians in Corinth were all too ready to be proud of their personal achievements, of their human wisdom (1 Corinthians 3:18), and to boast about their worldly distinctions and achievements (2 Corinthians 11:18). Thus it seems strange that Paul would instruct the

Corinthians to 'earnestly desire' or to strive after the gifts of God, as he appears to do in 1 Corinthians 12:31.

The answer to this difficulty probably lies in faulty translation of one word. It is the word *zēloute* which comes from the verb *zēloō*, meaning to have 'strong affection for' or to 'desire earnestly'. The difficulty arises from the fact that the form of the verb *zēloute* is exactly the same for the second person plural present indicative, for the second person plural present imperative and for the second person plural present subjunctive. Nobody knows for sure how to translate this word. Most English translations have made it an imperative, thus following the King James Version, 'but covet earnestly the best gifts'. But this contradicts all the rest of Paul's teaching on the subject. If, however, we translate it as a simple present indicative, we would have 'but you are earnestly desiring the greater gifts'. The only major translation to show any recognition of such an alternative rendering is the New International Version (NIV) where it is a marginal note.

If we accept the above rendering, there still remains the apparent difficulty of 14:1. But here the word is not 'charismata' but 'pneumatica' and pneumatica literally means 'spiritual'. There is no mention of the word 'gifts'. It is an interpretation not a translation to render 'pneumatica' as 'spiritual gifts'. Literally, it means that we should desire spiritual things, i.e. expressions of the Spirit. Thus in 12:31 and 14:1, Paul is speaking about two things that are quite distinct although clearly related, despite the fact that in English they have usually been rendered in the same words. In 12:31 where he had been speaking about the major ministry gifts within the Church, such as apostle, prophet, teacher, he concludes by rebuking the Corinthian Christians for striving after these higher gifts and seeking status within the Church. He says, 'And now I will show you the most excellent way', and then goes on to speak about love within the Body.

It is clearly love that was lacking in Corinth, as witness the divisions amongst them and even jealousy and strife (1

Corinthians 3:1–4). It seems highly unlikely that Paul would tell such carnal Christians as there were in Corinth to strive after the higher gifts. They were loveless and divided, they were full of pride and arrogance, they were worldly and even got drunk at the Eucharist (1 Corinthians 11:21). Paul rebuked them severely for despising the Church and for humiliating one another (11:22). Thus it would be entirely in accord with the context of the whole passage if we read Paul in 12:27–31 as reminding them that they were each members of the Body of Christ, and that it was God who had appointed men to different positions within the Church according to the ministry gift that he had given. He then asks the rhetorical questions, 'Are all apostles? are all prophets? are all teachers? do all work miracles? do all possess gifts of healing? do all speak with tongues? do all interpret? But you are each of you striving after the higher gifts to give you status in the church. But I will show you the most excellent way of all, it is the way of love.' Then after the beautiful love poem of chapter 13, Paul returns to the same theme. This time, instead of speaking about the major ministry gifts, he reminds them that they can all share in spiritual things, and that within the Christian community each individual may express some manifestation of the Spirit.

Because God had poured out his Spirit upon the whole Church and made them his people of the new covenant, heirs of the promises, it was possible for every Christian to enjoy certain manifestations of the Spirit. They could each one exercise the gifts of the Spirit and it was possible for each one, under the inspiration of the Spirit, to exercise the gift of prophecy. That is, *not* the ministry gift but the prophetic expression of the Spirit. This may in some way be akin to the difference between the canonical prophets and the Nebiim of the Old Testament. Paul's teaching in 1 Corinthians 14 is that God speaks to *all* his people and he would like every one of them to be able to prophesy under the inspiration of the Spirit (v. 5). But although it was possible for each individual to speak an occasional word from the Lord under the inspiration of the Spirit, within the worshipping life of the

Body, the gift of a regular prophetic ministry was something that God only bestowed on certain individuals.

The regular prophets were second in authority to the apostles within the Church and their task was to bring the Word of God to his people. This, of course, included prophetic preaching, i.e. the application of the unchanging truth of God's Word to the contemporary situation both within the Church and within the world. No doubt, the prophets of the early Christian Church did on occasions foretell future events, as we know that Agabus did, but just as with the Old Testament prophets this was almost of secondary importance compared with the major task of bringing the Word of God to bear upon the contemporary scene.

Spiritual Authority

The Old Testament prophets and the Christian prophets were appointed by God. In the Old Testament the prophet, unlike the priest, did not come from a special family of prophets. The testimony of Amos is interesting in this respect. There was an occasion when Amos was bringing a word from the Lord that was unpopular with the king. Amaziah, the priest, as an upholder of the establishment, told him to get out, 'Don't prophesy any more at Bethel because this is the king's sanctuary.' But Amos answered, 'I was neither a prophet nor a prophet's son, but I was a shepherd, and I also took care of sycamore trees. But the Lord took me from tending the flock and said to me, "Go, prophesy to my people Israel." Now then, hear the Word of the Lord!' (Amos 7:12–16). Amos was affirming that he did not have to seek the approval of either king or priest before bringing the Word of the Lord, because his authority was from God who appointed him. In the same way, Paul affirms that the gift of prophecy is from God himself. It is he who appoints in the Church apostles, prophets and teachers. But the prophet is under discipline and so subject to the discernment of the Church. The task of the prophet was to proclaim faithfully the Word of the Lord. But prophets had to be subject to the Lord within the Body of Christ. 'The spirits of prophets are subject to prophets' (1 Corinthians 14:32). This instruction of Paul's in regard to the exercise of the gift of prophecy was evidently generally accepted throughout the churches, for in the literature of the early Church after the period of the New Testament, we find that prophets are an accepted part of the ministry of the Church.

The gift of prophecy appears to have been clearly linked with the task of prophetic preaching or the expounding of the Word under the inspiration of the Holy Spirit. In the Didache[2], which is usually dated by most scholars around the end of the first century or early second century AD, there are references to travelling apostles and prophets who used to visit the churches, travelling from one town to the next bringing the Word of God to each assembly of Christians. The apostles were really missionaries or missioners whose task was primarily evangelism, while the task of the prophet was the prophetic exposition of the Word of the Lord. Prophetic preaching, however, was not the sole task of the prophet, who apparently was sometimes so moved by the Holy Spirit that he spoke under the inspiration of what appeared to be a kind of trance. The Didache gives strict instructions that a prophet who is speaking under such inspiration is not to be interrupted, since to do so is to utter blasphemy against the Holy Spirit. The actual quotation is as follows:

> While a prophet is uttering words in a trance, you are on no account to subject him to any tests or verifications; every sin shall be forgiven but this sin shall not be forgiven (Matthew 12:31). Nevertheless, not all who speak in trances are prophets, unless they also exhibit the manners

---

[1] It was originally entitled 'The Teaching of the Law to the Gentiles through the Twelve Apostles', but is nowadays known simply as 'The Didache', i.e. 'the Teaching'.

and conduct of the Lord. It is by their behaviour that you can tell the impostor from the true. Thus, if a prophet should happen to call out for something to eat while he is in his trance, he will not actually eat of it; if he does, he is a fraud. Also, even supposing a prophet is sound enough in his teaching, yet if his deeds do not correspond with his words, he is an impostor. Or again, a prophet, thoroughly accredited and genuine, may set forth some mystery of the church by his actions, and yet fail to teach others to copy his example. In that case, you are not to judge the man yourselves; his judgement lies with God. The prophets of old used to do things of a similar kind.

(The Didache, section 11)

Testing Prophecy

Clearly, the practice in the early Church beyond the period of the New Testament was to hold in high regard those whom God had called to a prophetic ministry, but also to test the word of the prophet. The whole Christian community was a prophetic people to whom the Lord had given gifts of discernment (see 1 Corinthians 14:29). They were thereby able to understand the ways of the Spirit and to know for sure those things that were of the Spirit and those things that were false. Their practice was to weigh carefully the words of the prophets. The instructions of Paul in 1 Thessalonians 5:19–21 were clearly being recognized and were carried out in many of the churches at the time of the writing of the Didache. Paul said, 'Do not put out the Spirit's fire; do not treat prophecies with contempt. Test everything. Hold on to the good. Avoid every kind of evil' (NIV).

Paul's injunction not to quench the Spirit or to despise prophecy was evidently adhered to for many years in the Church. There were, no doubt, those who were afraid of prophecy and who wished to suppress it on the grounds that false messages could be given to the Lord's people. But Irenaeus of Lyons gives us an insight into the practice of the

Church in the late second century. He wrote a strong denunciation of those Christians who wished to suppress prophecy:

> Others, again, that they might set at nought the gift of the Holy Spirit, which in the latter times has been by the good pleasure of the Father, poured out upon the human race, do not accept that Gospel of John in which the Lord promised that he would send the Paraclete; but set aside at once both the Gospel and the prophetic Spirit. Wretched men indeed, who in order not to allow false prophets set aside the gift of prophecy from the church; acting like those who, on account of such as come in hypocrisy, hold themselves aloof from the Communion of the brethren. We must conclude, moreover, that these men cannot admit the Apostle Paul either. For in his epistle to the Corinthians, he speaks expressly of prophetical gifts, and recognizes men and women prophesying in the church. Sinning, therefore, in all these particulars, against the Spirit of God, they fall into irremissible sin.
>
> (Irenaeus, Adversus Haereses III, 11,9)

Irenaeus was concerned that the efforts of those who, very rightly, were attempting to guard the Church against being misled by false prophets, were, in fact, suppressing the presence and the power of the Holy Spirit among his people. Irenaeus' strong condemnation was because he saw that to 'set at nought the gift of the Holy Spirit' was, in fact, to set aside the Gospel. No doubt Irenaeus knew the teaching of Jesus in Matthew 10:40–42, where our Lord clearly envisaged the continuing ministry of prophets within the Church. Jesus' words make it clear that he saw the prophet exercising an itinerant ministry and moving from church to church, bringing the Word of God to the contemporary scene for the building up of God's people.

Of course, there would be false prophets. There were from the very beginning. Paul and Barnabas had occasion to deal with one on the first missionary journey. It was in the coastal town of Paphos, on the Island of Cyprus, where they encountered a false prophet named Bar-Jesus who actually had the ear of the Proconsul and was influencing him away from the faith. Paul, as usual, didn't mince words, but 'being filled with the Holy Spirit looked intensely at him and said "You son of the devil, you enemy of all righteousness, full of all deceit and villainy, will you not stop making crooked the straight paths of the Lord?"' (Acts 13:9–10). Paul knew how to deal with impostors!

Clearly, the early Church expected false prophets. They were prepared to have to combat the harm that they did in undermining the true faith and in misleading even God's own people as well as those new to the faith. Whenever there is spiritual activity, or any manifestations of the Spirit, it is an occasion for the enemy to get in, possibly simply through men's pride and desire to elevate themselves above others. But God, in his wisdom, has made provision for just such eventualities. In giving the Paraclete to the Church, he safeguarded the Gospel and guaranteed the integrity of his Word.

Through the gift of the Spirit to the Church he gave to his people a measure of his own wisdom. He gave the gift of discernment through which all those who have the Spirit are able to discern those things that are of the Spirit and those things that are false. The spirit of discernment is open to all, not just to one or two, but to all those who are filled with his Spirit. It is available according to the measure of our openness to the Lord, according to our faithfulness in listening to him, according to our personal humility and Christ-centredness. Of course a Christian can be misled if he or she is not listening attentively to God and exercising his *mind* as well as his feelings. But that is precisely why God has given to us the gifts of the Spirit to give us wisdom and discernment as well as dynamic power.

The New Testament Church was not afraid to have prophets amongst its numbers. They rejoiced in all the manifestations of the Spirit because they knew that God had guaranteed the faithfulness of his Word. Paul clearly was aware of the possibility of the misuse of the gifts. He shows this not simply in 1 Corinthians 14 where he spells out very explicitly the way in which the gift of prophecy should be exercised within the Church, but also in passages such as 2 Corinthians 11:4–6 and 12–15, also in Romans 12:3–8. Paul was anxious to make it clear that the gifts of the Spirit had to be exercised with the utmost humility. No one should think too highly of himself. There had to be love and brotherly affection within the fellowship or they would be overcome by evil (Romans 12:3,9 and 21).

John also was deeply concerned, not to suppress the Holy Spirit, but that Christians should know how to deal with false manifestations of the Spirit among them. In 1 John 4:1, he exhorts the Christians not to be so naïve that they believe everything they hear, but to 'test the spirits to see whether they are of God; for many false prophets have gone out into the world'. He then tells them how to distinguish between that which is of the Spirit of God and that which is of the spirit of Antichrist.

It is clear from the evidence of the New Testament that the early Church was composed not only of inspired souls but also of saints with clear judgement. Ecstasy and discrimination were brought together for the building up of the Body of Christ. Our humanity can so easily lead us astray even at the moment when we are being strongly led by the Holy Spirit. We need the discernment and the correction of other Spirit-filled Christians within the Body of Christ for the right exercise of the gifts that he has given to his Church. In this connection an interesting passage occurs in the Journal of John Woolman, the American Quaker. He records how, on a mission tour, he would often sit quiet while a friend spoke. 'As for me, I was often silent during the meetings and when I spoke, it was with care that I might speak only what truth opened. One day,' he humbly confesses, 'being under strong exercise of the Spirit, I stood up and said some words in a meeting, but not keeping to the Divine opening, I said more than was required of me.'

Doubtless this was the kind of thing that Paul had in mind

when dealing with the local situation at Corinth, although he was no doubt also dealing with the specific situation of disorderly conduct within the church, where they used to interrupt one another and possibly even shout each other down. Hence Paul says they must speak one at a time and not interrupt. 'For God is not a God of confusion but of peace' (1 Corinthians 14:26–33). The gift of prophecy was being misused and the prophets had to be subject to the Church. Their ministry was to be received with discernment by the whole Body of God's people. Even this injunction had its obvious dangers and could give occasion for some individual to show off his own acuteness or simply to gratify the love of fault-finding. But despite all the warnings and rebukes the teaching of the New Testament is clear that the gift of prophecy is not to be suppressed.

Summary

In summary, the teaching of the New Testament is that the Holy Spirit is poured out upon all God's people. All have access to him through the Spirit and may manifest the evidence of spiritual things within their lives and within the corporate spiritual life of the Christian community. God has also given particular gifts of ministry to certain individuals, both men and women, both Jew and Gentile, both rich and poor, for he gives his gifts as a pure act of his grace and according to his own wisdom. Those who receive his gifts are stewards and not possessors. The gifts can be misused and those who have particular ministry gifts must stay very close to the Lord and exercise them with great humility and only under the clear direction of the Holy Spirit. The gifts are given for the building up of the Body of Christ.

In addition to the ministry gifts God gives the manifestation of the Spirit for the spiritual enlightenment and strengthening of all his people. It is open to all Spirit-filled members of the Body of Christ to exercise the gifts or to bring a prophetic word from the Lord or to have the spirit of discernment. All the gifts are the manifestation of the presence and the power of Christ within his Church through the ministry of the Holy Spirit. But love within the Body is *essential*, for love binds the members together and ensures unity, humility and a true openness to the Lord and to each other.

The early Church had the faith to believe that God would guard them against the dangers of being misled by false prophecy. But over the years the mainstream churches have neglected the gift of prophecy through fear of false prophets. In so doing, they have not only been going against New Testament teaching and practice, and against the teaching of the fathers of the early Church, but they have also been in danger of suppressing the Holy Spirit.

If we don't *expect* God to speak to us, we won't hear him when he does. God is longing to communicate with his people just as any human father longs to communicate with his children.

God has not changed over the centuries and we are the inheritors of the covenant and the promises. His precious Paraclete is amongst us today, but all too often Christians have their ears closed to the voice of God through fear that they may be misled through the wrong exercise of the gifts. The safeguards that God gave to his Church in the first century are available to us today in just the same way as the whole power of the Holy Spirit and the spiritual manifestations of his presence among his people are available to us today.

It is unbelief that suppresses prophecy and it is unbelief that suppresses the Holy Spirit. It is also a lack of openness to God or of expecting him to do as he has promised in his Word. If we are closed to the Holy Spirit through fear, or unbelief, or lack of trust, or for any other reason, he cannot work out his perfect will amongst us. If we do not expect God to do mighty things, we shall see no mighty works. Jesus himself was unable to do any mighty work, we are told, in Nazareth, through the hardness of heart and unbelief of the people there.

Listening, Looking, Discerning

God is longing to speak to his people today in the critical times in which we live, days of mounting world tension and international crisis. These are days when the very structure of society is breaking down in country after country; where the family in Western nations is weakened by divorce, lack of discipline among young people, lawlessness and violence of every kind; where urbanization is changing the nature of society in Third World nations; and where the lack of trust between East and West, and between North and South, grows increasingly serious. Under these circumstances, as the world moves towards a holocaust of violence and destruction, it is of the utmost urgency that Christians should listen to what God has to say to them, and through them to the world today.

We do not have to rely solely upon prophecy, although in times of great crisis God does send prophets among his people to speak to them directly, to build up faith and to bring them back to faithfulness to his Word. But in addition to prophecy, there are three major ways in which we may discover what God is saying to us today:

1. through study of the Bible;
2. through prayer;
3. through studying empirical evidence.

1. Studying the Bible makes us familiar not only with the Word of God to former generations but with his unchanging nature and his eternal Word for his people, for all mankind and for all ages.
2. 'Pray without ceasing' was Paul's instruction to the Christians in Thessalonica. Unceasing prayer opens us up to God and enables him to communicate with us. We need not only praise and adoration but unceasing intercession, actively waiting upon God in prayer. This feeds and nourishes our spiritual lives and moulds us into the stature of

a man or woman in Christ Jesus, until we reach the point where God can fulfil his good purposes in our lives and in the fellowship-life of his people.

3. We need also to study the empirical evidence, that is, the actual facts of what is happening in the world generally and of what God is doing amongst his own people. A careful study of what is happening in the world around us and of the activity of the Holy Spirit in our generation enables us to do what Jesus told us to do, that is, to interpret the signs of the times.

These three things, studying the Bible, constant prayer and studying the signs of the times, are not alternatives. They are all three necessary if we are rightly to hear and understand what God is saying to us in our present generation. We are bidden in Scripture to do all these three things, to study his Word, for it is the Sword of the Spirit, and to be a watching, praying people. All three are important also for confirming the prophetic word. If prophecy is genuinely of God, it will be confirmed by all these three essential elements of the spiritual life. God is a God of order, not of chaos. If the prophetic word is out of harmony with the witness of Scripture or with the witness of prayer or with the witness of the Spirit, it is false. But if it is in agreement, it should be listened to and heeded.

God is longing to speak to his people in every generation and particularly at certain critical periods in the history of mankind. Through giving his Holy Spirit to the Church, he has guarded his people against being misled and given them the means of testing the contemporary prophetic word. The people of God, those who are in Christ, will know what is of the Spirit, as the sheep know the voice of the shepherd and as the servant knows the master's voice.

Jesus said, 'The shepherd calls his own sheep by name and leads them out . . . his sheep follow him because they know his voice. But they will never follow a stranger; in fact, they will run away from him because they do not recognize a stranger's voice' (John 10:3–5).

Vision for Today

We are all of us limited in our vision and understanding of events in the world around us. Usually we can't see beyond our own neighbourhood or family or nation. We find it hard, if not impossible, to appreciate events that are taking place across the other side of the globe even if they are fully reported in the news media. We become immersed in the pressing problems of the moment in our own lives, which act as blinkers upon our scale of vision. Thus we often miss the significance of events in other countries or in parts of the world remote from us.

The task of the prophet is to give vision; to lift the awareness of people above the immediate and the particular to the global, the universal. The task, if faithfully carried out, not only brings awareness and understanding of wider issues but it gives deeper appreciation of local and particular issues because they are seen within the global setting and therefore appreciated in the context of the whole. For example, imagine a man being presented with a jigsaw puzzle of 1000 pieces which are just tumbled together out of a box on to the table and the man is told to fit them all together. He will have considerable difficulty if he has no idea of the end product. But if someone shows him the picture of what the completed puzzle becomes he knows what he is working towards and he can begin to see where the pieces of different colour and shape fit together.

The prophet helps others to see the overall picture as it has been revealed to him. This enables them to see the significance of local events in the light of wider issues, and to see what is happening in other parts of the world in the context of the overall picture.

The modern prophet is like a man with a newspaper in one hand and a Bible in the other. The prophet sees a picture of God's overall purposes for mankind which he translates into the context of the course of history and current world events.

It is this vision that he conveys to others that enables them to interpret and to understand the contemporary scene.

It is our task in this book to attempt to look at the contemporary world scene in the light of the Word of God from Scripture. It is our belief that the current international situation is so serious that understanding it in a biblical context is the most urgent task confronting Christians today.

History shows that there are some periods when there are few significant changes that take place. There are other periods when momentous events occur that change the course of mankind for generations to come. During such periods of change both the opportunities and the challenge are very great. In such times wrong decisions can result in enormous harm to mankind, while right decisions can bring untold blessings.

The challenge to mankind has never been greater than it is today. International relationships are fraught with danger. Never has there been greater need for the Word of God to be heard with clarity and conviction among the nations. Never has there been greater need for Christians as the people of God to be a prophetic people bringing the Word of the Lord to their generation. Never has there been greater need for the vision of the Lord to be among his people. It is our task to attempt to discover that vision and to see whether there is a special word from God to our generation.

CHAPTER TWO

The Prophetic Word: Isaiah 24–27

Part 1

The task of the prophets from their earliest appearance in the history of Israel was to bring the Word of God to the nation. Usually that word was to the particular circumstances of the day in which the prophet lived and worked. Because he was a man of God, with a special anointing of the Holy Spirit that endued him with the power to discern beyond the ordinary everyday events that were the boundaries of most men's vision, he was able to speak with divine authority as to the consequences of different courses of action. The prophet was a man who lived within the presence of the living God and yet a man of contemporary knowledge and experience who was intimately aware of the social, political, moral and spiritual state of the nation. The prophet was thus a man who lived in two worlds, the sacred and the secular. His ability to know the Word of God depended upon the quality of his spiritual life and his close and vital communion with God, while his ability to bring God's Word to men and to communicate it with relevance and timely application depended upon his living within the community and being in touch with all that was happening within the life of the nation.

Three Levels of Prophecy

Within the writings of the prophets it is possible to discern three levels of prophecy. These relate in the first place to the immediate present; secondly, to events that are likely to happen in the near future; and thirdly, to events in the far distance. Often these latter are eschatological in nature, that is, they are concerned with the last days or the end of the age, or the final judgement of the nations and the victory of God over evil and his reign in glory.

1. Most of the prophetic writings are at the first level of prophecy, in which events in the immediate present are being subjected to the scrutiny of the Word of God. Where there is injustice or oppression or a lack of faith among the political leaders, or immorality amongst the people, or idolatrous practices in the life of the nation, the prophets declare with forthright vigour the judgement of the Lord upon the evil they see around them. It is because they were men of their times, intimately concerned with the life of the nation in their own day and age, that prophecies of this type occupy most of their attention.

2. A second, and very important, part of the task of the man of God was to discern where the chosen path of the nation was leading and to attempt to redirect the people when they saw that national policies were clearly leading to disaster. Many of the most significant prophetic utterances are at this level.

3. The third level of prophecy concerns the far distant scene where the man of God attempts to show what has been divinely revealed to him and to interpret it to human understanding.

Sometimes we see the three levels of prophecy woven into a number of oracles in the same book, or within two or three chapters, thus forming a single bloc of prophecy but with different levels woven into the whole. When we read them together it is rather like looking at an oil painting of a landscape scene, where there is the immediate foreground with close attention being given to detail, and then the middle ground where there is a considerable amount of vividly portrayed material, but not in the same detail as for the foreground. Finally there is the distant scene where, although a great deal is clearly discernible and the scene is not just hazily sketched in, the fine detail is missing and what the eye beholds often has to be interpreted within the mind of the observer.

A good example of the three levels of prophecy occurring in close proximity is found in the early chapters of Isaiah where in 2:6–11 there is a revealing description of life in eighth-century Jerusalem, with its wealth, its interest in the occult, its idolatry and its lack of concern for the true worship of God. In 5:26–30 there is a vivid description of what will happen if the nation does not turn to God in penitence: he will use the Assyrian army to bring punishment upon his own people. The picture of the all-conquering Assyrian army on the march even comes across with terrifying precision in the English translation: 'None is weary, none stumbles, none slumbers or sleeps, not a waist-cloth is loose, not a sandal thong is broken. Their arrows are sharp, all their bows bent, their horses' hoofs seem like flint, and their wheels like the whirlwind.' It is a graphic scene that was enough to bring terror to even the stoutest heart. Then in 2:1–4 we have an example of the prophet looking into the far distance when God 'shall judge between the nations, and shall decide for many peoples; and they shall beat their swords into ploughshares, and their spears into pruning hooks'. The picture of God establishing his reign upon the highest mountain and all the nations flowing to it, followed by a time of universal peace, is a beautiful and as yet unrealized hope. The detail is missing, as we would expect when the divine truth that is being revealed by the prophet is in the far distance, but the scene is nevertheless clear to those with the eyes of faith, able to discern the ultimate purposes of God from his Word and from his revelation of his nature and his ways.

For those who wish to know the Word of God to the nations in our own time and are prepared to accept the spiritual discipline required in discerning the signs of the times through being a watching and praying people, as Jesus told us to be, the unfulfilled prophecies in the oracles of the great prophets are of priceless value. One of the most outstanding of such passages in the Old Testament is to be found in Isaiah, chapters 24–27. It is the present writer's belief that God has given this passage to our own generation with a special significance. It is there for us to read, to study and to understand its message if we have the eyes to see, the ears to hear, and a mind open to God to receive and accept what he is saying to the nations of the world in our generation.

The message of this book is based upon this passage of Scripture, so it is right that we first spend some time looking closely at the chapters themselves, before proceeding to examine their application and relevance to the events of our own time.

The 'Isaiah Apocalypse'

Chapters 24–27 of Isaiah are frequently referred to as the 'Isaiah Apocalypse'. This is a misleading description because they are not really apocalyptic in the strict sense. One of the essential features of apocalypse is its visionary nature. It is mysterious, a closely guarded secret in heaven that is revealed to the seer in the language of imagery and symbolism. This element is largely missing from this passage; so too are all the six main features of apocalyptic writing noted by Klaus Koch in *The Rediscovery of Apocalyptic*. Paul Hanson in *The Dawn of Apocalyptic* rightly emphasizes that the task of the prophets was to translate God's cosmic will into the historical context of the day, but he fails to recognize the extent to which the prophets, as men inspired by God and therefore in touch with the source of ultimate reality, were able to transcend their immediate environment. He writes: 'After 587 BC the picture changes. Israel's political identity as a nation comes to an end. The prophets no longer have the events of a nation's history into which they can translate the terms of Yahweh's cosmic will. Hence the successors of the prophets, the visionaries, continue to have vision but they increasingly abdicate the other dimension of the prophetic office, the translation into historical events' (p. 16). Hanson says that at this point we enter the period of the transition from prophetic into apocalyptic eschatology.

It is doubtful whether the experience of the exile is such a watershed in changing the whole type and tenor of prophecy in Israel as Hanson suggests. There are few prophets with a higher degree of historical contextualization than Haggai, yet Haggai is one of the writings that we may firmly date in the early post-exilic period. There is wide agreement amongst scholars for the dating of Haggai at around 520 BC. This was a time before the work of reconstruction had begun and when the social and economic life of the nation lay in ruins. Yet Haggai was no mere vague visionary, he was a man with a message directly related to the conditions of his day, and intimately aware of the historical situation.

What we are attempting to demonstrate is that it is entirely false to categorize types of prophecy merely on the strength of their emanating from a particular historical period. Certainly the prophets were men of their own day who reflected the historical conditions of their age and spoke in contemporary language and imagery, but they were also men of God who at times were caught up in the Spirit to such an extent that they glimpsed the ultimate purposes of God and were able to speak of the far distant scene that they had been permitted to glimpse. There is inevitably an eschatological element in such revelations but this does not remove it from the realm of prophecy into the realm of the apocalyptic.

Hanson himself notes a distinction between prophetic eschatology and apocalyptic eschatology. The former he defines as 'a religious perspective which focuses on the prophetic announcement to the nation of the divine plans for Israel and the world which the prophet has witnessed unfolding in the divine counsel and which he translates into terms of plain history, real politics and human instrumentality'. The emphasis here is upon the contextualization of the eschatological message in terms of an actual historical setting, rather than the language of imagery. Hanson further defines apocalyptic eschatology as 'a religious perspective which focuses on the disclosure (usually esoteric in nature) to the elect of the cosmic vision of Yahweh's sovereignty – especially as it relates to his acting to deliver his faithful – which disclosures the visionaries have largely ceased to translate into the terms of plain history, real politics and human instrumentality due to the pessimistic view of reality growing out of the bleak post-exilic conditions within which those associated with the visionaries found themselves. These conditions seem unsuitable to them as a context for the envisioned restoration of Yahweh's people.'

Even a cursory reading of Isaiah 24–27 reveals that we cannot read this passage as apocalyptic eschatology. It contains a mixture of prose and poetry linked around the central theme of a time of catastrophic destruction coming upon the world, which God will use to bring punishment upon mankind for gross wickedness. Through this event God restores order out of chaos, establishes his own authority not only over disobedient mankind but also over the spiritual forces of wickedness. He conquers all his enemies, including the last enemy, death, and establishes his reign of peace and justice which inaugurates a time of great joy and gladness for the righteous.

What we are taking issue with is the widespread predisposition amongst scholars to label 'apocalyptic' anything that they cannot readily pin to a particular set of historical circumstances. This is done despite the absence of the language of allegory and apocalyptic imagery. It is our contention that what we have in the so-called 'Isaiah Apocalypse' is not apocalyptic at all, but pure prophecy that is, in fact, unfulfilled. Yet its basic nature as prophecy clearly relates to an historical period as yet unreached. While we are prepared to accept the adjective 'eschatological' because of the nature of its substance, we nevertheless do not wish to detract in any way from the basic prophetic character of the passage we are examining.

The view we are taking is shared by a number of modern scholars, amongst whom Edward Young may be taken as representative. He writes: 'Among the literary traits [of apocalypse] are pseudonymity, symbolism, re-written history, written visions . . . If we read 24–27, however, we note that pseudonymity is entirely lacking. The writer does not take some figure of old and make him the recipient of angelic revelations. Nor do these chapters present themselves as revelations to a select group of initiates, nor as containing hidden secrets preserved by angels. For that matter there is nothing in these chapters that can specifically be identified as visionary, such as is true of portions of Daniel, Ezekiel, and Zechariah. Some symbols are present, it is true, but a comparison with Enoch or the Apocalypse of Baruch or some similar work shows how completely diverse they are. There is symbolism, but historical names also appear. Nor are the other supposed elements of apocalyptic present. Isaiah 24–27 is pure prophecy' (*The Book of Isaiah*, Vol II, p. 260).

Any discussion of dating this passage would not really be relevant for our present purposes. It is, however, interesting to note how in recent years there has been a reaction to the radical dating of such scholars as Duhm and Marti who place this passage well into the Maccabean era. In any case such a view is hardly tenable now that we know that the position of these chapters within the Isaiah scroll was firmly established in the scroll used by the Qumran community (as shown by the Dead Sea Scrolls). Otto Kaiser is aware of this point and nevertheless maintains that an early second-century dating is possible (*Isaiah 13–39*, p. 179). We do not have to rely entirely upon conservative scholarship for an early dating that would place this passage well within the Isaiah period, and it is worth noting that an immediate post-exilic dating is favoured by many scholars today.

A good summary of the literary problem and the difficulties of establishing any firm dating of these chapters is given by R. E. Clements in *The New Century Bible Commentary, Isaiah 1–39*, who follows Wildberger 'in recognizing that the chapters [Isaiah 24–27] have acquired their present form as the result of a long process of growth' (p. 199). Another useful summary of the debate is to be found in *The Broadman Bible Commentary* edited by Clifton Allen (pp. 259–60). Yet we wish to establish that for our purposes the actual dating of this passage is relatively unimportant. The problem only arises because in the view of some scholars it clearly stands out from the total book of Isaiah largely due to the position it occupies within chapters 1–39.

It is, however, the nature of the message that is significant for our present purposes. God has sent to the world a message of immense significance through this passage which has perhaps not as yet been fully recognized. Scholars have for many years attempted unsuccessfully to relate it to the realm of fulfilled prophecy, by linking specific references to historical events in the life of the nation Israel and events in the life of her neighbouring nation states.

A number of scholars have attempted to interpret the passage by identifying the unnamed city whose overthrow is described in Isaiah 25:1–5. Duhm related this to the destruction of Samaria by John Hyrcanus in 107 BC. M. L. Henry identified the fall of the unnamed city with the fall of Babylon to Cyrus in 538 BC. J. Lindblom argued that it was to be connected with the conquest of Babylon by Xerxes I in 485 BC. W. Rudolph connects the unnamed city with the capture of Babylon by Alexander the Great in 332 BC. These views are well summarized by Clements (p. 198). Clements himself takes the view that it is fruitless to try to identify the unnamed city since it cannot be linked with any historical event. He says 'the lack of identification of the hostile city which is to be destroyed and the failure [of the prophet] to identify the inhabitants of the earth who are to face divine judgement must be regarded as deliberate. The author is concerned with all nations and with the entire earth rather than with one specific hostile neighbour of the Jewish community . . . There could be no point, therefore, in seeking to identify the city whose destruction is foretold in 25:1–5.

Rather it stands as a thematic representation of the forces of evil arrayed against God's faithful people.'[1]

Even though scholars such as John Mauchline and Edward Young see apocalyptic elements in these chapters, they nevertheless recognize their basically prophetic nature and that they contain within them prophecies that are so far unfulfilled. This gives us further encouragement in taking the view that what we have in Isaiah 24–27 is a prophetic revelation of tremendous importance to mankind because of its unfulfilled nature and the possibility of its application to events in our own age.

It is the purpose of this book to examine such a possibility and to discover whether God is speaking to us today through the greatest of all prophetic books of the Old Testament. Through such mighty passages as Isaiah 53 God spoke of his purposes of redemption that were to be accomplished through Jesus. Thus it would indeed be fitting if God chose to speak in a very special way through this same source at what may prove to be one of the most momentous times in the history of mankind. We are not looking for any easy mechanical interpretation of Scripture, but we are seeking to know the meaning of a particular passage that may well have a special relevance for our generation. Our aim is to try to understand the message of the prophecy at the time when it was written, and then to turn to an examination of the world situation in our age and seek to discover whether there is evidence that the prophecy is applicable to us today.

[1] *Ibid.*, pp. 198 and 199. A further useful discussion of this point is to be found in Kaiser, *op.cit.*, pp. 176–9.

Isaiah 24–27

We are adopting a thematic method of exegesis in examining these chapters. In order to identify the major themes it may be helpful if we first summarize the subject matter of the passage. These four chapters are composed of a collection of poems and songs around a central theme of world-wide destruction and universal judgement brought about by man's sinfulness and wilful disobedience. God uses the destruction to punish mankind, to break the power of the evil forces opposed to him, to save a faithful remnant from destruction and to establish his glorious reign upon earth. The main themes of the passage are all found in chapter 24 and may be summarized as follows.

1. World-wide Destruction: vv. 1,3,19,20. God reveals to the prophet that destruction on a world-wide scale will sweep across the earth.

2. Universal Suffering: vv. 2,17,18. All classes will be affected without exception and there will be no escape from the forces of destruction.

3. Cause of the Disaster: vv. 5,6. The pollution of the earth by man will cause a universal curse to fall upon the world.

4. Desolation of the Countryside: vv. 4,7–9,11. Vegetation will wither and die. The vineyards will be destroyed and there will be an end to merrymaking.

5. Destruction of the City: vv. 10,12,13. The city likewise will be laid in ruins. Its walls will be thrown down, its houses emptied and its gates broken.

6. Overthrow of Opponents: vv. 21,22. The prophet announces that God will break the power of all those who oppose him. The oppressors on earth and the spiritual forces of evil in the heavens will be overcome.

7. Survival of Remnant: vv. 14–16a. Only a small remnant among the nations will survive the holocaust. Of the survivors those in the West will be the first to begin praising God.

8. Glorification and Reign of God: v. 23. After overthrowing all the forces opposed to him the Lord will establish his own reign in glory, his reign of justice and peace.

We shall work our way through chapter 24 noting the links with similar elements in chapters 25–27 as we proceed.

1. World-wide Destruction 24:1,3,19,20

> Behold, the Lord will lay waste
>   the earth and make it desolate
> and he will twist its surface
>   and scatter its inhabitants.
> The earth shall be utterly laid waste
>   and utterly despoiled;
>   for the Lord has spoken this word.
> The earth is utterly broken,
>   the earth is rent asunder,
>   the earth is violently shaken.
> The earth staggers like a drunken man,
>   it sways like a hut;
>   its transgression lies heavy upon it,
>   and it falls, and will not rise again.

The passage opens with the shattering announcement that 'the Lord will lay waste the earth and make it desolate'. The announcement is preceded by the word 'Behold' which is characteristic not only of Isaiah but also of all the major and many of the minor prophets of Israel. It is used particularly where they are about to bring a word from God that is of great significance to their hearers; as, for example, when Isaiah announces the birth of Emmanuel (Isaiah 7:14), or when Jeremiah announces the Word of the Lord to Israel following his visit to the potter's house (Jeremiah 18:6), or when Ezekiel in the valley of dry bones announces God's intention that they should live (Ezekiel 37:5). The intention here clearly is to bring a word from God that no one can afford to ignore.

The picture presented is one of unparalleled and catastrophic destruction that will engulf the whole of the world. It will 'twist the earth's surface and scatter its inhabitants'. Such incredible destruction on a world-wide scale that will actually disturb the surface of the earth, laying waste much of the world and lifting up whole populations and scattering them across the earth, is a scene that is as impossible to portray adequately in words as it is difficult for the human mind to conceptualize destruction on such an enormous scale. But this, in fact, is what the prophet has seen revealed to him and what he is trying to describe.

The word picture that the prophet is using may be drawn from a very severe earthquake that not only shakes the earth but actually twists its surface. The language of cosmic convulsion is sometimes used in Scripture to denote the devastation caused by invasion and war; as, for example, when Jeremiah in 4:23–26 probably draws upon the scenes of desolation he had already witnessed to warn Judah of what was coming to them as a consequence of the nation's sinfulness. Again cosmic disturbance can be a picture of divine intervention of a quite different kind; as, for example, in Peter's quotation of Joel 2:28–32, with its 'blood, and fire, and vapour of smoke', as denoting the outpouring of the Holy Spirit and attendant events upon the first Christian Pentecost. The theme of cosmic catastrophe depicted in Isaiah 24:1 and 3 is shown as something which takes place

43

that actually reverses the process of creation and returns the earth almost to the kind of primitive chaos that existed at the beginning of creation. 'The earth which is "filled with the glory of God" will be emptied and the work of creation will be undone; the surface of the earth will be upturned as in an earthquake and all the works of man demolished and the inhabitants scattered.'[2] Other commentators see the destruction as an act of judgement by God which is implied in the Hebrew text where the simile of the laying waste of the earth ('emptying', AV) is that used for the cleaning of a dirty dish. Hence Leupold writes, 'A scene of judgement on the broadest possible scope is depicted, a judgement that lies entirely in the future. The Lord is the one who presides at the judgement, even for that matter, disposes of it all alone in his own sovereign authority. In verse 1 the figure seems to be that of a man cleaning a dirty vessel, the bowl is the earth, men are the filth in it that must be removed. With consummate ease the judge picks up the vessel, turns it upside down, and empties it.'[3]

The theme of destruction is continued in verse 3 where it is said that the earth shall be utterly laid waste and utterly despoiled. The language used may at first sight suggest a vast army of soldiers moving across the land, pillaging, plundering and leaving behind them a trail of utter destruction. But there is nothing here to suggest a human agency at work. The plundering or despoiling of the earth is the outcome of a cosmic catastrophe, and this is confirmed by verse 19, where the Hebrew construction is so emphatic as to be almost untranslatable. Each phrase begins with an infinitive absolute and then the thought is repeated to give it a double emphasis. A literal translation would read

> Broken – broken lies the earth
> Cracked – cracked through is the earth
> Shaken – shaken violently is the earth.

[2] Edward Kissane, *The Book of Isaiah*, Vol. 1, Browne and Nolan Ltd., Dublin, 1950, p. 271.
[3] H. C. Leupold, *Exposition of Isaiah*, Vol. 1, Evangelical Press, London, 1974, p. 377.

It is no ordinary earthquake that is being depicted but a cosmic event whereby destruction comes to the earth from out of the wider universe. There is a progression in the thought of each of the phrases with an increasing intensity of the violence that is depicted. The first phrase describes some great convulsion that hits the earth with such shattering force that pieces of it are broken off. The second shows the surface of the earth cracking and splitting, while the third shows the whole globe being shaken violently. In his search for similes to describe what he has seen coming to the world, the prophet uses two more in verse 20, when he says that the earth staggers like a drunken man and sways like a flimsy watchman's hut hit by a hurricane. The word used for a hut indicates a light, frail shelter, probably made of thin canes and leaves, such as a watchman might use as a shelter from the sun but which would be tossed into the air and smashed in a storm.

Verse 20 concludes with a statement as to the reason why the terrible destruction comes upon the world. The prophet sees the earth staggering and reeling under the weight of its transgressions. He sees the people of the earth reaching such a point of rebellion against God that the earth can no longer contain the weight of their sins: 'So heavy upon it is the guilt of its rebellion that it falls – never to rise again' (NIV). Marti suggests that the guilt of the people is all the unjust blood that they have spilt upon the earth that brings to pass the shaking of the world which is the only way that God can cleanse the earth of the polluting effects of man's sin.[4] The language of this verse bears striking similarity with Amos 5:2, where the finality of judgement is pronounced against Israel. In this case it is the sinfulness of the whole of mankind that brings judgement upon the world through the gigantic cosmic convulsions which strike staggering blows at the surface of the earth.

---

[4] Young, *op. cit.*, p. 177.

2. Universal Suffering 24:2,17,18

> And it shall be, as with the people,
>   so with the priest;
>   as with the slave, so with his master;
>   as with the maid, so with her mistress;
>   as with the buyer, so with the seller;
>   as with the lender, so with the borrower;
>   as with the creditor, so with the debtor.
> Terror, and the pit, and the snare
>   are upon you, O inhabitant of the earth!
> He who flees at the sound of the terror
>   shall fall into the pit;
> and he who climbs out of the pit
>   shall be caught in the snare.
> For the windows of heaven are opened
>   and the foundations of the earth tremble.

The prophet declares that the destruction will affect all people. No distinctions of social rank will protect them from the desolation and destruction that is coming upon the earth. In the list of contrasts given in 24:2 the highest social ranking is that of the priests. The absence of any mention of the monarchy or the nobility is often advanced by scholars as indicating a post-exilic date when both the monarchy and the nobility had disappeared from the nation. But this is an argument from silence and not conclusive. In any case, to follow this argument through fully we would want to urge an early post-exilic date before the appointment of a governor and the restructuring of the social order with the rise of the new nobility. This would give us a date well within the Isaiah period. However, our concern here is not with the date of the passage but with its meaning and significance.

The prophet uses the contrasts of slave and master, maid and mistress, to show that there will be no distinctions of social ranking that can save anyone from suffering in the great devastation when it comes upon the earth. It will affect all people regardless of who or what they are. Social distinctions will be meaningless, the rich and poor will alike suffer. The message that social distinctions will be of no avail in saving anyone from the suffering and tribulation that is to come upon the earth is also given by the prophet Zephaniah in 1:18. He says, 'On the day when the Lord shows his fury, not even all their silver and gold will save them. The whole earth will be destroyed by the fire of his anger. He will put an end – a sudden end – to everyone who lives on earth.'

Both Isaiah and Zephaniah appear to be saying that the devastation that will come upon the earth will be so enormous and so all-encompassing, bringing about such general destruction, that everyone will be affected: not only the rich and the poor but also the good and the bad alike. Whether God will intervene and snatch the righteous out of the cauldron of destruction we shall have to assess in a later section, but for the moment we must note that the message of this passage is perfectly clear: that all alike will be caught up in the chaos and confusion of the world-wide general convulsion that will descend upon the earth.

Jesus also, in Matthew 24:22 and 23 and in Mark 13:19 and 20, refers to the time of general destruction coming upon the earth that the prophets foretell, but he indicates that the Father, in his compassion for 'the elect', will shorten the days. The meaning of this phrase is perhaps brought out a little more clearly by the Good News Bible translation: 'For the trouble of those days will be far worse than any the world has ever known from the very beginning when God created the world until the present time. Nor will there ever be anything like it again. But the Lord has reduced the number of those days; if he had not, nobody would survive. For the sake of his chosen people, however, he has reduced those days' (Mark 13:19 and 20). What Jesus is saying is that the coming destruction will be so widespread that everyone will be affected, but because of God's deep love for those who love him, and his great concern for them, he will intervene and stop the destruction so that the whole human race is not wiped out. He does not, in fact, say that none of the righteous will suffer, but that God will heed their prayers and for their sake will intervene and see that the destruction does not lay waste the entire earth and all its inhabitants.

To return to our passage in verses 17 and 18: the prophet emphasizes that even those who try to escape will simply find themselves running from one part of the destruction to another. He says it will be as though someone were running through a forest and fell into a ditch, then managed to climb out of that only to be caught in a trap. He thus emphasizes the general nature of the destruction he is foretelling and the fact that from it there will be no escape for anyone, although some will survive.

The message of these two verses is that the judgement will be universal. The imagery attempts to convey the absolute terror that will be struck into the hearts of all the earth's inhabitants – hence the imagery of the hunter and the hunted. When the calamity falls people run away blindly, but there is no escape, for 'he who flees at the sound of the terror shall fall into the pit'.

To clinch the point the prophet uses language reminiscent of that used in Genesis 7:11 and 8:2 to describe the universal calamity of the flood, from which only Noah and his family were saved. Kaiser believes 'this means a new flood and the abrogation of what Yahweh had created at the beginning of the third day of creation' (p. 191). But Young (p. 175) and Leupold (p. 384) both take a contrary view. Young says: 'Isaiah does not teach that there will be a repetition of that flood, for it was expressly revealed (Genesis 8:21) that such a means of universal destruction would never be repeated. The words teach that when the power of heaven acts the very foundation of the earth is affected. The truth is expressed poetically. The "windows from on high" are the windows through which the power from on high will flood.' The words are an attempt to express in pictorial language the universal calamities the prophet sees coming upon the whole earth.

3. Cause of the Disaster 24:5,6

> The earth lies polluted
>   under its inhabitants;
> for they have transgressed the laws,
>   violated the statutes,
>   broken the everlasting covenant.
> Therefore a curse devours the earth,
>   and its inhabitants suffer for their guilt;
> therefore the inhabitants of the earth are scorched
>   and few men are left.

Why Will It Happen?

The prophecy makes it clear that the devastation coming upon the earth will be as a direct result of the sinfulness of mankind. It is not just one nation, but all the nations of the world who have sinned against God, and the desolation of the earth will follow as an inevitable consequence of their evil ways. Verse 5 states: 'The earth lies polluted under its inhabitants; for they have transgressed the laws, violated the statutes, broken the everlasting covenant.' It is here that we find the key to an understanding of the entire passage. The pollution that is referred to here is that of the earth and not of individual human beings. Scripture is consistent in its declaration of what causes the pollution, or the defiling, of the earth. There are two things:

a) blood-guiltiness; and
b) idolatry.

a) BLOOD-GUILTINESS

When the anger and violence of man leads to murder, the blood of the victim pollutes or defiles the land. Numbers chapter 35 lays down a number of regulations concerning the various circumstances surrounding murder, manslaughter or accidental death. The passage makes it clear that there is an intimate relationship between the lifeblood of a man and the land in which he lives. When a man's blood is spilt upon the ground so that he dies from some form of violence, the land itself is polluted and can only be cleansed by some form of expiation being made by the person who was responsible for the victim's death. Numbers 35:33 says, 'You shall not thus pollute the land in which you live; for blood pollutes the land and no expiation can be made for the land, for the blood that is shed in it, except by the blood of him who shed it. You shall not defile the land in which you live.'

b) IDOLATRY

In Jeremiah 3:1–19, strictures are brought against both Judah and Israel for idolatry. Despite the terrible punishment that had befallen Israel, the northern kingdom, through being overrun by the Assyrian armies, which Jeremiah saw as a direct result of their evil ways, Judah did not learn the lesson and turn in penitence to God. She also continued to practise all kinds of idolatry. 'She saw that for all the adulteries of that faithless one, Israel, I had sent her away with a decree of divorce; yet her false sister did not fear, but she too went and played the harlot. Because harlotry was so light to her, she polluted the land committing adultery with stone and tree. Yet for all this her false sister Judah did not return to me with her whole heart, but in pretence, says the Lord' (Jeremiah 3:8–10). It is this spiritual adultery of worshipping other gods that is so abhorrent to God.

Psalm 106 verses 34–39 brings together, within the setting of a psalm that reviews the history of God's dealings with his people, these two outstanding sins of idolatry and blood-guiltiness. Not only had the Jewish people, who were in a covenant relationship with God, broken the first commandment and put other gods before him, they had also actually indulged in child sacrifice as part of their worship of pagan idols. These disgusting practices, which were seen as the height of sin, were roundly condemned from the time of Moses, throughout the period of the Judges and by all the prophets. Psalm 106:35 graphically portrays the abhorrence with which these terrible practices were regarded in the true religious tradition of Israel. 'They mingled with the nations and learned to do as they did. They served their idols, which became a snare to them. They sacrificed their sons and their daughters to the demons; they poured out innocent blood, the blood of their sons and daughters, whom they sacrificed to the idols of Canaan; and the land was polluted with blood. Thus they became unclean by their acts, and played the harlot in their doings.' Thus the land itself was polluted by the evil actions of the people. The Psalmist goes on to recall the terrible consequences of this evil-doing: 'Then the anger of the Lord was kindled against his people, and he abhorred his heritage' (v. 40).

The significance of these passages for the study of Isaiah 24:5 and 6a lies in the fact that although Numbers 35, Jeremiah 3 and Psalm 106 were written for the Jewish people living under the old covenant, their message is applicable to the whole of mankind. Our prophet says that the whole earth lies polluted under its inhabitants. The whole of mankind has transgressed God's laws and violated his statutes. In Genesis 3:17 God tells Adam that his wilful disobedience has resulted in a curse coming upon the earth: 'Cursed is the ground because of you.' Then, following the murder of Abel by Cain, God said, 'The voice of your brother's blood is crying to me from the ground. And now you are cursed from the ground which has opened its mouth to receive your brother's blood from your hand' (Genesis 4:10 and 11). That curse and its consequences are extended to cover the whole world, 'Therefore a curse devours the earth and its inhabitants suffer for their guilt' (Isaiah 24:6a).

The consequences of fundamental and wilful disobedience to God, and the breaking of the commandments and the spurning of his statutes, are spelt out in Leviticus 26:14–35. God says that everything will go wrong in the life of the nation: there will be disease and national misfortune of

many kinds. If, despite the warnings that these consequences of wrong-doing are intended to bring, men continue
to walk contrary to God's laws he says that he himself will
come upon them in fury and chastise them himself (v. 28).
Finally, 'I will lay your cities waste, and make your
sanctuaries desolate . . . I will devastate the land so that
your enemies who settle in it shall be astonished at it' (vv. 31
and 32).

The consequence of the curse that comes upon the earth is
all-consuming. It is like a fire that sweeps across the land
devouring everything and leaving behind it a trail of
devastation and destruction. 'For my decision is to gather
nations, to assemble kingdoms, to pour out upon them my
indignation, all the heat of my anger, for in the fire of my
jealous wrath all the earth shall be consumed' (Zephaniah
3:8). The whole of Scripture bears witness to the terrible
consequences of lawlessness and disobedience to God. There
are numerous passages in Isaiah that speak of the result of
this curse on the inhabitants of the earth, coming like fire
burning and devouring as it moves across the face of the
earth – see, for example, Isaiah 1:31; 5:24; 9:18; 10:16 and 17;
29:6 and 30:27. Thus the prophecy of fire sweeping across the
earth, that is depicted by the prophet, 'therefore the
inhabitants of the earth are scorched and few men are left'
(24:6), is in accord with numerous other passages of
Scripture where the fire is depicted as cleansing the earth
from the pollution caused by man.

Paul lends substance to the view that the whole of
mankind has deliberately rebelled against God. There is no
question of ignorance of the law providing sufficient grounds
for innocence. Paul declares in a forthright manner that the
natural created order is sufficient to give mankind a general
knowledge of the nature of God 'for what can be known
about God is plain to them, because God has shown it to
them. Ever since the creation of the world, his invisible
nature, namely, his eternal power and deity, has been
clearly perceived in the things that have been made'
(Romans 1:19 and 20). This general knowledge of the nature

of God has given man something akin to an intuitive knowledge of right and wrong, of goodness and evil. Paul is saying that although mankind as a whole has not had the supernatural revelation of himself and his Word that Israel has had throughout her history, nevertheless, the whole natural order of creation bears witness to God's truth in the conscience of man. In this Paul is reflecting the thought of Psalm 19. He is therefore able to say that 'men are without any excuse, for although they knew God, they neither glorified him as God nor gave thanks to him, but their thinking became futile and their foolish hearts were darkened' (Romans 1:21, NIV).

This paves the way for Paul's argument in Romans 2 that the whole of mankind has sinned, and that there are no special privileges given to the Jew that will allow him to escape 'the tribulation and distress' that will come upon 'every human being who does evil, the Jew first and also the Greek' (v. 9). Indeed, the Jew is no better off than the Gentile, for all alike are under sin (Romans 3:9). The only advantage of the law is that it spells out clearly what constitutes sin. But the Gentiles too are without excuse and 'all who have sinned without the law will also perish without the law, and all who have sinned under the law will be judged by the law' (2:12).

The only hope for mankind is reconciliation with God, and this is not attained through merit as a reward for righteous living. It is the pure act of the grace of God. The argument that Paul develops from Romans 1:16 and through chapters 2, 3 and 4 finds its climax in chapter 5, where Paul shows that we are made right with God only through faith in the Lord Jesus Christ. He is thus able to urge that all men need to be put right with God through the death of his Son, and that this is the only way of being delivered from 'the wrath of God [which] is being revealed from heaven against all the godlessness and wickedness of men who suppress the truth' (1:18, NIV).

For Paul, the wrath of God is not something he deliberately sends upon man as an act of violent and aggressive vengeance or the outcome of irrational rage. It is the natural outcome of the wrong-doing of mankind. Unrighteous behaviour breaks the moral code of the universe with inevitable consequences. These consequences can already be seen, as Paul outlines in a few graphic sentences in Romans 1:24–32. Throughout this passage the disastrous outcome of evil in society is shown to be the result of man's sinfulness rather than the direct intervention of an angry God. God revealed himself to man through his works in creation. But men by their own determined action refused to worship him and so were driven by powers of evil. Their minds became perverted and so too did their behaviour in society, including their sexual activity. 'Therefore God gave them over in the sinful desires of their hearts to sexual impurity for the degrading of their bodies with one another. They exchanged the truth of God for a lie and worshipped and served created things rather than the Creator' (vv. 24 and 25). The act of God was no more than abstention from interference with men's free choice. He 'gave them up', left them to themselves, with the inevitable consequence that they 'received in themselves the due penalty for their perversion' (v. 27). The phrase 'he gave them up' occurs three times in six verses in this passage, thus emphasizing the terrible effects of God's withdrawing from the arena and leaving man to be driven by the forces of darkness.

The Good News translation of Romans 1:18 and 19 tends to miss some of the impact of what Paul is presenting in this passage. The translators insert into verse 19 the words 'God punishes them', which are not found in any manuscript of the Greek and which tend to change the meaning of the passage. The GNB also uses the words 'God's anger' in verse 18 rather than the biblical term 'the wrath of God', which implies an inevitable consequence rather than the active emotion or passion of anger. Paul often uses this theological concept in an impersonal sense, as when he refers to 'vessels of wrath' (Romans 9:22) or 'children of wrath' (Ephesians 2:3) or the 'day of wrath' (Romans 2:5). He uses the term to describe what happens when man deliberately turns his back upon righteousness in a world created by a holy God.[5] The wrath comes upon man as a consequence of sin, and in the gospels, e.g. John 3:16 and 17, and in Romans, it is set in vivid contrast to the action or activity of God, which is directed towards saving man from the effects of human sin. The contrast is clear if the two verses Romans 1:17 and 18 are read consecutively. Paul says that the Gospel reveals the righteousness of God, but the wrath of God ('divine retribution', NEB) is revealed by the wickedness of men. The message of the New Testament is that God has stepped into the arena of human history to set man free from the enslavement of sin, as a man may enter a slave market and pay the redemption price for a slave and then set him free. The wages of sin is death, but the free gift of God is life. Man cannot earn his salvation. The only thing he deserves is death, but, because God is love, he is longing to save mankind from the consequences of their own folly in the exercise of free will. God knows what will happen to us if he simply 'gives us up' to be driven by the forces of evil. The end result is inevitable.

God, who is holy, and who created man in his own image, has so created the world that man can know God and know what he requires of him. But we have the freedom to reject God's will. Our freedom is either to choose to do his will or to be driven by the evil forces that both Paul and Jesus describe as the 'rulers of this world' (Ephesians 6:12 and John 14:30). The New Testament thus confirms the message that we are examining in Isaiah 24. Verse 6 says that 'a curse devours the earth and its inhabitants suffer for their guilt'. The inhabitants of the earth are suffering because of their own actions. The suffering is a punishment in the sense that it is richly deserved, it is divine retribution because men have

---

[5] I am well aware that some theologians take a contrary view. Leon Morris, for example, says, 'While disaster is regarded as the inevitable result of man's sin, it is so in the view of the Old Testament, not by some inexorable law of an impersonal Nature, but because a holy God wills to pour out the vials of his wrath upon those who commit sin.' Leon Morris, *The Apostolic Preaching of the Cross*, Tyndale Press, London, 1965, p. 152.

chosen to ignore God, and it is something that they have brought upon themselves rather than a direct action of an outraged God. God's desire is not for the death of the sinner but that all men should be saved. Men have disregarded the commandments of God, they have transgressed his laws, violated his statutes and broken the everlasting covenant (v. 5).

Most commentators believe this covenant to be the one made with Noah (Genesis 9:11–17), a covenant that did not simply apply to Jews, as did the covenant established with Moses. It was a covenant with the whole world and with every living creature upon the earth. Young says that this reference to an eternal covenant cannot be that which was made with Noah because 'it was an unconditional covenant. It involved no commandment whose fulfilment or obedience was required for the promise to be fulfilled. How, therefore, could one break or violate the Noahic covenant?' (p. 157). Young claims to be following Calvin in linking this covenant with 'the covenant of grace made with the fathers', the origins of which he traces back to God's giving of his law and ordinances to Adam and in Adam to all mankind (p. 158). Young, however, overlooks the fact that the covenant established with Noah, which was said to be 'an everlasting covenant between God and every living creature of all flesh that is upon the earth' (Genesis 9:16), undoubtedly did have a condition that was a prohibition upon the shedding of blood (Genesis 9:6). Undoubtedly this regulation prohibiting bloodshed can be traced right back to Adam. But the reference here in Isaiah 24:5 is that, due to man's wilful disregard of this regulation prohibiting bloodshed, he has broken the everlasting covenant established between God and mankind. Therefore he has brought upon himself a curse, and through him this curse extends to cover the whole earth.

'Therefore a curse devours the earth and its inhabitants suffer for their guilt.' The ground that was cursed because of Adam (Genesis 3:17) will eventually be purged when fire devastates it and the earth is scorched (Isaiah 24:6), disclosing the blood shed upon her (Isaiah 26:21).

CHAPTER THREE

The Prophetic Word: Isaiah 24–27

Part 2

4. Desolation of the Countryside 24:4,7–9,11

> The earth mourns and withers,
>> the world languishes and withers;
>> the heavens languish together with the earth.
> The wine mourns,
>> the vine languishes,
>> all the merry-hearted sigh.
> The mirth of the timbrels is stilled,
>> the noise of the jubilant has ceased,
>> the mirth of the lyre is stilled.
> No more do they drink wine with singing;
>> strong drink is bitter to those who drink it.
> There is an outcry in the streets for lack of wine;
>> all joy has reached its eventide;
>> the gladness of the earth is banished.

This passage adds further detail to the scene of universal destruction. It presents a horrifying picture of the entire world of nature mourning and withering and drying up as the shock waves of devastation begin to subside and there dawns upon the survivors ('few are left', 6b) the terrible realization of what has happened. The picture of the earth withering, linked with 'the inhabitants of the earth are scorched' (6b), suggests that the surface of the earth has been subjected to an enormous temperature that has set fire to much of the natural vegetation.

This picture of fire, with tremendous heat devastating all living matter, occurs in a number of other passages in Scripture that refer to a time of universal judgement.

Zephaniah refers to the 'fire of God's wrath consuming all the earth' (3:8). Malachi speaks of a 'burning oven that consumes like stubble' (4:1). Peter sees 'fire spreading across the sky and dissolving the whole earth so that every thing upon it is burnt up' (2 Peter 3:10). He says 'the physical elements of the world will actually melt with fire' (v. 12). Jesus also refers to the end of the age as a time of fire that will burn up the evil in the world (Matthew 13:40).

Verse 7 that says 'the wine mourns, the vine languishes' refers to the juice of the grape drying up on the vine so that no wine can be made. The blast effect of the holocaust of destruction that will come upon the earth will cause the natural vegetation of the countryside to wither and die. The vine thus dries up and this is used by the prophet as a pictorial means of expressing the terrible shock that comes upon the remnant of earth's inhabitants after the destruction. All joy and merrymaking disappear from the earth. The gladness of the earth dries up along with the world of nature.

As the fallout from the waves of destruction settles upon the earth the whole world of nature gives the appearance of mourning. Death and destruction are everywhere to be seen. Mirth, jubilation and gladness are also dried up in the parched throats of the survivors and 'all joy has reached its eventide' (v. 11). It is a bleak and terrifying scene that the prophet depicts. This is no ordinary drought but the after-effects of a furnace of heat that has blasted the surface of the earth and stripped the whole natural order of creation of its life-giving properties.

5. Destruction of the City 24:10,12,13

The city of chaos is broken down,
    every house is shut up so that none can enter.
Desolation is left in the city,
    the gates are battered into ruins.
For thus it shall be in the midst of the earth
    among the nations,

as when an olive tree is beaten,
    as at the gleaning when the vintage is done.

The prophet now turns his attention to the next part of the results of the cataclysmic destruction that will come upon the world. He sees the great centres of civilization being shattered. 'The city of chaos is broken down, every house is shut up so that none can enter' (24:10). The term 'city of chaos' is significant, for the word used here is *tohu*, which is the same word used in Genesis 1:2 and which most translators render 'void'. In Genesis it is used to describe the state of the earth when it was simply formless substance before God created the natural order of material creation. Jeremiah uses the same term, also translated 'void' in the RSV, in 4:23 to describe the devastating trail of destruction that he saw was coming upon the earth when 'the whole land shall be a desolation' (v. 27).[1] The term 'city of chaos' thus serves to describe a situation of indescribable devastation, where there is a complete lack of form and order so that the city is left utterly desolate. The phrase 'every house is shut up so that none can enter' is difficult to interpret. It is not clear whether the inhabitants had barricaded themselves inside their houses in a vain attempt to try to protect themselves from the descending destruction, or whether they had either fled the city or been wiped out along with everything else there. Their homes now lie shattered as unrecognizable heaps of rubble that no one could enter.

Through the sins of its inhabitants there had been introduced into the city the forces of desolation and confusion. These forces had been let loose with such terrifying fury that the very nature of the city itself was transformed into a desolation. It reverted to the original formless void that was unfit for man as a dwelling place before God put order into the material creation and saw that

---

[1] Some scholars believe this vision is based upon the plundering of the land by the Scythian invasion of 626 BC that Jeremiah saw. But historians are by no means unanimous that there was a Scythian invasion at that period.

it was good. The prophet sees that the end result of man's sinfulness seems to reverse the fundamental process of creation with such terrifying consequences that it renders the earth incapable of supporting life.

Isaiah continues the scene in verses 12 and 13, where he notes that once the devastation is let loose upon the city its defences are rendered useless: 'the gates are battered into ruins' and its inhabitants are left entirely helpless in the face of the onslaught. Verse 13 indicates that it is not just one city that will be engulfed in destruction, but many, probably most of the major cities of the world. 'For thus it shall be in the midst of the earth among the nations.' Although only one city is mentioned here it is understood as being representative of the cities of the world.

This does not mean that every city dweller throughout the world will be annihilated. The prophecy indicates that although the cities themselves will suffer enormous destruction, some of the inhabitants will escape. There will be a small remnant. Verse 6b states that there will be few men left, and this is reinforced in 13b with the simile of the olive harvest. This illustration is doubtless drawn from 17:6 where the picture is slightly clearer, showing men climbing into the branches of the olive trees with long sticks to beat down the remaining olives that could not be picked by hand. Even when this is done a few still remain in the topmost or outermost branches that cannot be reached. But in comparison with the size of the olive harvest gathered from each tree, the few that remain beyond the reach of the flailing sticks are very few indeed.

There have been many attempts by biblical scholars to locate the city of chaos to which we have already referred in chapter two. The identity of the city has given rise to much speculation amongst scholars, and many suggestions have been made, the favourite being Babylon. Others have been Jerusalem, Nineveh, Tyre, Sidon, Samaria, Carthage and even Rome. The most widely held view amongst modern scholars is to interpret the city symbolically as the personification of all the evil cities of mankind.

Representative of this view is Young, who summarizes his own exegesis in the following terms: 'It is an exalted city (26:5) inhabited by rejoicers who love wine (24:7–9). The inhabitants are haughty (25:2). It is a brave city (25:2; 27:10). It has a robust people (25:3) who considered it impregnable. It is razed to the ground (26:5) and left desolate (27:10). It is the city of chaos (24:10), where animals pasture (27:10). God is to be praised for its destruction (24:14). In accomplishing its overthrow God has manifested his justice (26:7; 27:11), his faithfulness to his promises (25:1), and his zeal for his people (26:11). More than this, one is not warranted in saying. The prophecy is vague in its references to the city. In the overthrow of the city, probably a representative of the power of man in opposition to God, God has triumphed gloriously' (pp. 260–1).

There is further mention of the city in 25:2, a clear reference to the destruction of a city that is the capital of a world super power.

> For thou hast made the city a heap,
> the fortified city a ruin,
> the palace of aliens is a city no more,
> it will never be rebuilt.

Clearly it is not Jerusalem that the prophet has in mind, for no Jew would rejoice over the destruction of the Holy City, and this is the context of this passage (vv. 1–5). These verses constitute a song of praise to God for carrying out his purposes. Even if a Jew could trace the hand of the Lord in the destruction of Jerusalem, as undoubtedly both Jeremiah and Ezekiel did, no true Israelite could ever make the statement 'it will never be rebuilt'! Even to consider the permanent destruction of Zion, the city of God, would be to contradict the whole nature and purpose of God and would thus be utterly unthinkable. Probably the most convincing argument that Jerusalem is not the place intended is the reference to the 'palace of aliens'. It was unthinkable that such a place could exist in Zion!

What is in fact envisaged in verse 2 is the destruction of a city that not simply symbolizes but is in very fact the centre of government of a world power that holds an evil sway over the nations. It is a highly fortified city protected by enormous force of arms, and contains at its centre some kind of castle that is thought to be impregnable, the palace of aliens, i.e. its centre of government.

God's power will be seen when this world capital of evil falls. Its destruction has been planned for a very long time (v. 1b). This demonstration of God's power will open the eyes of the nations who look to the world power, or who now rely upon their own power, and they will become aware of who is the real Lord of the nations. As they recognize God's sovereign power and his lordship among the nations they will pay him due honour and exalt him, abandoning for ever their own rule by force. The destruction of the wicked capital of the world will also be seen as a demonstration of God's care for the poor and needy. In some way the prophet envisages God intervening in the midst of the destruction to protect the defenceless poor who are his own people. To them he is seen as a stronghold and a refuge, 'a shelter from the storm and a shade from the heat, for the blast of the ruthless is like a storm against a wall, like heat in a dry place' (v. 4).

The prophet sees God working out his own purposes, plans formed from the beginning of time, amidst the chaos and destruction wrought by the sinfulness of mankind. God's purposes, far from being thwarted by man's sinfulness, are in fact carried out because it is his intention that the evil forces let loose into the world by that sinfulness will be overcome. The prophet thus rejoices in the fall of the capital city of the world powers of evil. He sees in this the fulfilment of God's intentions and he sees him intervening in the midst of the desolation to save his own people.

6. Overthrow of Opponents 24:21,22

> On that day the Lord will punish
>   the host of heaven, in heaven,
>   and the kings of the earth, on the earth.
> They will be gathered together
>   as prisoners in a pit;
> they will be shut up in a prison,
>   and after many days they will be punished.

The next phase of the prophecy follows naturally upon the fall of the world's capital. The prophet sees that once the period of world-wide destruction has begun a chain of events will be set in motion. He says that God will punish the host of heaven and the kings of the earth. He thus turns from the theme of general destruction and universal punishment to the particular judgement that will fall upon those primarily responsible for the catastrophe that has befallen the earth.

a) WORLD POWERS BROKEN

The phrase 'kings of the earth' clearly refers to world rulers, although there is no clue given to their actual identity. The meaning is conveyed that they are those men who have been primarily responsible for the chaos upon earth that has resulted from their evil rule. They had practised injustice, exploitation and bloodshed on a vast scale. This passage says that the day will come when the world rulers will be called to account for the power and authority that they have exercised upon earth. The phrase 'they will be gathered together as prisoners in a pit' does not indicate Sheol, neither is it intended to convey any particular physical area where all the world rulers will be brought together. It is intended to reinforce the following phrase 'they will be shut up in prison' and the two phrases together primarily indicate that there will be no escape for these wicked rulers. They have misused their power, misled the people and been the cause of enormous suffering and bloodshed which has polluted the earth. As men thrown into a dungeon or shut up in a maximum security prison, there will be no escape for them when God acts in judgement.

The phrase 'after many days they will be punished' is difficult to interpret. Young links this with the judgement and refers to 2 Peter 2:4, Jude 6 and Revelation 21:6 (p. 181). There is no general agreement amongst commentators. Perhaps the most ingenious suggestion comes from Kissane, who says: 'We should probably read "blood" (*damim*) instead of "days" (*yamim*) here.' He believes that the main burden of this passage is the charge against the world rulers that they have defiled the earth through bloodshed and thus offended against the holiness of God. He suggests that what the prophet is saying is that the world rulers will be brought to judgement and punished 'after much bloodshed' rather than 'after many days' (p. 275).

b) SPIRITUAL POWERS BROKEN

Just as the world rulers are to be punished 'on the earth', so the host of heaven will be punished 'in heaven'. This indicates two phases in the judgement of those responsible for world chaos that has led to the holocaust, according to the prophet. There seems no justification for Kaiser's interpretation of the 'army of the height' as referring to the physical heavenly bodies or the stars in the universe (Kaiser, pp. 194, 195). Most commentators agree that the 'host of heaven' refers to spiritual powers of evil that have been influencing the world rulers and attempting to encompass their downfall, and with them the annihilation of the whole of mankind. Taken in context with the whole passage we are studying this would appear to be the right interpretation.

The general content of chapter 24 prophesies that the evil of mankind will reach the point where it is so enormous that it will bring about destruction upon a world-wide scale of such enormity that it will engulf the whole of mankind, the majority of whom will be killed. At that point God will step in and punish those primarily responsible for the terrible things that are happening upon the earth: 'The Lord will punish the host of heaven in heaven.' The phrase refers to the existence of spiritual powers of evil that are outside the physical realm of the earth. The prophet clearly sees these forces as influencing events upon earth through the power that they exercise over world rulers. It is no coincidence that the host of heaven and the kings of the earth are linked in verse 21. Those who exercise the greatest influence through their positions of worldly authority are most exposed to the influence and the attacks of the spiritual powers of evil from outside the world. This is precisely the point of Paul's stern warning to the Ephesians that the real nature of the battle facing humanity is not simply a struggle against each other, but spiritual warfare, and to understand the nature of spiritual warfare we have to recognize the main source of the attack. It comes not from a human source or from the world of physical creation, but from the spiritual hosts of evil outside the earth's domain. Paul says 'for we are not contending against flesh and blood but against the principalities, against the powers, against the world rulers of this present darkness, against the spiritual hosts of wickedness in the heavenly places' (Ephesians 6:12).

The idea of spiritual warfare is a concept that many Christians find difficult to comprehend. Yet we live in an age when there is greater interest in the occult than at probably any previous time in recent history. Despite the sophistication of the Western world it is here that we find the greatest proliferation of occultic practices in recent years, and the publication of numerous books and magazines on the subject. It would appear that non-Christians find it easier than many Christians to believe in the existence of paranormal powers of evil existing outside the human sphere and having an influence over our lives.

Jesus clearly believed in the existence of spiritual powers of evil. He saw them at work in human lives and he exercised his power and authority over them to cast them out and to bring deliverance to those who were in bondage. Jesus also believed that the powers of evil have their own hierarchy, and he was confident of his own victory over them: 'Now is the judgement of this world, now shall the ruler of this world be cast out' (John 12:31). Jesus clearly saw his victory as being through the cross, a victory that all can enter into. Hence his very next words were 'I, if I am lifted up from the earth, will draw all men to myself' (v. 32). Paul graphically describes the victory of the cross over the powers of evil in the heavenly realms: 'He disarmed the principalities and powers and made a public example of them, triumphing over them' (Colossians 2:15).

That victory of the cross, although complete, is not finally consummated until the day when God brings all things into subjection under the Son and when 'before him every knee shall bow, in heaven and on earth, and under the earth, and every tongue confess that Jesus Christ is Lord, to the glory of God the Father' (Philippians 2:10). Jesus himself speaks of the day when he will finally defeat the powers of the heavens, and he clearly links this with the times of tribulation and world-wide destruction that he says are to come upon the earth (Matthew 24:29 and Luke 21:26).

Thus Jesus confirms the prophecy of Isaiah 24:21 which foretells the overcoming of the powers of evil by God at the time of the great destruction that will come upon the earth. Clearly the spiritual powers of evil will be within sight of achieving their ultimate objective – the complete annihilation of mankind and the utter destruction of the earth – God's spiritual and physical handiwork. But it is not within the purpose of God that this should succeed. His purpose is that good will overcome evil. Hence the prophet foretells, and Jesus confirms, that in the time of the world-wide destruction God will step in to prevent the complete destruction of the world and the absolute annihilation of mankind. He will use this occasion to punish the powers of evil that have brought the world to this point through the influence and sway they have exercised over mankind. Their power will be broken. God will accomplish this and, in some wonderful way that none of us can yet comprehend, God intends to use his people, those who are utterly committed to him, his true Church, to demonstrate his power over the forces of evil. This is what Paul says in Ephesians 3:10. He states that it is God's purpose 'that through the church the manifold wisdom of God might now be made known to the principalities and powers in the heavenly places'. He further states that this has been part of God's intention from the beginning of creation. Indeed this is God's plan that had been hidden for ages but was revealed through the Lord Jesus Christ – that God intended through Jesus to raise up a people of spiritual power to work with him in overcoming the spiritual forces of evil that are driving the world and mankind towards destruction.

God has provided not only the archetype of the victory, the cross of Jesus, but he has also given to his people the power whereby evil may be overcome. It is the power of the Holy Spirit that was given at Pentecost and is God's gift to his people through the Church in every generation. The victory is his, and the day will come when the whole of creation will see it and will join in wonder and praise that the prophecy of Isaiah 45:23, repeated in Romans 14:11, will be fulfilled: 'As I live, says the Lord, every knee shall bow to me, and every tongue shall give praise to God.'

7. Survival of Remnant 24:14–16a

> They lift up their voices, they sing for joy;
>> over the majesty of the Lord they shout from the west.
> Therefore in the east give glory to the Lord;
>> in the coastlands of the sea,
>>> to the name of the Lord, the God of Israel.
> From the ends of the earth we hear songs of praise,
>> of glory to the Righteous One.

At first reading these verses appear uncharacteristic and out of place. They form a little song of praise in the middle of a chapter of unremitting gloom foretelling world-wide destruction and desolation. But the placing of this song immediately following the simile of the olive tree gives a clue as to its meaning. We have already seen that the picture of the few olives left on the trees beyond the reach of the reapers at the time of the harvest symbolized the small remnant that the prophet says will be left after the destruction. The song begins 'They lift up their voices, they sing for joy over the majesty of the Lord'. The 'they' referred to here are no doubt the small remnant who will be left on the earth at the time of God's intervention to stop the destruction.

a)   THE RIGHTEOUS WILL REJOICE

The prophet sees the whole remnant of the inhabitants of the earth giving praise and glory to God when he has established his power over heaven and earth. He sees the song of praise beginning in the west. He therefore turns to the east and commands them also to give glory to God. As their songs of praise join with those in the west they are echoed right around the world. 'From the ends of the earth we hear songs of praise, of glory to the Righteous One.' Perhaps it was a small foretaste of this universal adoration of God that the shepherds glimpsed when they heard 'the multitude of the heavenly host praising God and saying "Glory to God in the highest and on earth peace among men with whom he is pleased!"' (Luke 2:13 and 14).

The prophet continues this theme in 25:9 when he states 'It will be said on that day, "Lo, this is our God; we have waited for him, that he might save us. This is the Lord; we have waited for him; let us be glad and rejoice in his salvation."' He is seeing the time of universal glory to God which is glimpsed by so many writers in Scripture; the time when all the nations will acknowledge the power and supremacy of God and give him the glory due to his name. Psalm 96 beautifully catches this theme. It foretells the day when all the peoples will sing to the Lord a new song and the whole earth will bless his name. Among the nations they will say 'The Lord reigns'. Similarly Psalm 97 looks forward to the time when the heavens will proclaim God's righteousness and all the people will behold his glory. Psalm 98 rejoices in the victory that the Lord has won and that 'he has revealed his vindication in the sight of the nations'. Therefore the Psalmist says 'Make a joyful noise to the Lord all the earth, break forth into joyous song and sing praises! . . . for the Lord comes to rule the earth. He will judge the world with righteousness and the peoples with equity.'

Although verses 14-16a do not clearly state either the identity of those who are rejoicing or the reason for their joy, the context of the passage gives ground for a fairly confident interpretation. We have already stated the view that 'they' who sing for joy are the remnant who survive the world-wide devastation. The reason for their rejoicing is no doubt initially the very fact that they have been preserved alive and have escaped the ravages of the holocaust that has been let loose upon the earth. But there is a much deeper reason than this, and the clue to it is found in the final line of verse 16a where we see that the songs of praise are giving 'glory to the Righteous One'. This is the RSV rendering which is favoured by most scholars, although it is worth noting that the most reliable Hebrew texts only speak of 'glory to the righteous'.

There is no justification for the Good News translation which inserts the words 'Israel' and 'nation', arriving at 'we will hear songs in praise of Israel, the righteous nation', which is misleading since 'Israel' and 'nation' do not appear in any Hebrew text. The prophet is certainly not seeing Israel as the one righteous nation that will survive the devastation unblemished. Neither is he implying that the remnant who survive will be drawn solely from the ranks of Israel. The remnant is from all the nations of the world, and the significance of this passage is that they all join in songs of praise. Certainly they would not be praising righteous men and women. The prophet is far too conscious of the sinfulness of mankind to suggest such a strange notion. He clearly intends the word 'righteous' to apply to God. He is foretelling the time when all mankind will give glory to God because they recognize him as 'the Righteous One'. This recognition comes out of the experience of suffering.

The survivors of the holocaust realize that it is the collective sinfulness of mankind that has brought about the world-wide destruction from which they themselves have somehow miraculously escaped. As the shock waves of horror and suffering that have engulfed all men and women begin to subside, the survivors not only recognize that the destruction which has come upon the earth was richly deserved but they also recognize the wonderful mercy of God in stepping in to prevent the total annihilation of mankind and the full disintegration of the physical earth. In the events that have overtaken the world they see God's hand both in judgement and in mercy. The judgement is seen in that man, by his own evil ways, brought the destruction upon himself and his world. God acted in perfect justice in allowing man to endure the consequential suffering of his own wickedness, but God in his love and mercy stepped into the chaos with a word of command like the stilling of the storm and brought peace to the earth. The prophet sees that in the calm which follows men will turn to God in wonder and awe, seeing him as the Righteous One who has acted to save his people and to restore unto them the joy of their salvation. Those who rejoice are no doubt themselves righteous, but only in the sense that they have recognized the righteousness of God and that they have been brought into a right relationship with him solely through what he has done for them.

b)   THE POOR AND THE LOWLY EXALTED

The theme of rejoicing in the wonderful act of God in saving the world from utter destruction is continued in 25:1–5. The prophet himself joins in the exaltation:

> O Lord, thou art my God;
>   I will exalt thee, I will praise thy name;
> for thou hast done wonderful things,
>   plans formed of old, faithful and sure.

He has been given a revelation of what is to happen at the climax of history when the forces of evil will reach the point of almost complete victory. But just when all appears to be utterly hopeless for mankind, when evil is about to triumph finally over good and there appears to be no hope of saving the human race from absolute extermination, God acts to break the powers of evil and overthrows the forces that have conspired to destroy the world. God had his plans formed from before the beginning of creation itself. His plans for the nations were good, just as were his plans for Israel, plans to 'give a future and a hope' (Jeremiah 29:11).

The 'wonderful things' that have happened are things that only God could have done. He has accomplished the destruction of the enemies of the earth, the real enemy of mankind. He has established himself as the ultimate power in the universe and he has shown himself to be the deliverer of mankind. In order to achieve this, God had to break the secular powers of the nations (24:10) and the spiritual powers that have been directing them (24:21). As the revelation of God's purposes is unfolded before the eyes of the prophet he himself cannot refrain from joining in with the whole company of survivors from all nations in praising God for the amazing things he has done.

The reason why God is to be praised is given in 25:2. The prophet recalls the destruction of the world capital whose downfall symbolizes the full and final end of the kingdoms of the world that have been ruled by oppressors and tyrants, to the extent that they have become closely identified with, and willing agents of, the spiritual forces of evil that have purposed the destruction of mankind. The downfall of the world city is so complete that 'it will never be rebuilt'. As a result 'strong peoples will glorify God' (v. 3). The united power of the nations had to be broken so that man could learn the lesson that it was futile to trust in his own powers and useless to put his trust in material things. The nations had to learn that God is Lord of all the earth before they could turn to him and praise him and give him the glory.

Those who thought themselves to be strong would now recognize their own inherent weakness and would turn to God and glorify him. People from the ruthless nations would look to God with a sense of awe as they contemplated the vast demonstration of his power in overcoming the destructive forces that were sweeping across the face of the earth. Man can let loose forces of destruction, but he finds himself unable to control them. He can change the city into a heap of ruins, but it takes a greater force to stem the tide of destruction and to deliver the remnant of mankind from the fate of their own folly. Even those who boasted in worldly strength can now only stand in reverential awe before the majesty of God.

One of the consequences of God's action and the establishment of his power in the world, his kingly reign, will be the turning upside down of human values. Whereas formerly men stood in awe of human strength and the power of material things, whose possession gave honour and status to men as individuals and to the mighty nations, now it is the poor who are exalted. Those who are lacking in worldly status and who were needy in terms of material possessions, but who were strong in faith and their trust in God, will be exalted above all others: 'For thou hast been a stronghold to the poor, a stronghold to the needy in his distress, a shelter from the storm and a shade from the heat' (25:4).

God is a God of justice, so that in the days when he establishes his power in the world the oppressors of mankind will be overthrown and the poor and the needy will be uplifted. Jesus confirms this in his paradoxical statement that it is the meek who will inherit the earth (Matthew 5:5). Jesus also confirms God's deep compassion for the poor and tells them that the kingdom of God is theirs (Luke 6:20). Isaiah sees this coming about in the day when God breaks the power of human empires. In 26:5 and 6 he sees how those who are rich in the possession of material goods, status and power are not only overthrown but their humiliation is completed by the feet of the poor trampling over the ruins of their great cities that once symbolized the affluence of the mighty men of the world.

There are many other witnesses throughout Scripture to the fact that this is the determined purpose of God. He will one day put down the rich and the powerful and exalt the lowly poor and the humble faithful. Zephaniah said that on the day that God acts neither the silver nor the gold of the rich will be able to deliver them (1:18). Jesus warned of the dangers of riches keeping a man out of the kingdom (Mark 10:23), while James spoke in his customary forthright terms concerning the last days: 'Come now, you rich, weep and howl for the miseries that are coming upon you. Your riches have rotted, your garments are moth-eaten. Your gold and silver have rusted, and their rust will be evidence against you, and will eat your flesh like fire. You have laid up treasure for the last days' (James 5:1–3). Perhaps Mary was catching a glimpse of the times of which Isaiah speaks at the end of the age when the work of Christ will reach its climax and fulfilment. As she magnified the Lord before the birth of Jesus, Mary said, 'He has shown strength with his arm, he has scattered the proud in the imagination of their hearts, he has put down the mighty from their thrones, and exalted those of low degree; he has filled the hungry with good things, and the rich he has sent empty away.' (Luke 1:51–53).

Thus the New Testament confirms the message of the prophet, in the day that God acts to break the unrighteous power of the nations and to establish his own authority in the world. The humble, poor and needy with whom Jesus had such a strong affinity throughout his earthly life will be raised up and exalted and will lead the praises of God among the survivors of the nations.

8. Glorification and Reign of God 24:23

> Then the moon will be confounded,
>   and the sun ashamed;
> for the Lord of hosts will reign
>   on Mount Zion and in Jerusalem
> and before his elders he will manifest his glory.

Chapter 24 reaches its climax with this final verse. Once all the powers of this world have been overthrown and the rulers of the kingdoms of mankind have been removed, there will be nothing to prevent the full and complete establishment of the reign of God. In this verse the prophet is thrown back upon symbolic language to describe the glory of God that he sees revealed in the time of God's final and complete victory. He says that the moon will be confounded and the sun ashamed. By this he simply means that there will be no need for the moon to give light to the world by night and the sun to give light by day, because the glory of God will be so bright that it will outshine the sun and the moon and the stars, which, after all, are only the work of God's own creation. In Revelation 21:23 we are told that in the city of God there will be 'no need of sun or moon to shine upon it, for the glory of God is its light and its lamp is the Lamb'.

God's glory will be so bright and so clearly revealed that all other sources of light will pale into insignificance, just as all other powers will have been swept aside. When the kingdom of evil is finally put down the kingdom of God will be universally established for all to see. The spiritual hosts of wickedness that opposed God will also have been destroyed so that he truly will be seen to be Lord of lords and King of kings.

The centre of God's reign is said to be upon Mount Zion and in Jerusalem, but this does not mean that it will be established upon the physical site of Jerusalem. Again, this is figurative language that would be the natural means of expression to an Old Testament prophet describing the revelation of the ultimate things that God permitted him to see. Zion and Jerusalem symbolized for all the prophets the seat of God's power and the city where his presence was revealed to his people. It was the place hallowed by the Temple, the sacrificial system and the worship of God that had continually been offered up since David established Jerusalem as his capital and brought the ark into the city centre amidst national rejoicing.

The elders referred to in the final part of this verse are the leaders of the people of God, before whom the very presence and the glory of God are revealed. What is being foretold is the presence of God within the assembly of his people. The true people of God are those who inherit the covenant and the promises, those who accept Jesus as Lord and Saviour and thus through Christ enter into a new and right relationship with God. As Paul says, 'It is not the children of the flesh who are the children of God, but the children of the promise are reckoned as descendants' (Romans 9:8). What Israel failed to obtain through her reliance upon the law, the believers in Christ have obtained through the pure act of the grace of God. God established a new basis for his people that opened the way to peoples of all nations. The way of salvation was not through works of the law but purely through faith in Christ, so that 'everyone who calls upon the name of the Lord will be saved' and thus there was 'no distinction between Jew and Gentile' (Romans 10:12 and 13).

In speaking of God being with his elders in glory the prophet is referring to the Church as the assembled people of God, with the elders of the people worshipping the Lord. In Revelation 4:4 there is a similar picture painted: 'Round the throne were twenty-four thrones and seated on the thrones were twenty-four elders clad in white garments with golden crowns upon their heads.'

This theme of God reigning in glory in the presence of his people continues in chapter 25 in verses 6–9, where immediately the scene is set for a great feast. It was normal to follow the coronation of a king with a feast that he provided not simply for the nobility or the elders of the people, but for all the people so that the whole nation could join in rejoicing at the beginning of the reign of their king. With the kings of Israel it was customary to regard the feast that was part of the coronation festivities as a sacrificial meal. It had religious as well as social significance, binding the king and his subjects to God as well as creating a kind of communal solidarity between king and people. As they ate together under the blessing of God, giving thanks for the food which he had provided, they were bound to him as their God. (See, for example, Adonijah's futile attempt to establish himself as king in succession to David by carrying out the customary religious and social festivities in 1 Kings 1:9,19,25 and 41).

The feast which God provides to celebrate the beginning of his reign, the establishment of his kingdom upon earth, is for all peoples. 'On this mountain the Lord Almighty will prepare a feast of rich food for all peoples, a banquet of aged wine – the best of meats and the finest of wines' (25:6, NIV). As God's reign is to be universal so also is the feast. No nation is to be excluded from the blessings which the Lord brings. Even those who had formerly been enemies of God now that their power has been broken will be invited to the feast, and because all men now look upon God with reverential awe they will come to the feast in his honour, to give him the full glory due to his exaltation.

The banquet is going to consist of all the most choice foods and drink that can be offered. God will provide the very best and he will take great delight in having the people come to enjoy the great feast with him. It will be God himself who will preside at the feast, and around him will be gathered the people of his family, drawn from all the nations of the world, who in that day look to him and to him alone as the supreme authority. The prayer that Jesus taught his disciples and that has been prayed by his people for nearly 2000 years will come true, 'Thy kingdom come, thy will be done, on earth as it is in heaven' (Matthew 6:9–13).

The things that God has to offer at his table are those which alone can quench the thirst and satisfy the hunger of needy men and women. They are the things the world cannot give. They are the wine and milk offered without money and without price (Isaiah 55:1). Jesus himself, knowing the Father's intention, offered the invitation 'If anyone thirst, let him come to me and drink' (John 7:37), and he spoke of himself as 'the living bread which came down from heaven; if anyone eats of this bread he will live for ever and the bread which I shall give for the life of the world is my flesh' (John 6:51). God has provided for the Lamb's great feast of festal joy foreshadowed in Revelation 7:13–17, where those who have come out of the great tribulation enter into the presence of God and hunger and thirst no more 'and God will wipe away every tear from their eyes'.

The next two verses are amongst the most beautiful of the entire passage. 'And he will destroy on this mountain the covering that is cast over all peoples, the veil that is spread over all nations. He will swallow up death for ever, and the Lord God will wipe away tears from all faces, and the reproach of his people he will take away from all the earth; for the Lord has spoken' (25:7 and 8). For the feast of the Lord to be enjoyed for ever, those things which prevent men from enjoying it must first be removed. The darkness both of ignorance and sorrow which now covers the earth must be taken away.

The word rendered 'destroyed' in verse 7 perhaps is best translated by the words 'swallowed up'. The prophet uses this term to stress the fact that God completely takes away the covering or the veil that is spread over all mankind. This is the veil of mourning that was commonly used in his day as a sign of sorrow in the presence of death. No one can be in mourning at a coronation feast. This is a time for rejoicing, for celebrating the reign of the king. It is death that has held sway over the whole of mankind and that is the last enemy that God has to tackle. The victory was already assured in Christ, as Paul states emphatically, 'Death is swallowed up in victory. O death, where is thy victory? O death, where is thy sting? The sting of death is sin and the power of sin is the law. But thanks be to God who gives us the victory through our Lord Jesus Christ' (1 Corinthians 15:54–57). Death came into the world through sin, but life has come through Jesus Christ, 'For as in Adam all die, so also in Christ shall all be made alive' (1 Corinthians 15:22).

Mankind, now set free from the bondage of sin, will, in the time foreseen in Isaiah 25:7, be released from the grip of the final enemy, death itself. Having conquered the powers of evil on the earth and in the heavens, death will actually be swallowed up in God's final victory. Although Christ overcame death through the cross, the effects of sin remain active in the world and it is only with the second advent of

Christ that we will see the promised blessings realized to their full. Then will be fulfilled the promise of the ages that nothing shall be able to separate us from the love of Christ . . . neither death nor life, nor angels nor principalities nor powers . . . nor anything else in all creation will be able to separate us from the love of God in Christ Jesus our Lord (Romans 8:35–39).

In the act of swallowing up death for ever so that it can never again hold sway over mankind, God will remove the veil of tears and suffering that has overshadowed mankind throughout the pages of history. Like a loving parent who hurries to a child frightened by the darkness and not only surrounds him with the loving arms of security and comfort, but also wipes away the tears from his eyes, so God will wipe away the tears from the eyes of his people. He will remove from all faces the signs of suffering and take away the reproach of his people from all the earth. The New Testament makes it clear that God has already done this in the person of his Son but it is here in the climax of the ages that the victory of the cross becomes accepted by all people. When all the nations are brought in subjection before him and all opposition is subdued, then God's redeeming love will be accepted by all mankind. This is not simply a vain hope of some vague day of blessing that may or may not come. It is the sure and certain hope of mankind established firmly in the Word of God, for it is he himself who has promised it. Verse 8 ends with the emphatic 'for the Lord has spoken'.

Finally, 'It will be said on that day, lo this is our God; we have waited for him that he might save us. This is the Lord, we have waited for him, let us be glad and rejoice in his salvation' (25:9). This beautiful little song of thanksgiving sets a seal on the entire prophecy. Its inclusion is seen by some scholars as countering the doubts aroused in the minds of the hearers of the prophecy by the contrast between their present situation and the extraordinary things prophesied. The assurance is given in the form of a song of anticipation and thanksgiving that those who put their trust in God and see in him the hope of mankind will not be waiting in vain. The hour of fulfilment of the hopes of mankind will certainly come. The time of world-wide salvation is drawing near. The climax of the ages will be hastened by the gathering gloom of the forces of evil as they seek to accomplish their unholy purposes in the destruction of mankind and the whole created order of the physical world, but in the time of greatest evil God is at work. In the fullness of time he will act. Those who put their trust in the Lord will not be ashamed. He will indeed save them. He who is a stronghold to the poor and the needy will shelter them from the storm and from the blast of the ruthless (25:4).

God warns his people that the coming times of tribulation will indeed be terrible, when the forces of destruction let loose by sinful mankind will wreak a terrible havoc throughout the world. He bids them seek refuge in him.

> Come my people, enter your chambers,
>   and shut your doors behind you;
> hide yourselves for a little while
>   until the wrath is past.
> For behold, the Lord is coming forth out of his place
>   to punish the inhabitants of the earth for their iniquity,
> and the earth will disclose the blood shed upon her,
>   and will no more cover her slain.
>
> (26:20 and 21)

Those who wait patiently for the Lord will not be dismayed. They will see him step into the world's scene in such an amazing way, never before seen and beyond even the imagination of man to depict or the tongue of man to describe – but the result will be clear for all mankind to see. It will be the victory of God over all the forces that have opposed him and sought to frustrate his will and his good plans for the whole of his creation, both material, in the world of nature, and for his own family of mankind.

Once God has acted decisively there will be no more doubts, for even the unrighteous who survive the times of destruction will be forced to acknowledge God and will join in the songs of praise. But the righteous who have waited patiently upon the Lord and whose faith has not been overcome will rejoice mightily.

In that day they will say, 'Surely this is our God: we trusted in him and he saved us. This is the Lord, we trusted in him; let us rejoice and be glad in his salvation.' (Isaiah 25:9, NIV).

CHAPTER FOUR

Isaiah's Vision of the End of the Age

The prophecy of Isaiah 24–27 is unique in character. Although amply confirmed in other parts of Scripture in both the Old Testament and the New, there is no single prophetic utterance dealing with the end of the age which is quite so vivid and explicit. There is nothing unusual in prophecies of doom and destruction. They occur throughout the works of the writing prophets but usually refer to Israel and Judah, or more specifically to the coming destruction of Jerusalem or Samaria. These prophecies have already been fulfilled and it is not difficult to trace the threads between the words of the prophets and events in the history of Israel and Judah. But it is not the prophecy of world-wide destruction that makes Isaiah 24–27 unique. There are other prophecies, such as Zephaniah 1, which speak of the destruction of the whole world. These chapters do not in fact speak of the destruction of the world. They refer to a cataclysmic event from which the world will survive, as also will a remnant of mankind.

What makes the vision of Isaiah unique is its clarity and lack of apocalyptic or extravagant language. Despite the vivid and horrific scenes it depicts, there is a sense of restraint and a lack of emotionalism about the account that carries with it a quiet authority. The prophet clearly is a man acting under direction. He calmly records the revelation he has received and reports what he has been told. He does so within the context of a deep personal faith and utter conviction in the absolute control of God, whose good plans for mankind can be thwarted by sin for a time but whose overall purposes are sure. These he will work out in spite of all the wickedness of mankind and the spiritual powers of evil arrayed against him.

World-wide Destruction

Despite the unemotional, almost matter-of-fact, presentation, what is depicted is a scene of world devastation on a gigantic scale, and it is perhaps hardly surprising that most scholars have regarded this passage as apocalyptic in nature. It has been generally thought that the prophet was using visionary or symbolic language to describe some scene far removed from ordinary everyday human experience, and which requires a spiritual rather than a material interpretation. Today we know that mankind possesses the power to cause an explosion so immense that it can 'lay waste the earth and make it desolate and twist its surface' (Isaiah 24:1). We have the capability of causing a nuclear holocaust so immense that it could, in fact, make 'the foundations of the earth tremble' and shake the earth so violently that 'it staggers like a drunken man' (Isaiah 24:19 and 20).

The world's super powers now have atomic weapons so powerful that by comparison they make the atomic bomb which devastated the city of Hiroshima in 1945 look like a mere firework. Just one of the modern strategic nuclear bombs on each city could lay waste every major city in the world! Two countries alone, the United States and Russia, have between them more than 20,000 nuclear weapons!

It is now recognized by scientists, politicians and military experts that there is a real possibility of most of the civilized world being laid waste in the event of an all-out exchange of nuclear weapons.

God's Good Purposes

The prophecy of Isaiah 24–27 is that the wickedness of man will bring upon the world an event of enormous destruction. The prophet speaks about God laying waste the earth (24:1), because he believes that God is the God of the whole of history and that nothing happens outside his sovereign control. This does not mean that God wishes it to happen, or that God actually sets the events in motion. The whole of Scripture bears witness to the fact that God's desire for mankind is for his good and not for evil, for his welfare not for his downfall. Through the prophet Jeremiah God spoke a message to the people of Jerusalem in exile in Babylon. 'I know the plans I have for you, plans for good and not for evil, to give you a future and a hope' (Jeremiah 29:11). Similarly, he sent a message to the Christians in Rome through Paul, assuring them that 'in everything God works for good with those who love him' (Romans 8:28). Peter reassured the Christians in the early Church that 'The Lord is not slow in keeping his promise, as some understand slowness. He is patient with you, not wanting anyone to perish, but everyone to come to repentance' (2 Peter 3:9) NIV.

Jesus himself assured us that God has good purposes for the whole world. John 3:16 and 17 declares God's universal love and desire that every individual 'should not perish but have eternal life'. Jesus assures us that God's purpose in sending the Son into the world was 'not to condemn the world but that the world might be saved through him'. In the same passage Jesus refers to the central tragedy in the history of mankind 'that the light has come into the world and men loved darkness rather than light, because their deeds were evil' (John 3:19). Thus at one and the same time Jesus speaks both of the love of God and of judgement. God's purposes for the whole of mankind are good because of his great love for all men and women who are his children, his own creation, whom he longs to embrace as beloved children within his family.

The free will that God has given us enables us to come freely to him and to be able to enter into the full relationship of sonship, but it also carries with it the possibility of deliberate rebellion and rejection. When we reject God we are rejecting the good, we are choosing the darkness rather than the light, we are turning our backs upon love, for God is good. He is the essence of light; his nature is love. To reject goodness, to walk in the darkness, is to turn our backs upon love, which is the essence of sin. It leaves us without protection and totally exposed to the forces of evil that hold sway in this world. We become children of darkness who hate the light and do not come to the light in case our evil deeds are exposed (John 3:20). Once men choose darkness and reject the light they are no longer led by the Spirit of the Lord as sons of God, but they are driven by the forces of evil as children of darkness, with inevitable consequences in a world order that is controlled by the laws that God has laid down from the foundation of the universe.

The nature of God's creation of the universe is such that there is an intimate relationship between the spiritual and the physical worlds. There is a metaphysical relationship between man as a spiritual being and the physical world in which he lives and moves and has his being. We see the same kind of relationship existing within each man as an individual since we have both a spiritual and physical nature. Our spiritual nature and our physical body are closely related; indeed they are indivisible during our earthly lives. Whatever affects one part of our being also affects the other. Thus physical disease causes mental anguish and may even cause spiritual suffering. In reverse, spiritual disorder may be a cause of physical disease. There are certain types of physical ailment, such as skin diseases, that are known to be closely related to our spiritual and psychiatric health.

In the same way, there is a strong relationship between the moral and spiritual health of a community and the natural order of the physical environment in which they live. This in turn affects the physical health and wellbeing of each individual member of the community. For example, it is known that children growing up under the shadow of a motorway complex, where the atmosphere is constantly polluted by the exhaust fumes of motor vehicles, suffer from abnormal levels of lead poisoning, that stunts their physical growth and affects their glandular development and bodily health in a variety of ways.

Man's Sinfulness

The prophecy of world-wide devastation in Isaiah 24–27 states that this will come upon the earth as the result of the universal sinfulness of mankind. The three charges that are brought against men are:

1. They have polluted the earth.
2. They have transgressed God's laws and violated his statutes.
3. They have broken the everlasting covenant.

(Isaiah 24:5)

We shall be examining each of these charges in some detail in the following chapters, with the purpose of discovering whether or not this is the Word of God intended for our own day and age. If we do find that the prophecy is relevant for this present generation we shall want to enquire whether the destruction it foretells is inevitable or whether its primary purpose is to serve as a warning to mankind. For the moment, however, it is right that we emphasize the witness of Scripture, that God's purposes for mankind are for good and not for evil, but due to the very holiness of God's nature we can only enter into the fullness of fellowship with him as we are perfected through Christ. The power of sin in our lives is only broken through receiving what he has done for us through the cross.

The inevitable conclusion of this is that the vast majority of mankind, who do not know salvation in Christ, are driven by the forces of evil that Scripture tells us are the rulers of this world (Ephesians 6:12), the forces of darkness that are driving mankind towards self-destruction. It is as though a self-destructive madness had gripped mankind, and like the Gadarene swine we are being driven helplessly towards the edge of the precipice. There is an unbreakable bond that links mankind together, not simply because we share the same nature as part of the same order of creation, but because we live in the same natural environment and what one part of the community does affects the others. When one member of the community pours lead poisoning into the atmosphere, we all suffer from the resultant pollution. When the rulers of two nations go to war, all the citizens of those nations are affected. We are bound together as members of a family, a neighbourhood, a community, a nation, and as members of the race of mankind. No man is an island! We cannot live to ourselves alone. What we do affects others. Modern technology has given us the power of communication so that what happens in one part of the world can be instantly heard and seen by whole populations ten thousand miles or more away. Science has succeeded in transforming the world into a neighbourhood, but we have not thereby become better neighbours – only more dangerous enemies!

Despite the witness of the New Testament to God's great love for the whole of mankind, the witness of Scripture is equally strong that God will allow man the unrestrained exercise of the free will he has given him. God did not even intervene to prevent evil men from crucifying his own Son, but delivered him up for all. In allowing man the freedom to crucify Christ the purpose of God was not frustrated but fulfilled. God used the very occasion of man's most heinous crime for his own most glorious act of salvation. He turned the cruelty and death of the cross into the glorious new life of the resurrection. The cross and resurrection reveal not only the great love of God and the lengths to which he will go in order to save those of his own creation upon whom he lavishes his love, but they also reveal his purpose. His ultimate purpose for mankind is not to condemn and to destroy, but to save and to bring them into a glorious new love relationship with himself.

According to Isaiah 24–27, we may expect God to act in exactly the same way at the end of the age, when the time of the fulfilment of his purpose underlying the whole of creation draws to a climax. The day will come when the sinfulness of mankind will reach the pinnacle of evil. This will be the point at which man is capable of the ultimate blasphemy, that of the destruction of the creation that God brought into being with his own hands and saw that it was good, and the annihilation of man whom God created in his own image. At that point God will act in precisely the same manner as he acted at the time of the crucifixion. He will allow the sinfulness of mankind to go just as far as will fulfil his purpose, and then he will step in and bring about his own mighty act of salvation. He allowed Jesus to go to the cross, not sparing him the suffering of scourging and nailing to the tree. But although he allowed Jesus to die, he did not allow a bone of his body to be broken, neither did he allow his body to suffer corruption in the tomb. At that point the Father intervened with the mighty act of the resurrection that triumphed over death. In the same way God will allow man the freedom to vent his unbridled cruelty upon his fellow man. Nation will rise against nation and there will be let loose into the world terrible suffering that will encompass the whole of mankind.

Isaiah prophesies that no one will be spared the destruction that lays waste to the land. When the times of tribulation come upon the world and the forces of destruction sweep across the surface of the earth, no one will be spared. All will suffer. Even the righteous will be affected. They will not be *spared* the suffering but will be *brought through* it. None will be lost because the Father knows each one by name. The very hairs of their heads are numbered. They belong to the Son, therefore they belong to the Father. He has put his seal upon them, they bear his name, therefore they cannot be lost. But the Word of the Lord does not guarantee that they shall be spared physical suffering and death. He who spared not his Son but delivered him up for us all, guarantees eternal life to all those who turn to him, but nowhere does he guarantee to take them out of the world, only to keep them safe from the evil one while they are in the world. 'In the world you have tribulation; but be of good cheer, I have overcome the world' (John 16:33).

God's way is to save and to redeem through suffering. This is revealed to Isaiah in the greatest of all prophetic passages in the Old Covenant – Isaiah 53 – where he describes God's plan of salvation for mankind. He saw that at the right time God would send his Messiah who would be 'despised and rejected by men . . . but he was wounded for our transgressions, he was bruised for our iniquities; upon him was the chastisement that made us whole, and with his stripes we are healed.' In the same way, God would cleanse and heal his people through suffering. Isaiah saw that the destruction was inevitable because of the corruption and evil that had crept into the national life of God's people. But he saw that the future hope of Israel lay in a renewed remnant who would survive the destruction and return to God with whole-hearted commitment. 'In that day, the remnant of Israel and the survivors of the House of Jacob will not lean upon him that smote them, but will lean upon the Lord, the Holy One of Israel, in truth. A remnant will return, the remnant of Jacob, to the Mighty God. For though your people Israel be as the sand of the sea, only a remnant of them will return. Destruction is decreed, overflowing with righteousness' (Isaiah 10:20–22). The survivors of the exile would come back to their own land with great rejoicing as a spiritually renewed and cleansed people, 'and the ransomed of the Lord shall return, and come with singing to Zion; and everlasting joy shall be upon their heads; they shall obtain joy and gladness, and sorrow and sighing shall flee away' (Isaiah 51:11).

Similarly, Jeremiah saw that the exile was a necessary evil to get rid of the corrupting forces that had come into the life of the nation. He had a vision of two baskets of figs, one full of good figs, the other full of very bad figs. Those enduring the suffering of slavery and exile in Babylon were like the good figs whom the Lord would one day bring back and use to rebuild Jerusalem and to rebuild a new and holy nation. 'I will build them up, not tear them down; I will plant them, and not uproot them. I will give them a heart to know that I am the Lord; and they shall be my people and I will be their God, for they shall return to me with their whole heart' (Jeremiah 24:6 and 7).

Jeremiah shows that those who teach that God's people will be spared the suffering that will come upon mankind because they belong to the Lord, are false teachers. There were plenty of false teachers around in the last days of the old Jerusalem, who spread a false complacency amongst the people and removed from them a sense of urgency for repentance and openness to the Word of God. 'Thus saith the Lord of Hosts; "Do not listen to the words of the prophets who prophesy to you, filling you with vain hopes; they speak visions of their own minds, not from the mouth of the Lord. They say continually to those who despise the Word of the Lord, 'It shall be well with you'; and to everyone who stubbornly follows his own heart, they say, 'No evil shall come upon you''" (Jeremiah 23:16 and 17).

God does not change. His ways are the same today as they were in the days of Jeremiah. In the passage we have been studying, Isaiah clearly states that when the destruction comes upon the earth, no one will be spared: 'It shall be as with the people, so with the priest' (24:2). He says that if anyone escapes suffering in one part of the world, he will be caught up in another (24:18). Jesus did not promise his disciples a life of tranquillity, but persecution and suffering. He clearly foretold that 'They will deliver you up to tribulation, and put you to death; and you will be hated by all nations for my name's sake. And then many will fall away, and betray one another, and hate one another. And many false prophets will arise and lead many astray. And because wickedness is multiplied, most men's love will grow cold. But he who endures to the end will be saved' (Matthew 24:9–13). Jesus went on to speak of the coming destruction in the last days which will encompass the whole of mankind. 'For then there will be great tribulation, such as has not been from the beginning of the world until now, no, and never will be. And if those days had not been shortened, no human being would be saved; but for the sake of the elect, those days will be shortened' (Matthew 24:21,22).

The promise of Scripture is not that the righteous are spared the suffering that is common to the whole of mankind, but that they have the power to overcome all things and that God is with them under all circumstances and is actually involved with them in the suffering. That is the message of the cross, and it is through the cross and the resurrection that we have the victory. This is the message that Paul underlines with such power and conviction in Romans 8: 'Who shall separate us from the love of Christ? Shall tribulation, or distress, or persecution, or famine, or nakedness, or peril, or sword? . . . No, in all these things we are more than conquerors through him who loved us. For I am sure that neither death, nor life, nor angels, nor principalities, nor things present, nor things to come, nor powers, nor height, nor depth, nor anything else in all creation, will be able to separate us from the love of God in Christ Jesus our Lord' (35–39).

The message of Scripture is clear: God does not shield us from suffering, he enters into it with us and gives us the victory! In 1 Thessalonians 5:3 Paul warns against the false complacency of those who proclaim peace and security. He says that 'Sudden destruction will come upon them as travail comes upon a woman with child and there will be no escape'. In the previous chapter, Paul says that at the second coming of Christ, which will inaugurate the new era at the end of this age, there will be a joining together of the saints who have fought the good fight and are in glory with the Lord as the Church triumphant, and those who are left in the world at the time of the latter days and the fulfilment of all that is prophesied. He says that those who are alive 'who are left, shall be caught up together with them in the clouds to meet the Lord in the air' (1 Thessalonians 4:17). Perhaps the clouds will be the mushroom clouds of destruction that will cover the earth and blot out the light of the sun, when the evil of mankind lets loose the holocaust and destruction sweeps across the surface of the earth. Those who belong to Christ and have put their trust in him and who suffer and die in the tribulation of those terrible days will be caught up, as it were, between earth and heaven, plucked like brands from the burning, to link up with the saints in glory and to swell the shout of the Church triumphant at the coming of the King to overcome the powers of evil and to establish his reign of peace upon earth. As he comes to shorten the days, for the sake of the elect, and to quell the forces of destruction, their shouts of praise and adoration shall put a ring of glory around the earth that will herald the triumph of the Lord over the great enemy of mankind.

Perhaps the words of John in Revelation 7:14, 'These are they who have come out of the great tribulation', refer to those who are faithful to the Lord, who love him and trust him and who are brought through the terrible times of destruction to link up with the Church triumphant.

It may be of great significance to notice the presence of the little word 'the' in Revelation 7:14 in reference to the word 'tribulation'. The King James Version omits this and translates, 'These are they which have come out of great tribulation', which could mean any kind of personal trouble. But the Greek text uses a construction that very emphatically includes the definite article. It states: 'These are they who have come out of THE great tribulation.' This clearly refers to some great and catastrophic world event through which the faithful have lived and died. But it is an event that they have been brought through in triumph without the loss of their faith.

We are not, however, putting forward these suggestions as confident interpretations of Scripture. We are here moving in a realm of which no one can speak with certainty. There is no certainty that the second coming of Christ is to be linked with the world-wide destruction prophesied in Isaiah 24–27. We can, however, say with confidence that when the holocaust is unloosed and the times of tribulation come upon the earth, God will not allow the physical world to be finally destroyed, neither will he allow the whole of mankind to be annihilated. He will intervene at the right moment. He knows the exact moment when to act. At that point, just as when the soldiers came to the foot of the cross to break the legs of Jesus they found that God had already begun to act, so it will be when the holocaust of destruction descends. When the point is reached where the earth is about to be broken asunder and the whole of mankind is on the brink of annihilation, God will begin to act. According to the vision of Isaiah 24–27, when man lets loose the holocaust, God will do four things.

God's Action

First, he will break the world powers that are warring and threatening the ultimate destruction of the physical creation. He will break them finally and completely and so utterly decisively that the world capitals will never again be rebuilt, neither will the dominion of man's political rule ever be reestablished. The unjust regime will be at an end, the violent nature of man will be tamed and the way will be open, the stage set, for God to establish his own reign of peace and justice, of harmony and love in the world, that his will may be done on earth as it is in heaven.

Secondly, God will break the spiritual powers of evil, the unseen forces that have been driving mankind for thousands of years and influencing the course of history. They have been stirring up the violence and hatred within the nature of man which have led to all the cruelty, oppression and injustice that have left a trail of violence, destruction, human suffering and misery across the pages of history. How God will accomplish this no one knows, and there is no word throughout the Bible to suggest exactly how it will happen. There is, however, a small glimpse of these events that Paul refers to when writing to the Christians in Ephesus. He tells them in chapter 3 about the tremendous revelation of God's ultimate purposes that he has been permitted to see. Then he makes the almost incredible statement that at the climax of history, God will fulfil his purpose to break the spiritual forces of darkness by using the Church, the great company of the redeemed, the Body of Christ, to make known to the principalities and powers in the heavenly places the manifold wisdom of God.

It is of course Christ, and he alone, who will take on and defeat the spiritual powers of darkness, and his victory is already assured through the cross. There can be no doubt that God's mighty act of redemption is already being witnessed to the principalities and powers and has been witnessed to them for nearly two thousand years. This, Paul tells us, is the plan of the mystery hidden for ages in God who created all things (Ephesians 3:9). That great act of salvation will reach its fulfilment at the end of the age when the evil of mankind explodes into the greatest act of human violence, letting loose the holocaust into the world, and then God steps into the battle arena to hurl back the destruction and defeat the powers of evil both on earth and in the heavens. It will be through the great company of the redeemed on earth and in heaven, who will be rejoicing in the manifold wisdom and glory of God, that his great purpose will be unfolded to the principalities and powers (Ephesians 3:10). In the moment of their ultimate defeat there will come the realization and acknowledgement of the stupendous purposes of God for the whole of his creation, and especially for man made in his image. His saving purposes will be made known and his glory revealed to the entire universe.

The third thing that will happen is that God's kingdom will be established. Having broken the powers of evil that have held the whole created order in chains of bondage throughout the generations of mankind, God will now establish his own authority within his own creation. The tragedy of the incarnation is beautifully expressed in the Prologue of John's Gospel: 'The Word was in the world, and though God made the world through him, yet the world did not recognize him. He came to his own country but his own people did not receive him' (John 1:10–11). This tragedy will now be reversed. God's purpose in sending the Son, which was to make known his saving purposes, to accomplish his salvation and to make it available to all men, will now be fulfilled in the establishment of his reign of peace and justice in the world. His reign will be irresistible because there will be no powers to stand against him. All those who survive the devastation will see the establishment of God's reign upon earth, and beginning with the righteous who have been waiting for him and who shout with joy as they realize what has happened – that their God has indeed come to their aid and has won the victory – the praises of God will be sung right around the world until the whole world is ringed with praise and adoration. All mankind will at last accept God and acknowledge him to be the Lord, the King of Kings and Lord of Lords, Sovereign of all creation.

The fourth and final thing that will happen is that when the whole of mankind has accepted God and he is glorified in the world he will gather the nations to him and he will bless the whole family of mankind. God will lift the veil of suffering and take away mourning and sorrow from every heart. He will wipe away the tears from every face and there will be no more death. He will so bless his children that he himself will feed them with food that he provides: without money and without price. His love for his children is so great that he will provide the finest food for the greatest feast that he has had planned from the beginning of time. Then shall the wilderness and the dry land be glad and the desert will rejoice and blossom. The reign of God upon earth and his glorification will transform the whole of the created order that has been polluted and marred by the sinfulness of man.

Such is the revelation of the things that are to come that are prophesied in Isaiah 24–27. What we now have to do is to ask whether the circumstances leading up to the events foretold in these chapters correlate with the circumstances of the times in which we live. There are two sentences in the prophecy (24:5 and 6a) that provide a key to the understanding of the passage:

The earth lies polluted
  under its inhabitants;
for they have transgressed the laws,
  violated the statutes,
  broken the everlasting covenant.
Therefore a curse devours the earth,
  and its inhabitants suffer for their guilt.

In the next six chapters we shall be examining the charge that Isaiah brings against mankind that

a) Man has defiled or polluted the earth;
b) Man has disobeyed God's laws and violated his statutes;
c) Man has broken the Everlasting Covenant with God.

Our examination of the present world situation will of necessity be sociological in character. Its emphasis will, however, be upon empirical evidence rather than theoretical analysis. In two of the chapters, those on physical and moral pollution, the bulk of the illustrative material will be drawn from Britain because of the writer's familiarity with the British scene. This has been written, however, in the confidence that Britain is typical of the nations of the Western world and that similar material could be amassed for any of its other nations. The other four chapters are fully international in their illustrative material.

When we have completed our examination, if we find the case against man to be proven and 'therefore a curse devours the earth and its inhabitants suffer for their guilt', as Isaiah declares, we shall then seek for a word from the Lord to the nations of the world and to his Church.

CHAPTER FIVE

Pollution: The Physical World

Biblical Evidence

'The earth is the Lord's and the fullness thereof, the world and those who dwell therein' (Psalm 24:1). This is the central conviction that runs right the way through Scripture, that 'the Lord is the everlasting God, the Creator of the ends of the earth', as Isaiah put it (40:28). The Bible affirms that God is the creator of the whole universe, he created the earth out of a formless void (Genesis 1:2), he separated the sea from the dry land, he planted natural vegetation upon the land and gave the power of life to the natural environment. He created men and women and gave them life and 'dominion over the fish of the sea and the birds of the air and over every living thing', and he also gave them 'every plant yielding seed which is upon the face of all the earth' (Genesis 1:26,29).

It was this that caused the Psalmist to marvel that God, who created not only the world but the farthest galaxies of the universe, should care so much for man as to give him power over the natural order of creation.

> When I look at thy heavens, the work of thy fingers,
>> the moon and the stars which thou hast established,
> what is man that thou art mindful of him,
>> and the son of man that thou dost care for him?
> Yet thou hast made him little less than God,
>> and dost crown him with glory and honour.
> Thou hast given him dominion over the
>> works of thy hands;
>> thou hast put all things under his feet.
>
> (Psalm 8:3–6)

The power that God has given to man to exercise over the

physical environment is not simply a privilege, it is also a responsibility. God makes it clear throughout Scripture that he retains the ownership of the land. Each successive generation of man is like a tenant farmer who has temporary jurisdiction over the property, until one day he has to hand it on to others and is actually called to account for his stewardship during his time of occupation. The ancient Jewish laws of the 'Year of the Jubilee' ensured that this basic truth underlying the whole of creation was kept before the people, generation after generation.

At the end of every forty-nine years, the Year of the Jubilee was celebrated on the fiftieth. During this year all land that had passed into other hands through debt had to be returned to the original owners. This was not merely a social regulation aimed at curbing the acquisitive desires of the entrepreneurs and ensuring that the rich did not get richer at the expense of the poor, although God issued stern warnings against the monopolistic practices of the rich landowners: 'Woe to those who join house to house, who add field to field until there is no more room' (Isaiah 5:8). The major theological reason for the Jubilee was to serve as a constant reminder that the earth is the Lord's. He is the creator of all things. The land belongs to God not to man. God allows man to use the land and intends him to enjoy it. He gives us rain and fruitful seasons (Acts 14:17), but he does not intend man to despoil it.

Man has no permanent abode upon the earth, he comes from the earth and he returns to it, earth to earth, ashes to ashes, dust to dust. He will be called to account for his stewardship of the earth, for God watches over his creation and hates to see the natural beauty of the earth spoiled and disfigured: that which he created beautiful and perfect, scarred and marred by the wickedness and corruption of man. In the time of Noah it is said that 'The Lord saw that the wickedness of man was great in the earth . . . And the Lord was sorry that he had made man on the earth, and it grieved him to his heart. So the Lord said, "I will blot out man whom I have created from the face of the earth". And

God saw the earth, and behold, it was corrupt; for all flesh had corrupted their way upon the earth' (Genesis 6:5–7,12).

Empirical Evidence

'The earth lies polluted under its inhabitants'

The physical environment is the common heritage of mankind, it belongs to us all. This is both a blessing and potentially a source of great danger, since common property is always open to the abuse of those who do not have a high regard for the common good. Every advance in modern technology brings its own side effects, problems of waste disposal and dangers of poisonous pollution of the environment – of land, of water, of the air. In a world lacking strong international controls, men can exercise their own self-interest regardless of the consequences to others. What happens in one part of the world can affect the health and the livelihood of millions of people living thousands of miles away. Today, one of the greatest problems facing mankind is the devastating effects upon the environment of modern industrial processes, and the consequences of living in the great urban residential complexes in which more than half the world's population lives.

The problem of disposing of the waste from the world's ever-growing cities and the enormous pollution of the environment thereby caused is as great a problem as feeding the world's ever-expanding population. Potentially, it threatens the very survival of man when viewed alongside the present staggering growth of the world population. Over one million people are added to the population of the world every five days, which means that during the final twenty years of this century the world's population will actually increase by more than the total number of people who were in the world at the beginning of the century.[1] Nine-tenths of this population increase will take place in the third world,

---

[1] This will be dealt with at greater length in chapter 8.

where many countries will double in size. Nigeria and Bangladesh, for example, are expected to have as many people at the end of this century as the United States and Russia today, and India will have at least 1.2 billion inhabitants. Most of this third world population explosion is taking place in the cities, many of which are growing faster than the growth rate of the total population, and by the end of this century the largest of them will exceed thirty million. It is a mind-stopping exercise to try to imagine the amount of pollution pouring into the environment from such immense urban industrial conurbations.

In Britain there has been a growing consciousness of the increasing problems of pollution since the middle of the nineteenth century, when the dangers of bad water and the true implications of the industrial revolution were becoming clear. The rapid expansion of industrial towns meant that the meagre facilities for the disposal of waste simply could not cope. In Manchester, it is said, sewage ran in the gutters, and the life expectancy in the slums was not more than twenty years.[2] The Public Health Act, 1875 and the Rivers Pollution Prevention Act, 1876 began the process of controlling the unbridled pollution of the environment. But even so, it took four thousand deaths from London smog in 1952 to produce the Clean Air Act of 1956, and to have the whole of the city of London declared a 'smokeless zone'. Despite the enormous advances that have been made in the control of pollution throughout the developed world, the problem is one that is in fact increasing rather than diminishing, both due to the increases in population and to the advances in technology and the consequential problems of waste disposal. The three major areas of pollution of the natural environment are through water, upon the land, and in the air.

---

[2] Mabey, p. 17.

1. *Water Pollution*

In highly populated industrial societies, the easiest place to dump waste is in the rivers, but there can be no more deadly practice as this inevitably affects the health of the entire population and has untold side effects and repercussions throughout the world of nature. The two main sources of water pollution are 'people' and 'industry'. With people, the major problem lies in the disposal of sewage. Until the final quarter of the nineteenth century, it was common practice in Britain to dispose of raw sewage directly into rivers, with the consequence that many large cities had rivers running through them that were little more than foul open sewers. The stench of the River Thames through eighteenth-century London was notorious. It seems incredible that nothing was done about it until angling enthusiasts began to complain that fish were disappearing from the river. The last reported salmon in the Thames was in 1832!

(i) SEWAGE DISCHARGE

In Britain, more than 18,000 million litres of sewage effluent a day are discharged into rivers and streams. To this figure must be added a further 68,000 million litres of industrial cooling water, which of course is never returned to the river as clean as when it is drawn off. The river pollution survey of England and Wales published in 1972 showed that 60 per cent of the entire volume of waste discharged into British waterways consists of either raw sewage or insufficiently treated sewage effluent. The survey revealed that there were 437 discharges of crude sewage into rivers, although only 47 of these were into non-tidal waters. About half of all the industrial effluents released into British waterways were also considered to be unsatisfactory in terms of pollution.[3]

Some idea of the magnitude of the problem can be assessed when it is realized that many towns and cities in the

---

[3] Brooks, p. 44

UK are highly dependent upon rivers for their main water supplies. With the constant and increasing demands both from industry and for domestic purposes, our rivers would simply run dry in the summer months were it not for the recycling processes. This is a point made by environmentalist Peter Brooks: 'Our dependence on the return of effluents to rivers in order to maintain an acceptable extraction rate is strikingly illustrated by the situation that is existing along the non-tidal Thames. Every day, about 818 million litres of sewage effluents and 191 million litres of trade effluents are discharged into the river, from which each day the Metropolitan Waterboard draws off about 1364 million litres for purification prior to distribution in its mains.'[4] This means that Londoners are dependent for their drinking water upon purified sewage effluent, and it is estimated that every litre of water that flows down the Thames is actually recycled five times before it reaches the sea.[5]

It is not only our rivers and streams that are polluted, many coastal towns and cities discharge directly into the sea without any treatment. One of my own vivid memories is of a family holiday at a well-known Yorkshire seaside resort where my children and I were bathing in the sea, and suddenly found ourselves surrounded by large quantities of floating human excreta. It was a horrifying experience and I confess that, until that moment, I had no idea that it was permissible in Britain for towns to pump raw sewage direct into the sea where, given unfavourable conditions of wind and tide, it could be floated straight back on to the beaches. The practice is, however, not uncommon, as the map in Figure 1 indicates.

Peter Brooks notes that:

The simplest and cheapest method of disposal, is to discharge raw, untreated sewage and industrial effluent direct into the nearest water course or ocean. Although

---

[4] Brooks, p. 32.   [5] Mabey, p. 37.

FIGURE 1 *Discharges of Sewage to Estuarine and Coastal Waters of England and Wales.*

Million gallons per day (percentage untreated in brackets)

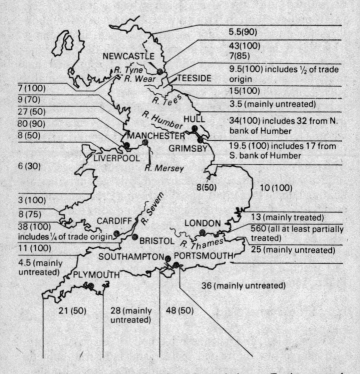

Source: Third Report of the Royal Commission on Environmental Pollution. Reproduced by permission of the Controller of Her Majesty's Stationery Office.

only a small proportion of the population's sewage is discharged raw into non-tidal waters, the sewage from about 30 per cent of the population draining to tidal waters was discharged crude at the time of the 1970 survey. Of the rivers receiving untreated sewage, the worst were the Tees (with about 500 discharges), the Tyne (with 270 outfalls), and the Severn (70 outfalls). So bad are the conditions on the Tyne that a new sewage scheme estimated to cost some 50 million pounds has been prepared, and a general cleaning up of the estuary as part of an urban renewal programme is also envisaged (*ibid.*, p. 46).

(ii) INDUSTRIAL WASTE

The map in Figure 2 gives an indication of discharges through industrial effluent into the river mouth and coastal waters around England, while the map in Figure 3 gives an indication of the overall position around the coasts of Scotland.

The problem of the disposal of industrial waste is a world-wide problem. It is also a very costly undertaking, and there are many private contractors who specialize in the business of the removal and the disposal of waste materials and substances. In Britain one national company handles some 9 million litres of liquid industrial waste every day. Much of this waste is taken in specially constructed and lined tankers and dumped at sea, just as most of the sludge from London's sewerage plants is taken by barge every day down the Thames and dumped into the North Sea.

The North Sea is in fact rapidly becoming one of the most polluted areas of water in the world. It receives not only the outfall of eastern Britain but also of western Europe. 'It has been estimated that some 5 million tonnes of sulphur dioxide, 1½ million tonnes of particulate matter, 1 million tonnes of nitrogen, 1500 tonnes of lead, 300 tonnes of DDT and 30 tonnes of mercury find their way into the North Sea

FIGURE 2 *Discharges of Trade Wastes to Estuarine and Coastal Waters of England and Wales.*

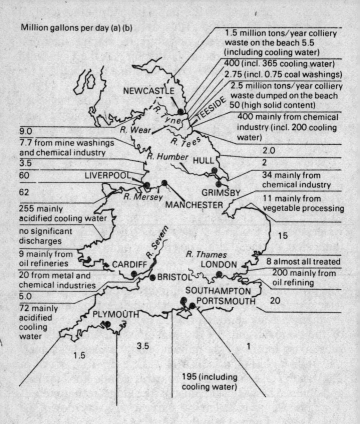

Million gallons per day (a) (b)

1.5 million tons/year colliery waste on the beach 5.5 (including cooling water)

400 (incl. 365 cooling water)

2.75 (incl. 0.75 coal washings)

2.5 million tons/year colliery waste dumped on the beach

50 (high solid content)

400 mainly from chemical industry (incl. 200 cooling water)

9.0

7.7 from mine washings and chemical industry

2.0

3.5

2

60

34 mainly from chemical industry

62

255 mainly acidified cooling water

11 mainly from vegetable processing

no significant discharges

15

9 mainly from oil refineries

8 almost all treated

20 from metal and chemical industries

200 mainly from oil refining

5.0

20

72 mainly acidified cooling water

1.5

3.5

1

195 (including cooling water)

NEWCASTLE

TEESIDE

R. Tyne

R. Wear

R. Tees

R. Humber   HULL

LIVERPOOL

R. Mersey   GRIMSBY

MANCHESTER

R. Severn

R. Thames

CARDIFF   LONDON

BRISTOL

SOUTHAMPTON

PORTSMOUTH

PLYMOUTH

(a) Excluding cooling water except where stated

(b) Except for solid discharges, which are expressed on a weight basis.

Source: Third Report of the Royal Commission on Environmental Pollution. Reproduced by permission of the Controller of Her Majesty's Stationery Office.

FIGURE 3 *Discharges of Domestic Sewage and Trade Wastes into Estuarine and Coastal Waters of Scotland.*

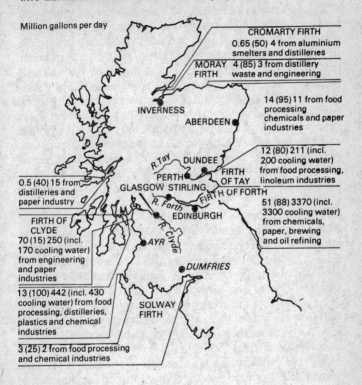

Million gallons per day

CROMARTY FIRTH
0.65 (50) 4 from aluminium smelters and distilleries

MORAY FIRTH 4 (85) 3 from distillery waste and engineering

14 (95) 11 from food processing chemicals and paper industries

12 (80) 211 (incl. 200 cooling water) from food processing, linoleum industries

0.5 (40) 15 from distilleries and paper industry

51 (88) 3370 (incl. 3300 cooling water) from chemicals, paper, brewing and oil refining

FIRTH OF CLYDE
70 (15) 250 (incl. 170 cooling water) from engineering and paper industries

13 (100) 442 (incl. 430 cooling water) from food processing, distilleries, plastics and chemical industries

3 (25) 2 from food processing and chemical industries

SOLWAY FIRTH

INVERNESS
ABERDEEN
R. Tay
DUNDEE
PERTH
FIRTH OF TAY
GLASGOW STIRLING
R. Forth
FIRTH OF FORTH
R. Clyde
EDINBURGH
AYR
DUMFRIES

Sewage discharges, percentage untreated (in brackets), and trade waste discharges

Source: Third Report of the Royal Commission on Environmental Pollution. Reproduced by permission of the Controller of Her Majesty's Stationery Office.

every year, all coming from the atmosphere and originating either in Britain or in other European countries.'[6]

The pollution of the River Rhine has on more than one occasion caused a European scandal, such as in June 1967 when one container of toxic material killed millions of fish. In 1972 a Dutch press photographer took a bucket of water from the Rhine delta near Rotterdam and had himself photographed with the bucket in his hand. He then developed the negative in the water! He was giving publicity to the fact that this chemically laden water is the source of the water supply for nearly half the population in Holland. As Britain and the rest of the European continent continue to pour pollution into the North Sea, which once yielded 5 per cent of the world's entire supply of fish, the fishing industry is shrinking since life in these once fruitful waters continues to decline.

(iii) POLLUTION OF THE OCEANS

Every year, the coasts around Britain and along the continent of Europe become more and more polluted with oil discharged from spillage or from the cleaning out of the tanks of the large number of giant tankers that use the Channel waters every day. The effects on marine life and upon sea birds are causing grave anxiety to conservationists. Not only are tens of thousands of birds every year destroyed by oil-soaked feathers, but they are also poisoned by eating affected marine life.

This is a problem that is not simply confined to the coastal waters of Europe, as Jacques Cousteau, the famous marine biologist, pointed out. He stated that during the past decade, life in the sea has decreased by 40 per cent. Thus the oceans of the world are becoming steadily polluted by the activities of man. The pollution stems not simply from the occasional oil-tanker disaster that spills millions of gallons of crude oil into the sea, causing untold damage to marine life and the devastation of miles of coastland waters when the oil slick eventually reaches land, but also from the millions of tons of

---

[6] Brooks, p. 39

rubbish that get dumped into the oceans of the world every year. Thor Heyerdahl, in recounting his voyage across the Atlantic in *Ra II* (1969–70), stated that they were never free from floating debris of all kinds, in complete contrast to his previous voyage in the *Kon Tiki* (1947), when floating rubbish was no cause for comment.

Water pollution is an immense problem in North America, where a great deal of industrialization has taken place around the Great Lakes during the past century. The effects upon the environment have been little less than disastrous in some places. It has been estimated that some 161 million kilograms of nitrogen, 27 million kilograms of phosphorus and 4082 kilograms of chloride are put into Lake Erie every year.[7] Reports from Ohio also indicate that there is so much oil on the surface of the River Cuyahoga, and so much inflammable gas floating up from the decaying sewage on the bottom, that it has been known to burst into flames![8]

Pollution resulting from the discharge of industrial waste is a continuous problem of world magnitude. With each new advance in technology, new difficulties for the disposal of waste are encountered as, for example, in the well-known problems of the disposal of radioactive waste, with its enormous potential hazards to human health and to life itself. The transportation of this waste presents considerable dangers, and there has been more than one major alert in recent years due to accidents whilst this waste is in transit. With the proliferation of nuclear power stations throughout the world, the problems of waste disposal are multiplied.

The problem of industrial pollution was highlighted as far back as the 1960s by what is now known as the classic case of mercury poisoning in Japan. Sometimes known as Minamata Disease, this occurred when quantities of methyl mercury compounds, formed during the manufacture of acetoaldehyde (a paint solvent), were discharged into Minamata Bay. The discharge contaminated fish which were

---

[7] Brooks, p. 36   [8] Mabey, p. 44

eaten by the local inhabitants. Many soon began to suffer from numbness in the lips and limbs, restricted vision, disorientation, slow and slurred speech, impaired hearing, constant trembling, loss of consciousness, and in some cases, death. The total number of people involved was in the region of a thousand.[9]

In a world where new industrial processes are constantly being developed, and with the rapid growth of cities during the final years of the twentieth century, a serious threat to the health of mankind is developing. It is estimated that by the year 2000, 50 per cent of the world's population of more than six billion will be living in cities of half a million or more. Unless there is firm international control of man's ever-increasing potential for polluting his own environment, there seems little hope that the situation will improve dramatically in the near future.

2. *Land Pollution*

There are many forms of land pollution, some of which result from modern methods of farming which include the widespread use of chemical sprays, pesticides and fertilizers. The farmer who accidentally allows half a can of pesticide to drain into a ditch may be starting a chain reaction as the ditch drains into a stream and the stream passes into a river. The pesticide which is poisonous to pests is also poisonous to marine life, to small animals and to fish. Young children are particularly vulnerable to chronic poisoning by pesticide and insecticidal residues. These produce a predisposition to cancer formation, and can also be the cause of cell damage and various illnesses. Much has been written about the DDT 'chains' by which DDT sprayed on to crops has found its way into soil and water. 'From water it has passed to the internal organs of aquatic creatures, who in turn have been eaten by fish which have been consumed by man –

---

[9] Brooks, p. 85

whose fatty tissues act as a store house for this chemical. The problems posed by chemicals generally are highlighted by the knowledge that DDT has been found in Adélie penguins and crabeater seals in the Antarctic, lindane in flour and other chlorinated insecticides in both human and cows' milk.'[10]

Modern methods of factory farming are also giving cause for widespread concern through a variety of side effects. This is particularly so in the use of antibiotics, which when added to pig and poultry feeds lead to faster growth rates and therefore to a reduction in the amount of food required per pound of live weight gain. This, of course, gives the farmer greater profitability through quicker turnover. In Britain, government controls have been brought in to prevent the use of such antibiotics, due to the fact that certain animal feeds may cause bacteria in the animal's body to become resistant to the antibiotic used. The resistant bacteria may then pass on their resistance to other bacteria of different types, which in turn may be transmitted to human beings who eat the animal flesh. These bacteria in man then become difficult to control with antibiotics, which in turn could pose serious problems for public health, particularly if there were an outbreak of such bacteria as typhoid.

There are therefore many forms of pollution which can be deliberately although inadvertently introduced by the widespread use of chemicals in the farming industry. Although the profitability of both arable and animal farming may be greatly increased by the use of chemical scientific technology, the dangers to mankind are also proportionately increased.

The application of contaminated fertilizers to the land can similarly produce infection. The bacteria can survive in the soil for a year or more, and they can be transmitted to animals through grazing on infected land. Infection can spread to farm lands from sewage sludge, effluents from cess-

---

[10] Brooks, p. 84

pools and septic tanks which can seep through the soil or through underground waterways.

(i) REFUSE DISPOSAL

A major form of land pollution is through the tipping of refuse. In Britain this is strictly controlled by national legislation, and supervised by Local Authorities to ensure that tips are on suitable sites with a minimal risk of pollution of underground water supplies through the tipping of household refuse in which the filtering action of the subsoil affects the processes of natural purification. The tips have to be adequately protected at the flanks, and covered at the end of each working day. 'By contrast, in the United States some 94 per cent of more than twelve thousand government-controlled tips are inadequate or inefficiently operated, and 70 per cent of 300 incinerators are without adequate pollution control devices.'[11]

Throughout the Western world the difficulties of disposing of refuse are compounded by the ever-increasing use of plastics and the notorious difficulty of getting rid of any plastic container after its use. In Britain, it is estimated that something like half a million tons of low-density and high-density polythene is used every year for disposable containers. These are used for food packaging, detergent and bleach bottles, as well as for a wide variety of container packs, plastic bags or agricultural sacks. There are great difficulties in disposing of all these containers since the plastics used are non-biodegradable. If they are buried in the ground they simply remain inert and indestructible, although the day is envisaged when a degradable plastic will be introduced, with all the consequent problems of additional pollution risks. Where a general policy of refuse tipping is not followed, and after sorting plastics are incinerated, there is the consequent problem of the production of noxious fumes.

---

[11] Brooks, p. 69.

(ii) INDUSTRIAL WASTE

It is, however, the dumping of industrial waste upon the land that is still the most serious problem of pollution. Such waste is often used for in-filling of land that has been taken for opencast coal mining, or for quarrying for sand and gravel. There are many other instances where disused mine shafts are used for the dumping of industrial waste that is otherwise difficult to dispose of. But always there are hazards of pollution involved. Even when harmless chemicals are dumped in this manner they can when mixed sometimes produce a chemical reaction that is highly dangerous and may poison the soil or seep into underground water systems, pollute vegetation or be eaten by wildlife.

With the expanding population of the world and increasing industrialization to meet expanding demands, the dangers of pollution of the earth increase daily. There are no really safe methods of disposing of many of the poisonous wastes produced by industry, but in addition to these known hazards, there is the constant problem of man's own untidiness and lack of concern for the natural environment. We pollute the land not only through the dumping of industrial waste but also through the fertilizers which the farmers use to make crops grow, and which sometimes cause pollution when the rain washes them into rivers. The chemical fertilizers make the water plants grow too quickly so that they choke the river and die. When they rot they take all the oxygen out of the water so that fish and marine life are killed.

Man is a problem to himself through his own careless misuse of natural resources, and through his predisposition to throw away things for which he no longer has a use. In Britain 700,000 motor cars are dumped every year in our throw-away society. Many of these are simply left on the roadside or dumped in the country, or left in lay-bys to rust and to rot, an eyesore and a hazard. The land that is such a precious natural resource – and upon which we are so completely dependent for our food and our health – we

111

constantly abuse and pollute with our manufactured poison and our domestic trash.

3. *Air Pollution*

Air is essential to life. Whereas we can reject food we know is unfit, or refuse to drink water which we believe is contaminated, we have no such choice with air. We breathe or we die. Even if the air is foul and we know it may be poisoning us, we can only hold our breath for a few moments before we are forced to allow our lungs hungrily to suck it in. For one period of my life, I used to walk along the Mile End Road in the East End of London daily during the morning rush hour, with three lanes of traffic in either direction pouring out noxious fumes. I used to try to measure my steps so that my air intake was minimal, but however hard I tried I couldn't help sucking in quantities of exhaust fumes, although I knew them to be highly polluted and poisonous to my body.

(i) SMOG
In Britain considerable strides have been taken in the past thirty years to rid the atmosphere of smoke pollution from domestic and industrial emissions. The London smog of 1952 was a national scandal that brought to a head the pressure to declare smokeless zones over our city regions. But while the burning of open coal fires and garden bonfires, plus the disappearance of coal-fired steam trains on the railways, and the strict control of smoke emissions from factories and public buildings, has done much to clean up the air over our cities, other forms of air pollution have been introduced in our ever-increasing technological society.

Aircraft and cars contribute considerably to the pollution of the atmosphere in all the major cities around the world. The Los Angeles smog in the USA is a well-known phenomenon. Three million cars are estimated to be on the roads of LA, and during the summer and early autumn high levels of air pollution are produced over the city that hang like a cloud, clearly to be seen by the naked eye. This is due to a heat inversion over the city that does not allow the exhaust gases from cars, and other polluting gases produced by the city, to escape into the higher atmosphere. 'The five million local inhabitants, half of whom live in the city itself, suffer intense irritation to the eyes, nose and throat, although this is neither long-lasting nor of permanent effect . . . It has been proved that the action of sunlight upon the air containing a high proportion of oxides of nitrogen and olefinic hydrocarbons has the effect of synthesizing them to ozone and nitro-olefins and these are the causative agents of the human symptoms.'[12]

The problem of motor vehicle pollution is a world-wide phenomenon. Exhaust fumes contain, in addition to water vapour, carbon dioxide, unburnt and partly decomposed hydrocarbons, carbon monoxide, oxides of nitrogen, lead, benzpyrenes and carbon particles. The diesel engine, by comparison with the petrol-driven engine, emits lower concentrations of pollutants, although if it is incorrectly operated and maintained, it can emit both smoke and offensive smells. The dangers of carbon monoxide emissions are, of course, well known. These increase during periods of acceleration and are invisible, odourless, tasteless and potentially lethal to human beings. Although on the city streets the safety level is rarely reached, people suffering from anaemia or heart diseases, as well as those who are heavy smokers, can be affected by much lower levels.

(ii) LEAD POISONING

The most dangerous form of pollution coming from vehicles of all kinds is that of lead poisoning, which comes from cars using petrol with an anti-knock compound tetraethyl of lead. In Britain, up until the announcement in the House of Commons in May 1981 of the phased introduction of new regulations to restrict the use of lead in petrol, the usual

---

[12] Brooks, pp. 115–16.

content of this compound was about three millilitres per gallon. It is combustion of this compound that produces a lead content in the exhaust gases, which in turn can be extremely injurious to health. Lead poisoning occurs when lead particles enter the body, usually through the lungs or digestive system. Even with relatively low levels of lead intake, the brain and the nervous system can be damaged. The symptoms of this are inability to concentrate, restlessness and poor learning ability. With higher levels, damage to the brain, heart and kidney is caused, sometimes resulting in death.

Young children are particularly vulnerable to lead poisoning because their brains and nervous systems are still developing. Children can absorb lead more easily and have less resistance to it than adults. Unborn children can be affected in the womb if the mother is exposed to lead poisoning through air pollution, resulting in serious damage to the child. The USA is probably ahead of the rest of the world in introducing controls on lead pollution emissions from cars. The Federal Government has, since 1968, successively been introducing measures to control the type of engine fitted to new cars and for the imposition of exhaust controls. Lead-free petrol has been available in the US for more than ten years, and considerable strides have been taken towards the elimination of this type of pollution. In Britain progress in this direction has been much slower, and although further restrictions were placed on the safe lead content of petrol in 1981 it has to be emphasized that there are no safe levels for lead intake to the human body.

Recent studies indicate that children's mental health is measurably affected at much lower levels than those previously thought to be dangerous. 'The two most thorough and significant studies are by Dr H. Needleman in Boston and Dr G. Winneke in Düsseldorf. Both measured lead levels in the teeth of children in urban areas and found differences in mental functioning; those with lower lead levels performed significantly better. Dr R. Stephens of Birmingham University was a member of the Department of

Environment working party which measured lead levels in the teeth of children living near Spaghetti Junction in Birmingham. Taking the results from Needleman and Winneke's studies into account, he calculated that it is likely that 20 per cent of children under thirteen in inner Birmingham are suffering from low level mental impairment as a result of their exposure to lead. Lead levels in Birmingham's air are typical for big cities, so the same proportion of children in other urban areas is likely to be affected.'[13]

The Birmingham studies are substantiated by research carried out in New York, where it was discovered that there is a highly significant correlation between the blood lead levels of children and the lead levels in petrol. This research was carried out over a six-year period of air pollution study. As the lead levels in petrol went up, so did the blood levels of the children, and both declined together as lead-free petrol was introduced. In Britain, about seven thousand tons of lead particles are discharged into the air from car exhausts every year. It is estimated that leaded petrol is responsible for at least 90 per cent of this atmospheric lead pollution in urban areas. Some of this lead is inhaled directly, while other particles settle as dust and can be taken up from the soil by plants. Professor D. Bryce-Smith of Reading University has calculated that for a person living near a motorway, some 80 per cent of the total lead intake is from leaded petrol.[14] This includes lead that is inhaled and dust that settles on food, cooking utensils and crockery. Corroborating evidence for this study comes from research in Denmark, which has revealed that airborne lead pollution affected grass up to one kilometre from the nearest road and was directly attributable to motor vehicles using leaded petrol.

The effects of pollution upon plants can also adversely affect human beings. Cattle grazing on grass near motorways absorb lead poisoning, while sulphur dioxide is readily

---

[13] Quoted from *Lead in Petrol*, Friends of the Earth, June 1980.
[14] *Ibid.*

absorbed through the stomata into the mesophyll of leaves and causes stunted growth or injury to many types of plants. In Los Angeles, locally grown crops of many varieties exhibit white or spotted areas on the surface through ozone injury, while throughout the world in many farming areas that are near industrial complexes, pasture land is contaminated by fluoride, which is eaten by cattle and adversely affects milk production and may be passed on to human beings.

(iii) INDUSTRIAL WASTE

The six most widespread air pollutants that are presently receiving intense international study by the World Health Organization are: 'sulphur dioxide; particles; carbon monoxide; oxidants; oxides of nitrogen; and lead'. (Brooks, p. 134). Industrial processes are responsible for most of these air pollutants, and they can often do immense damage over a very wide area. In Canada it was recently discovered that the very large Sudbury mining complex was emitting sulphur dioxide from its chimneys, and this was affecting forests of conifers in the surrounding area. Taller chimneys were then built to throw the poisonous fumes higher into the atmosphere. The result of this was simply to spread the pollution over a wider area. Prevailing winds carried the sulphur dioxide northwards and it settled on remote lakes a hundred miles away, forming sulphuric acid and destroying all life in lakes that were rich with different varieties of fish. This has been an ecological disaster of immense proportions in remote lakeland areas of hitherto unspoilt beauty.

Similarly, the Dryden Paper Company in northern Canada was found to be emitting inorganic mercury from the manufacturing of chlorine, and this was settling in rivers and lakes hundreds of miles away. The result was that mercury poisoning was found in fish in remote rivers and lakes renowned for their rich fishing grounds. All fishing of tuna and swordfish in these areas has now been banned, and many fishermen have lost their livelihoods. Marine life in some lakes from Winnipeg through to the Hudson Bay area has been severely affected, and it is said that it may be a thousand years before the lakes recover. The devastating effects of man's civilization upon the natural environment are incalculable.[15]

(iv) CITY ATMOSPHERE

Within the cities it is impossible to say how many of the diseases that afflict modern man are caused by pollution. It is well known that the lungs of city dwellers are much more dirty than those of people who all their lives have been breathing clean country air. The effect of air pollution upon city buildings should give us some idea of the potentially lethal effects of the air we breathe. In Britain the stonework of many buildings of great historical value is severely damaged by poisonous fumes in the air. York Minster, for example, which is constructed of magnesium limestone, has been badly damaged by sulphur dioxide in the atmosphere which, when it hits the damp surface of the stone, reacts with the limestone carbonate and sulphuric acid to form magnesium sulphate which is very soluble and easily washes away in the rainfall.

Similarly, damage to the limestone fabric of Cologne Cathedral has been blamed not just on industrial emissions but also on exhaust from railway engines in the nearby mainline terminal. Carbon dioxide in the air also assists in the corrosion of stone. The classic example of this is in London, where Cleopatra's Needle, which has been standing on the Embankment for little more than a century, has received greater damage from London's air in that short period than throughout the centuries it stood in the dry unpolluted air of Egypt. City dwellers similarly notice that clothes and fabrics, particularly net curtains, are attacked by acids in the air, and repeated washing of the materials spoilt by soot and smoke dramatically shortens their lives. Leather and bookbinding materials also suffer from sulphurous acids which they absorb, and precious books housed in city

---

[15] *Source:* Open University programme on Pollution, BBC Television, March 1981.

libraries throughout the world are often irreparably damaged.

(v) THREAT TO LIFE

It is, however, the damage to human life with which we are principally concerned, together with the long-term effects upon the physical environment that accrue from a combination of all forms of man's polluting activities.

The envelope of air which surrounds the earth is relatively thin, and about 95 per cent of this total air is concentrated in the first nineteen kilometres above us. The plain fact is that we simply do not know what are the long-term effects upon the natural order of mounting pollution on a world scale. There is accumulated evidence that the air around the earth has only a limited ability to disperse pollutants. Some scientists believe that irreparable harm is being done, which will prove to be a natural disaster of untold magnitude within the next few years. One expert writes: 'The more carbon dioxide there is in the air, the less the sun's warmth will be able to escape and the more the atmosphere will heat up. Since it is likely that the amount of carbon dioxide in the air will go up by as much as 25 per cent by the year 2000 there is good reason to be concerned. The earth will not have to heat up very much to melt large chunks of the ice caps causing weather changes, tidal waves and flooding all over the world. It is ironic that this particular pollutant, the one we can do least to control and know so little about, could turn out to be the cause of more serious changes to the world than any other man-made substances.'[16]

We have already begun to see the effects of some of these changes in the abnormal weather experienced in the northern hemisphere during the winter of 1981/2. The global rise in temperature caused ice to melt in the northern polar regions, which in turn caused the sea level to rise, which in turn caused cold air to be forced south bringing incredibly low

---

[16] Mabey, p. 90.

temperatures into Europe and North America. In some parts of Scandinavia and Britain, for example, temperatures were recorded lower than that of the South Pole. Throughout the northern hemisphere storms and flooding brought various degrees of havoc to areas unused to such climatic conditions.

4. *The Environment – God's Gift to Man*

The physical environment is man's common heritage, God's precious gift of natural resources that he has given into our human hands. Man's stewardship is not only selfish and irresponsible, but it may yet prove to be his own undoing. The earth lies polluted under its inhabitants.

Throughout the world, and especially in the industrialized nations, men are behaving with a reckless lack of concern for the natural environment and doing untold damage to the ecology of our planet. We are wasting precious natural resources, polluting the environment and defiling the whole created order of the world in which God has placed us.

In the crucial field of fuel energy, mankind still behaves as if all these resources – up to now so abundantly wasted – were renewable. The oil stock of our planet has been built up in a long process over millions of years, and is being blown 'up the chimney', within only a few generations. Exhaustion of these resources is foreseeable but their replacement by alternative fuels is not. Pollution and exploitation are all embracing, whether of the atmosphere, or soil, or the seas which are being over-fished with little regard to replenishment. Are we to leave our successors a scorched planet of advancing deserts, impoverished landscapes and ailing environments?

The grave consequences of increasing soil erosion and desertification should also concern all of us. Unchecked deforestation at its present rate, would halve the stock of usable wood by the end of this century (and deprive more than one billion poor people of their essential fuel for

119

cooking). The 'absorptive capacity' of trees, which check carbon dioxide pollution, would be reduced to a dangerous level. It is not just a risk to the environment, it is a plundering of our planet, without regard for the generations to come.[17]

The reckless policies of deforestation at present being pursued by mankind reduced the world's forest area by some 25 million acres during 1981. The continuation of such policies plus the ever-continuing expansion of world-wide urbanization and industrialization can only result in an ecological disaster of untold magnitude.

'The earth lies polluted under its inhabitants.' There is surely abundant evidence that this prophecy is being fulfilled in our own generation, not only by the kind of civilization that we have created but by the relentless pursuit of man's own self-interest and complete disregard for the consequences. Surely man has brought a curse upon the land. The world is part of God's own created order, that in the beginning he saw was good. It is we who have polluted the earth and thereby defiled the work of God's own hands. Can any man fail to fear the consequences?

---

[17] Brandt, pp. 19 and 20.

CHAPTER SIX

Pollution: The Moral World

Biblical Evidence

The Bible makes it clear that God created man to live within a moral order. Injustice, oppression, lies, and deceit are all roundly condemned throughout Scripture. They are seen as the kind of behavioural traits that act as corrupting forces in society. God reminds his people time and again that it is not possible to turn the moral code of the universe upside down without suffering the direst consequences. 'Woe to those who call evil good and good evil, who put darkness for light and light for darkness, who put bitter for sweet and sweet for bitter! . . . Therefore, as the tongue of fire devours the stubble, and as dry grass sinks down in the flame, so their root will be as rottenness, and their blossom go up like dust; for they have rejected the law of the Lord of hosts, and have despised the word of the Holy One of Israel. Therefore the anger of the Lord was kindled against his people, and he stretched out his hand against them and smote them, and the mountains quaked, and their corpses were as refuse in the midst of the streets' (Isaiah 5:20,24,25).

Hosea, similarly, speaks in the straightest terms of warning of the inevitable consequences of breaking the moral law that God has established upon the earth: 'Hear the word of the Lord, O people of Israel; for the Lord has a controversy with the inhabitants of the land. There is no faithfulness or kindness, and no knowledge of God in the land; there is swearing, lying, killing, stealing, and committing adultery; they break all bounds and murder follows murder. Therefore the land mourns and all who dwell in it languish' (Hosea 4:1–3).

Paul, with equal firmness, declares that the whole of mankind will be held responsible to God for their moral behaviour. He sees man being driven by the forces of darkness so that 'They were filled with all manner of wickedness, evil, covetousness, malice. Full of envy, murder, strife, deceit, malignity, they are gossips, slanderers, haters of God, insolent, haughty, boastful, inventors of evil, disobedient to parents, foolish, faithless, heartless, ruthless. Though they know God's decree that those who do such things deserve to die, they not only do them but approve those who practise them' (Romans 1:29–32).

When any society, nation or generation of mankind becomes so corrupt that the lives of men and women are given over to the kind of behaviour Paul was describing, they are not only in the gravest danger as individuals but the whole of their society is in danger of collapsing. They are breaking the moral code that underlies the whole social order of creation that God has willed for man whom he has created in his own spiritual image. Because God is holy and just, he cannot and will not protect a deliberately rebellious people who turn their backs upon what is just and right, and practise all manner of evil things thus bringing moral pollution and corruption into society. Through Jeremiah he warned the people of Jerusalem that their prayers and their religiosity would not save them from the consequences of their evil ways. Only repentance, coming before the Lord in humility and turning away from their wickedness would save them. 'Look, you put your trust in deceitful words. You steal, murder, commit adultery, tell lies under oath, offer sacrifices to Baal, and worship gods that you had not known before. You do these things I hate, and then you come and stand in my presence, in my own Temple, and say "We are safe!" Do you think that my Temple is a hiding place for robbers? I have seen what you are doing' (Jeremiah 7:8–11, GNB). Jeremiah then goes on to warn them in the sternest terms of the consequences of their folly and the destruction that will come upon their city.

In every generation the Word of the Lord is the same to a morally degenerate society. It is well expressed by Amos, who warned those 'who turn justice to wormwood, and cast down righteousness to the earth' to 'seek good, and not evil' that they may live. And he reminds them that God will not accept their worship or listen to their prayers until they turn away from the evil and corruption that has gripped the life of the nation. 'Take away from me the noise of your songs; to the melody of your harps I will not listen. But let justice roll down like waters, and righteousness like an everflowing stream' (Amos 5:7,14,23,24).

Empirical Evidence

'The earth lies polluted under its inhabitants'

A second, and equally deadly, form of pollution is moral pollution. Moral pollution rivals physical pollution in the swiftness of its effects upon human life and the depth of its penetration of every area of man's social and personal relationships. Twentieth-century man has polluted the world by his lack of moral restraint. Beginning as a Western phenomenon and closely linked to the rise of modern urban industrial city life, moral pollution has, in the closing decades of the twentieth century, spread to almost every part of the world.

Man's Enslavement

Millions of men and women, particularly those living in the world's great urban industrial complexes, find themselves enslaved or their lives in some way ensnared by some form of moral pollution. The high rates of marriage breakdown in most Western countries, with consequential weakening of family life and often devastating effects in the lives of children, are all attributable to the pollution of the moral world. Others are enslaved by some form of drug dependency, craving for their daily doses of nicotine, barbiturates, soft pot or the hard stuff, pep pills, tranquillizers, sleeping pills or alcohol – anything to counter the effects and enable us to cope with the demands of modern life.

By some strange and paradoxical twist of nature, perhaps only understood by Christians with their theology of man's sinful nature and God's plan of redemption, the present enslavement of mankind by forces generated within the moral world is a direct result of man's attempts to find freedom, true liberation and fulfilment for every individual within society. Most of the great social reforms undertaken during this century in Western countries have been enacted through basically humanitarian desires to give each individual greater freedom of choice in their lifestyles and liberation in the exercise of their individual abilities. But these humanitarian desires have been rooted in a basically humanitarian philosophy of life, that fails to understand the true nature of man and therefore has dismally failed to recognize the direction in which man would exercise his new-found freedom.

Alexander Solzhenitsyn, in his Harvard lecture, said, 'The tilt of freedom in the direction of evil has come about gradually, but it was evidently born primarily out of a humanistic and benevolent concept according to which there is no evil inherent in human nature.' It is this failure to take account of man's natural propensity to evil, and even to misuse something fundamentally good such as the freedom of the individual, that is the basic failure of humanistic attempts at social reform. It is this philosophical naïvety, characteristic of so many politicians in countries throughout the Western world, which has been responsible for the disastrous collapse in moral standards of life witnessed as each decade of this century has unfolded.

The lesson mankind has failed to learn, and still resists facing, is that you cannot have freedom without dealing with man's inherent drives towards evil. The lessons of history are perfectly plain. Men will exercise their freedom for their own self-interest, and under the guise of freedom men will engage in every form of self-indulgence, to the utter disregard of the interests of other individuals and the well-being of society as a whole. Hence unrestrained freedom both for the individual and for societies leads to moral pollution.

In the Western world humanistic naïvety has been compounded by the deliberate attempts of certain factions to undermine the moral stability of the nations as a means of achieving political ends. It is well known that there are two commonly practised techniques advocated by anarchists who wish to undermine the stability of a society. They are:

(1) to break down the cultural standards of morality by promoting pornography, and
(2) to discredit the family as an institution and encourage promiscuity and easy divorce.

Commenting on the present situation of moral values in Denmark, Dr Michael Harry, a Danish gynaecologist, traces a clear link between the free availability of pornography and the incidence of rape. He says, 'Since pornography became legal in Denmark the rate of rape has increased by 400 per cent and there is no telling of pornography's influence on promiscuity.'[1]

Similarly, Dr Olof Norgaard, who has carried out extensive research into the effects of sex education among children in Denmark, believes that there is a clear link between the type of sex education and promiscuity. He believes that where sex education deviates from a purely biological basis and teaches techniques of contraception it promotes sexual experimentation amongst children and leads to promiscuity. He states, 'Knowledge of contraception is an essential prerequisite to utilization, and it is unquestionable that increased knowledge causes increased use.'[2] Commenting upon this Dr Michael Harry adds' 'Contraceptive sex education increases unwanted pregnancies

---

[1] 'Ethics and Medicine 1980.' An address by Dr Michael Harry to the International Congress of the World Federation of Doctors Who Respect Human Life, University of Dublin, Trinity College, Eire.
[2] *Ibid.*

and abortions which would not occur under biological sex education.'[3]

Sex Offences and Rape

There has been a considerable amount of research in recent years on the incidence of sex offences, which supports the view that there is a clear link between the free availability of pornography and the occurrence of rape and violent crime. What the advocates of complete lack of moral restraints in society fail to realize is that indulgence in fact feeds the appetite, it does not satisfy it. With the gradual relaxation of the laws governing censorship in most Western countries over the past two decades, there has been a corresponding increase in crimes of violence. Removal of censorship governing the publication of literature and the showing of films in public or private cinema clubs has given an enormous boost to the production of pornographic magazines and books, often depicting scenes of sadistic sexual violence. When these scenes are also portrayed on the screen they feed the imagination and the passions, and arouse the most primitive urges even in normal human beings. With the paranormal they are highly dangerous and often lead to the most fearful crimes of violence.

It is difficult to obtain accurate figures for rape, since at least two out of every three cases are not reported to the police, either for fear of retribution, fear of publicity, a reluctance to talk about a horrifying experience, or simply due to the belief that the police won't be able to do anything about it anyway. Despite this large grey area of unreported crime during the decade 1964–74, the incidence of reported rape per 100,000 of the population rose in the United States from 11 to 26 per annum. During this same period the figures for England and Wales rose from 1.1 to 2.13, while in Australia they rose from 2.4 to 6.1 and, in New Zealand,

---

[3] *Ibid.*

from 4.4 to 9.1. This was of course the period during which relaxation of the laws governing censorship occurred. It was also the period during which the tidal wave of various forms of pornography that has engulfed most Western countries in recent years began to be generated.

Commenting on the link between pornography and rape, John Court states, 'There is not only a dismally similar upward trend in all places where pornography became widely available, but the increases show close proximity in time to relaxation of the pornography laws. The possibility that these trends might simply reflect general rises in the rate of violent crime has to be rejected, as I have shown that the growth curves for violent crime reports and for rape reports do not correspond at all well. For example, violent crime in the US rose on average 11 per cent per annum in the period 1960–72, with the rate reducing to 6 per cent per annum in the last three years of that period. Rape showed a 7 per cent annual increase over the same period but, by contrast, accelerated to 23 per cent in the years 1970–72. Pornography is the more strongly implicated in this acceleration when it is known that over the same period three countries which chose to take a firm policy against pornography (Singapore, Japan and South Africa) experienced no such increase. Indeed Japan achieved a significant reduction in its rape problem. This is of special interest in the light of an earlier cultural acceptance of rather violent sexual depictions, since it suggests that a curb on violent pornography can lead to a reduction in rape.'[4]

This phenomenon is perhaps most clearly discernible if we look at the increases in the rate of reported rape during the decade 1964–74 in terms of percentages.

---

[4] *Pornography: A Christian Critique*, pp. 50–51.

FIGURE 4[5]   *Increases in the Rate of Reported Rape*
1964–74

United States	139%
England & Wales	94%
Australia	160%
New Zealand	107%
Japan	−49%

Thus Japan, with its strongly restrictive policy restraining pornography, is the only country to have shown an actual decrease in the rate of reported rape during that period.

FIGURE 5   *Statistics for Rape and All Sexual Offences*

	Cases known to police of rape	Convictions for rape	Convictions for all sexual offences
1969	869	228	6500
1970	884	305	6660
1971	784	269	6760
1972	893	281	6475
1973	998	331	7169
1974	1052	343	7204
1975	1040	336	6800
1976	1094	330	6600
1977	1015	313	*7000
1978	1243	319	*7500
1979	1170	378	*7400

new basis introduced

Source: Criminal Statistics HMSO.

---

[5] *Ibid., p. 51.*

The above figure shows the situation in Britain in regard to cases of rape known to the police over the decade 1969 to 1979. It also shows the convictions in respect to rape and those in respect to sexual offences of all kinds. It indicates the steady increase in violence of this kind in British society. This is in line with what is happening throughout the Western world.

Violent Crime

We turn now to examine the situation in regard to violent crime. The following table gives the figures for crimes of violence in the UK.

FIGURE 6 *Crimes of Violence Known to the Police*

	1969	70	71	72	73	74	75	76	77	78	79
Homicide	392	393	459	476	465	600	515	565	482	532	629
Convictions for Murder	78	99	91	85	83	136	98	108	116	139	124
Convictions for Manslaughter	180	184	218	235	229	284	280	280	238	271	258
Violence against persons (1000s)	37.8	41.1	47.0	52.4	61.3	63.8	71.0	77.7	82.2	87.1	95.0
Convictions for violence against persons (1000s)	21.0	23.4	26.3	28.3	33.0	33.2	36.3	38.4	42.6*	42.6*	48.5*

*new basis

Source: Criminal Statistics HMSO

It must be emphasized that in all the above figures what we are considering is cases of violent crime actually known to the police. There is strong evidence to suggest that the actual rises in violent crime are much more considerable than are reflected in these figures. For example, research in the East End of London has shown that while cases of rape reported to the police in recent years have been falling, the actual occurrence of rape and attempted rape assaults have been increasing. For various reasons already referred to, women prefer not to tell the police. Another factor that is probably of even greater significance is the type of violence that is occurring. There is a considerable increase in recent years in street violence, in what used to be known as highway robbery but what is euphemistically referred to as 'mugging', i.e. robbery on the public highway with violence against the person. This is becoming increasingly common on the streets of all our major cities in Britain; so too is street fighting and gang warfare amongst youths. Often racialism is involved in these attacks, and many families belonging to racial minority groups are afraid to go out on the streets of British cities, especially after dark, because of savage attacks made upon them. Even in the shelter of their own homes many families live in fear, and it is not uncommon for a black family in the East End of London to be quietly watching television when a brick or a petrol bomb is hurled through the window. In most cases the police are totally unable to bring to justice the men of violence, which not only fans the flames of racial hatred but increases amongst ethnic minorities the sense of injustice by the police and by the whole of white society. From this arose the sense of outrage among the entire West Indian community in London over the unresolved mystery of the fire at a party in Deptford, at Christmas 1980, when a blazing inferno, started in suspicious circumstances, swept through the house and claimed the lives of thirteen black youngsters.

The high rates of vandalism, including arson, in most inner-city areas of British cities, causing millions of pounds' worth of damage to property annually, are a further indication of the rising tide of violence within British society. Violence against the person and violence against property have a similar root in the frustration experienced by the individual due to the conditions of modern life, together with the lack of moral restraint upon behaviour generally. This is compounded by the widespread social acceptability of violence in Western society. There is even an adulation of super-human strength and physical violence in many programmes on TV, including popular series screened at family viewing times and watched by millions of children and young people. Inner-city kids grow up with the idea that it is exciting to play real life 'cops and robbers', and to carry out in their own streets the daring exploits of terrorists and urban guerrillas that they see not simply in fictional entertainment programmes but in everyday occurrences on the TV news.

With such a permissive attitude towards violence throughout the Western world, it is small wonder that there has been a vast increase in the incidence of violence on city streets. The kind of mob violence that was seen in the riots in British cities in the summer of 1981 was both an expression of the pent-up frustration experienced by many young people in a situation of relative deprivation and high unemployment, and an indication of the social values that are becoming increasingly acceptable throughout the world. These values show a complete disregard for the sanctity of life, and a lack of respect for law and order. They permit the individual or groups of individuals, who have a real or supposed grievance against other persons or institutions, to take whatever action of a violent nature that they wish against other people or their property.

Throughout the world, violence is becoming commonplace. The world has grown used to scenes of rioting and looting on city streets; to scenes of hijacked airliners, with desperate gangs threatening to blow them up along with all their passengers. The news media give saturation coverage world-wide to the attacks of urban guerrillas upon foreign embassies, to the taking of hostages, to political massacres, to revolutionary coups, to the assassination of world statesmen, and to indiscriminate bombings and mass

131

murder. We live in an age where adults have become hardened to bloodshed and violence, and children grow up to believe this is normal behaviour. This is an attitude encouraged by the dramatization of violence in films and on TV, where violence, rape and murder are regularly offered as part of the diet of entertainment.

Drink and Drugs

The use and abuse of alcohol and drugs is also closely linked to the incidence of violent crime. It is well known that many of the most violent underworld vice rings are connected with the distribution and sale of drugs, where very large sums of money are involved. Police forces throughout the world devote a large proportion of their time and manpower to the uncovering and breaking of this type of crime, but although their efforts are not without success, all major Western police forces admit that they hardly skim the surface. The amount of undercover crime connected with drug abuse is a problem of staggering proportions in the modern world, bringing untold misery to millions of lives.

FIGURE 7 *Drug Statistics*

	1969	70	71	72	73	74	75	76	77	78	79
Registered Drug addicts	1466	1430	1549	1619	1818	1970	1952	1879	2023	2400	2810
Drug offence convictions -Indictable	NA	NA	NA	1216	1529	1547	1415	1593	1632	1740	NA
-Non-indictable	NA	NA	NA	11,490	11,988	9246	9067	9627	9667	10,292	11,711
Convictions for drunkenness offences (1000s)	77.0	78.1	83.0	88.2	96.8	97.9	99.7	103.2	99.9	98.0	105.6

Source: Home Office statistics.

The above figures for drug addicts, drug offences and drunken and drugged driving convictions give an indication of the current situation in Britain. The figures need to be treated with some caution, as only a small percentage of drug addicts actually register and are included in Home Office figures. The convictions for drug offences also only represent a small proportion of the actual crime committed. The figures are, however, useful if only as an indication of the steady increase in offences of this nature over the past decade. There is no doubt that drug abuse is a world problem of immense proportions, and is one of the reliable indicators of the level of corruption and decadence in the world today.

FIGURE 8 *Turnover on Gambling*

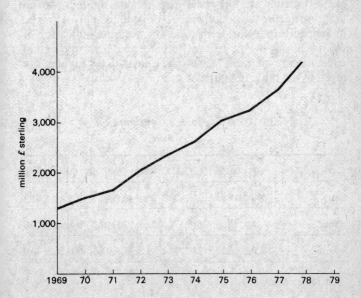

Source: Annual Review of the Churches' Council on Gambling

The graph in Figure 8 setting out the situation in regard to expenditure on gambling in Britain is a useful indicator of moral values in the nation. During a period of economic recession, when there have been stringent cutbacks in expenditure on the arts and many worthwhile social projects, the nation's self-indulgence in gambling has continued unabated. The figures show the staggering total of more than £4000 million, being the gross amount staked and representing annual turnover. The steady rise of more than 250 per cent over the decade is also an indication of declining moral standards and the desire to get something for nothing in an acquisitive society.

In an examination of the situation in regard to expenditure upon alcohol in Britain, the figures show a similar colossal increase year by year throughout the past decade. However, they are not given here because the increases in taxation during the period make it difficult to analyse the rise in expenditure in real terms. A more accurate indication of the situation in Britain can be perceived from the actual consumption of beer, wines and spirits. The Figures are given in the table in figure 9.

FIGURE 9 *Alcohol Consumption*

	69	70	71	72	73	74	75	76	77	78	79
Beer[1]	33.4	34.4	35.8	36.7	38.3	39.1	40.1	40.7	40.3	41.4	41.7
Wine[2]	44.8	45.8	53.9	61.9	78.5	82.5	77.5	80.7	78.4	92.4	100.0
Spirits[2]	17.5	20.1	21.1	24.2	30.1	33.2	31.6	35.6	30.1	36.5	40.0

[1]in millions of barrels

[2]in millions of gallons

Source: HM Customs & Excise.

The above figures show that while there has been a steady increase of 25 per cent in beer consumption over the decade, there has been a startling increase of 123 per cent in wine consumption and of 129 per cent in that of spirits. These massive increases underline the rapid increase in alcoholism in Britain. It is a serious social problem not simply in Europe and the West but in many other countries throughout the world.

Probably the most telling indicator of moral and social values in Britain is shown in the following figure, indicating that overall the British people spend more upon alcohol than they do upon basic foodstuffs.

FIGURE 10 *Relative Spending Patterns*

	1969	70	71	72	73	74	75	76	77	78	79
Basic foodstuffs in £1000m	2.45	2.6	2.82	3.01	3.56	4.16	4.9	5.58	6.41	7.31	8.36
Alcohol in £1000m	2.03	2.3	2.59	2.91	3.42	3.92	4.86	5.84	6.54	7.47	8.87

Source: Central Statistics Office

A further indication of the unsound basis of moral values in modern Britain may be seen in the nation's attitude towards smoking. There has been a great deal of research carried out both in Europe and in the USA over the past twenty-five years, which clearly shows a direct relationship between tobacco smoking and the incidence of lung cancer. Despite this, smoking is still socially acceptable amongst millions of people, and in spite of certain curtailments on advertising the tobacco trade continues to flourish unabated.

FIGURE 11 *Expenditure on Tobacco Advertising*

	1967	68	69	70	71	72	73	74	75	76	77
£millions	4.19	4.11	4.22	4.26	5.33	5.44	6.24	16.64	21.51	30.88	30.67

Source: Nationwide Festival of Light

The above figures show the tremendous increase in expenditure on tobacco advertising of some 632 per cent during the decade 1967–77. During the same period deaths due to lung cancer increased by more than 20 per cent. It seems incredible that in an intelligent society, where it is clearly proved that smoking is one of the causes of lung cancer, the effects of social education to try to dissuade people from damaging their health are deliberately undermined by advertising campaigns aimed at increasing nicotine dependence. Those who ignore the evidence and indulge in smoking and who contract lung cancer are not only recklessly throwing away their own lives, but also committing a sin against society in taking up hospital beds and being given medical care at the expense of the rest of the community. It is thus a moral issue.

A further indication of the disregard for life is seen in the figures for alcohol advertising and the convictions of drunken drivers.

The staggering increase of nearly 2000 per cent in expenditure on alcohol advertising during a ten-year period is not merely an indication of defective moral values, but it is a national scandal when seen in relation to the very clear link between alcohol consumption and road accidents. We continue to slaughter more than 7000 people on the roads of Britain annually, and in a high proportion of these road deaths, certainly more than half, the drivers involved have been drinking alcohol. The rise in the number of convictions

FIGURE 12 *Expenditure on Alcohol Advertising Related to Convictions for Drunken Driving*

	1967	68	69	70	71	72	73	74	75	76	77
Alcohol advertising (£millions)	1.99	2.23	2.49	3.03	3.21	4.17	14.74	27.91	32.98	37.60	40.09
Convictions for drunken driving	10.04	20.96	22.81	25.41	37.81	45.9	53.53	53.88	55.8	47.52	44.83

Source: NFOL

for drunken driving of more than 340 per cent during the decade 1967–77 is not simply an indication of changes in the law and more vigilant policing methods, it is also due to the actual increase in the incidence of drunken driving. This in turn is but one indication of the serious social consequences of the rising tide of alcoholism, not only in Britain and Europe, where these figures are matched, but also throughout the Western world. Yet society still tolerates vast expenditure on alcohol advertising, which encourages children and young people to become habitual drinkers and blinds them to the terrible dangers involved not only in drinking and driving but also to the dangers to physical and mental health.

Abortion

The disregard for the value of life that is one of the characteristics of twentieth-century man is nowhere seen more clearly than in the abortion of unwanted pregnancies. Many Western nations have made legal abortion easy to obtain, not simply on medical grounds due to the endangering of the life or health of the mother, or due to the risk of serious disease, or in the case of a pregnancy resulting from rape, but the conditions have been so liberalized as to provide virtually for abortion on demand. This is so in the cases of Britain and Denmark. The significance of the abortion laws of a country lies in the fact that they provide an indication of the value of human life in the general regard of that nation. Throughout history it has only been in the most corrupt societies that medical bodies have condoned or practised abortion, infanticide and euthanasia. The decaying Roman empire and the Nazi regime, where abortion techniques were developed on Jews and Gypsies, provide two such examples.

In 1948 the World Medical Association meeting in Geneva reaffirmed and updated the Hippocratic Oath which sets the standard followed by most medical practitioners. They did this following the second world war, when millions of innocent men, women and children had been slaughtered, as well as members of the armed forces, in the conflicts in Europe, North Africa and the Far East. It was a time when the world was reeling under the impact of man's inhumanity to man, and doctors were most conscious of the dangers of undermining respect for human life. The doctors made a solemn declaration: 'I will maintain the utmost respect for human life from the time of conception. Even under threat, I will not use my medical knowledge contrary to the laws of humanity' (Declaration of Geneva adopted by the World Medical Association, September 1948).

Underlying the social expediency and the personal indulgence of the pro-abortionists who campaign under such slogans as 'A woman's right to choose' is the fallacious argument that the unborn child is not really a human being, therefore only the mother has any rights. The unborn child is referred to as a 'foetus' rather than a baby, in order to play down the reality that in abortion a human life is being destroyed. The foetus is in fact a human being, and is recognizably so, from the moment of conception. At thirty

138

days, before most women even realize they are pregnant, the foetus has its liver, kidneys, lungs, a heart pumping blood, a brain of unmistakable human dimension and a distinct personality of its own.

The mystery of human life is one of the continuing miracles of creation, before which man in every generation stands in awe. David beautifully expresses this in Psalm 139: 'You created every part of me; you put me together in my mother's womb. I praise you because you are to be feared; all you do is strange and wonderful. I know it with all my heart. When my bones were being formed, carefully put together in my mother's womb, when I was growing there in secret, you knew that I was there – you saw me before I was born' (Psalm 139:13–15, GNB).

The biblical view is that all human life is sacred. The commandment 'Do not commit murder' (Exodus 20:13, GNB) does not simply apply to Jews or to Christians or to the religious, but to the whole of mankind. This is underlined by the story of God's reaction of abhorrence to the murder of Abel by his brother Cain in Genesis 4. But the biblical understanding of human life is also that it begins not at birth but at conception. This is clearly implied in the words of the Psalmist quoted above. He speaks of God knowing him before he was born, while he was being carefully put together in his mother's womb. This is a beautiful and inspired description of the creation of a human being, that not only reflects the spiritual truth of man being created in the image of God but is also physiologically accurate, although stemming from a period many hundreds of years before the development of modern medical science. What we know today underlines the accuracy of the Psalmist's words and supports the biblical view that human life begins in the womb and not simply at birth. The chart in Figure 13 shows the development of the unborn child from the moment of conception on day one through to the birth of the baby thirty-six weeks later.

FIGURE 13 *The First Weeks of Life*

Day 1	Conception – sperm and ovum meet in fertilization. Genetic make-up complete. Colour of eyes, hair, sex and even build determined. A unique individual is present in the womb.
Day 17	Development of own blood cells. Placenta established.
Day 20	Foundation of entire nervous system established.
Day 21	Heart starts to beat. This is at least as dramatic as birth.
Day 30	Regular blood flow within closed vascular system. Ears and nose start to develop.
Day 42	Skeleton complete and reflexes present. Liver, kidneys and lungs formed.
Day 43	Electrical brain wave patterns can be recorded.
Day 56	All organs functioning; growth and maturity are all that occur now, in the same way that a child grows into an adult.
Day 65	The baby can make a fist and will grasp an object stroking his palm; will also leap up and down in womb with movements co-ordinated.
Week 16	Baby is half birth length and its heart pumps 50 pints of blood daily.
Week 20	Hair appears on the head. Weight – 1lb. Height – 12 inches.
Week 28	Eyes open. Baby can hear mother's digestive processes and heartbeat. Social abortions performed up to this time in Britain.
Week 36	Birth – just another stage in an already well advanced process. From the above it is clear that the baby can feel pain at a very early stage. We are, therefore, destroying babies legally and painfully up to 7 months after conception.

Christian tradition has from the time of the early Church been firmly against anything that might undermine the sacredness of human life, including that of the unborn child. The Didache, one of the earliest known Christian writings outside the New Testament, clearly states: 'Thou shalt not kill the foetus in its mother's womb.'

In modern times both Protestants and Catholics have re-affirmed this view, although Catholics have probably been the most faithful to it. Pope John Paul II, speaking in Ireland in 1979 said, 'So I say to all, have an absolute and holy respect for the sacredness of human life from the first moment of its conception. To attack unborn life at any moment from its conception is to undermine the whole moral order which is the true guardian of the well-being of man. The defence of the absolute inviolability of unborn life is part of the defence of human rights and human dignity.' The same view was put forward by Protestants in Scotland: 'Though poles apart in vital doctrine from the Church of Rome, we yet join with them in this biblical regard for human life, including that of the unborn babe' (*The Monthly Record*, official organ of the Free Church of Scotland, May 1974).

The Lambeth Conference of the Church of England is also on record as taking the same view: 'In the strongest terms Christians reject the practice of induced abortion, or infanticide, which involves the killing of a life already conceived (as well as a violation of the personality of the mother) save at the dictates of undeniable medical necessity . . . The sacredness of life is in Christian eyes an absolute which must not be violated' (Statement of the Lambeth Conference of Bishops, 1958).

Despite all the assurances of pro-abortionists, there is massive evidence to show that the liberalization of the laws on abortion in fact results in the cheapening of the view of human life, and also plays a major role in undermining the basis of the moral order upon which the foundations of modern civilization rest. In Denmark, where precise statistics of abortion have been kept over a considerable period, careful research of this question has been possible. From 1939 the law permitted the termination of a pregnancy (1) to avoid serious danger to the mother's life or health, (2) after rape, incest or under-age intercourse, (3) where a distinct danger of inherited mental disease or deficiency, or severe mental or physical illness, could be ascertained. Then in 1970 the law was liberalized and in 1973 abortion on demand up to the end of the twelfth week of pregnancy was made lawful. Large increases in abortions occurred from 1970 onwards, that according to Dr Olof Norgaard were directly caused by the laws enacted by the Danish parliament. Danish figures also show that the legalization of abortion does not lead to a decrease in the number of illegal abortions. Writing in the *World Medical Journal* in reference to the Danish experience, Dr Norgaard has stated: 'We can therefore establish as a fact that liberalization of the last two abortion laws has evoked a vast increase in legal abortions without a simultaneous decrease in illegal abortions.'[6]

In Britain the Abortion Act became law in 1968, and during the first ten years of its operation over 1,300,000 unborn babies were killed in National Health Service hospitals and state-licensed private abortion clinics. Although it was never the intention of the legislators that Britain should have abortion on demand, figures show that 97 per cent of women who make use of the so-called 'pregnancy advisory services' do in fact have abortions. Moreover, although the intention of the legislature was to make abortion available to those with health or mental health problems or to give relief to those hard-pressed women with large families, statistics do in fact reveal that only about 2 per cent of the UK subjects who have abortions are women who come into these categories. Thus 98 per cent of those who have abortions are outside the 'hard cases' for whom the Abortion Act was supposedly intended.

The British experience is in fact that abortion has become respectable and a part of daily life at a time when medical, social and economic reasons for it are less urgent than ever before in human history. Moreover the free availability of abortion has not brought about the decline in illegitimacy

---

[6] *World Medical Journal*, Volume 26, No. 4, July/August 1979.

which was confidently forecast in 1967. In fact the rate of illegitimacy has actually risen in comparison with the general birth rate. Over the period from 1960 to 1977 the general birth rate fell from 90 per thousand live births to women of child-bearing age to 55 per thousand. During the same period the rate of illegitimacy rose sharply as the following graph indicates.

FIGURE 14 *Illegitimate Live Births (England and Wales)*

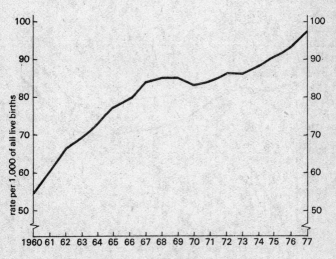

Source: Life publication, 'Save the Unborn Child'.

The graph in Figure 14 indicates a remarkable change in the moral values and behaviour of British society. The figures show that at a time when the overall birth rate has been falling sharply there has been a 3 per cent increase in the number of illegitimate births. This fact is the more remarkable when we consider that it is during this same period that there has been a greater emphasis upon sex education, enormous increases in the availability of contraceptive medication and devices together with the free availability of abortion. The figures reveal that illegitimacy no longer carries any social stigma, and that sexual promiscuity is becoming accepted as a normal part of everyday life for increasing numbers in Western society.

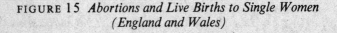

FIGURE 15 *Abortions and Live Births to Single Women (England and Wales)*

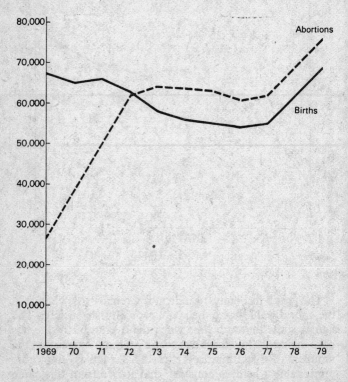

Source: NFOL

The graph in Figure 15 showing a comparison between the figures for abortions and live births to single women over the past decade indicates that while the number of abortions is rising so too is the number of illegitimate births. No doubt, the figures are also an indication that the family, built upon a stable marriage union, is no longer the bedrock of British society.

The following table sets out the statistics in relation to abortion in Britain:

FIGURE 16 *Legal Abortions (England and Wales)*

	69	70	71	72	73	74	75	76	77	78	79
To married women in 1000s	23.0	34.3	41.5	46.9	46.8	45.1	43.1	40.3	39.6	42.2	42.8
To single women in 1000s	27.0	41.7	53.5	62.1	64.2	63.9	62.9	60.7	62.4	69.8	76.2
Total in 1000s	50	76	95	109	111	109	106	101	102	112	119
To under 16s in 1000s	1.17	1.73	2.3	2.8	3.09	3.33	3.57	3.42	3.62	3.3	3.37

Source: Social Trends, HMSO

It will be seen from the above figures that while there was a fluctuation in the number of registered abortions during the period 1968–77 among married women, the overall increase was 86 per cent. Similarly there was a fluctuation in the annual figures over the same period for single women in England and Wales, but the overall rise was 182 per cent. Among girls under sixteen years of age, however, there was a remarkable increase of 722 per cent, from a mere 566 in 1968 to 3620 nine years later. When we consider the fact that these are schoolgirls below the age of legal consent for sexual intercourse some indication may be gained of what is happening to sexual standards of morality in Britain.

FIGURE 17 *Abortions, Live & Still Births for All Women, Single Women & Women Under 16 Years (England and Wales)*

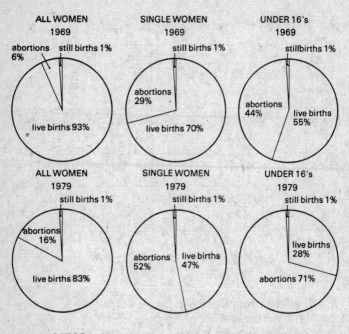

Source: NFOL

The charts in Figure 17 set out clearly the situation after ten years of legalized abortion in Britain. The Act that was designed to defend life and to be of particular help to older married women, and to cut out unwanted pregnancies within marriage, has had the opposite effect. There has been only a relatively small increase in abortions amongst married women but massive increases amongst single women and girls under sixteen. The Act has materially assisted in promoting sexual promiscuity due to the free availability of abortion, and it has undermined the sanctity of life as one of the basic values of civilized society.

FIGURE 18 *Ratio of Live Births to Abortions*

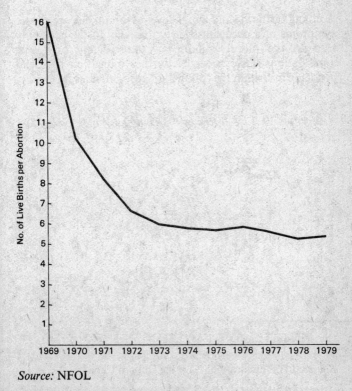

Source: NFOL

The above graph shows that during the decade 1969 to 1979, the ratio of live births to abortions in Britain fell significantly. The actual figures show that there was one abortion to every sixteen live babies born in 1969, whereas in 1979, there was one abortion for every five live births. This is a salutary and significant increase which should cause every thinking man and woman to pause and to consider seriously the inevitable consequences to life in Britain if this trend continues.

Falling Birth Rate

A falling birth rate and a high level of infanticide are classic symptoms of a decadent society that can, in the end, only lead to the moral collapse of that society or to its annihilation. If we needed a further indication of social genocide in Britain the following figure provides it.

FIGURE 19 *Live Births in England and Wales 1960–77*

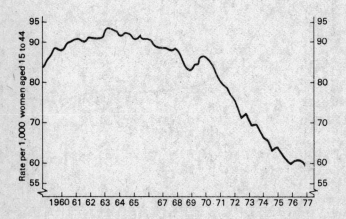

Source: LIFE publication, 'Save the Unborn Child'.

It is surely a sign of the moral decadence of our society that in Britain today we hold life so cheaply that we can kill a million unborn babies every six years. By the end of this century we shall have killed more infants than Hitler murdered Jews in the holocaust of Europe during the days of the Third Reich. But it is an even more remarkable fact, perhaps indicating some form of national genocide, that we should be killing our babies in such vast numbers at a time when there is a general fall in the birth rate in Britain. Even if we were to add all the legal abortions granted to British residents to the number of live births in England and Wales over the period 1968–77 there would still be a dramatic fall in the birth rate, as the following graphs indicate.

FIGURE 20 *Abortions Under the 1967 Act (England and Wales)*

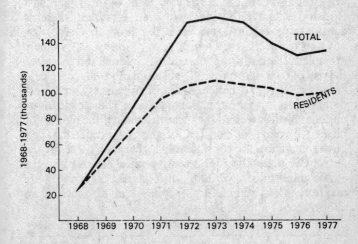

Source: Ibid.

FIGURE 21 *Live Births in England and Wales 1963–77 (thousands)*

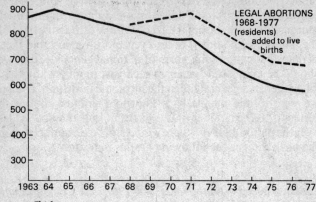

LEGAL ABORTIONS 1968-1977 (residents) added to live births

Source: Ibid.

We must also consider the decline in the birthrate amongst British residents, together with the fact that there is considerable medical evidence to show that abortion adversely affects the reproductive ability of women, prejudices the health of subsequent children and increases the risk of their deformity.[7] There is, on this evidence, a case for suggesting that there exists in British society an almost paranoic death-wish for national suicide. The decline in the national birth rate is all the more dramatic if the figures for births to women of non-UK origins are extracted. Their birth rate figures are considerably higher than those for the native UK population. For many women belonging to the ethnic minorities in Britain, their higher birth rates are due to religious and cultural factors which also include an abhorrence of abortion.

---

[7] See *British Medical Journal*, 1, 1976, p. 1303–4, 'A Study of the Effects of Abortion on Subsequent Pregnancy'. Also see *Royal Society of Health Journal*, August 1972 and *The Lancet*, October 1971.

In plain terms this means that while the non-white population continues to increase steadily there is a dramatic down-turn in the birth rate of the white population. This has been accelerated by a combination of the free availability of contraception and the legalizing of abortion. If this trend continues the effect will be a dramatic change in the racial balance of the British population so that by the end of this century some UK cities will have mainly non-white populations. It will be a strange quirk of history if during the century which began with Britain ruling over the most extensive empire in the history of the world, that same century ends with Britain being ruled over by the sons of those over whom she once ruled. From a Christian stand-point a man's racial origins are totally irrelevant, in the same way as social class distinctions and sex are irrelevant within the Christian community and in the eyes of God (Galatians 3:28). But while for the Christian social distinctions are meaningless, there is no doubt that for some British people such an eventuality would be considered a national disaster.

Family Breakdown

The moral pollution that has invaded the Western world, resulting in a decline in moral standards including the regard for the value of human life, has also affected personal relationships throughout society. There is no more sensitive area where the effects of this are clearly to be seen than within the family life of Western society. In almost every nation there has been a very large increase in the level of family and marriage breakdown. The tensions within the family stem from a complex interaction of moral and social forces of change that affect individual and community values. To this must be added the effects of the pop culture upon young people and the relaxation of discipline within schools, that have changed the attitudes of children and young people towards adults. But it is the general disregard not only for the sanctity of life but for the value of personal relationships,

151

personal integrity and faithfulness that have had the most devastating effects upon the family and marriage.

FIGURE 22 *Divorce (England and Wales)*

Year	Number of dissolutions
1936	5575
1940	6915
1947	47,041
1950	29,096
1959	25,689
1960	27,870
1970	58,200
1971	74,400
1975	120,500
1977	129,100

Source: Social Trends, HMSO.

The statistics in the above table in figure 22 show a dramatic increase of almost 120 per cent in the numbers of divorces granted in England and Wales during the seven-year period 1970 to 1977. If we look at the long-term trend from the pre-war years until the present, we see an even more dramatic change in attitudes towards marriage in Britain. One in every three marriages in Britain is now breaking down, with the inevitable result of producing basic instability of family life. When family life in a nation begins to break down it affects every aspect of the national life. The rearing of children in secure, loving family situations is essential to personal security and to the psychological, moral and spiritual health of the nation. With vast numbers of children experiencing the traumas of family breakdown, with the inevitable accompaniment of family rows and tensions, the future stability of the rising generation must be in jeopardy.

Despite the free availability of contraceptive devices and abortion, illegitimacy today is the highest on record in Britain. This again is a further indicator of the general breakdown of traditional family life and child-rearing practices. In 1979, nearly 17 per cent of all live births

FIGURE 23 *Extra-Maritally Conceived Live Births (England*

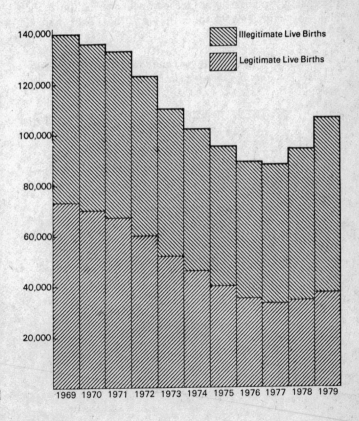

Source: NFOL.

to residents of England and Wales were extra-maritally conceived. This figure includes illegitimate live births and those which were pre-maritally conceived, i.e. live births occurring within eight months of the marriage of the parents. 'The above figure shows the number of pre-maritally conceived legitimate live births has been dropping steadily since 1969, with a slight increase in 1978 to 1979. This decrease of 94 per cent over the last decade shows that, increasingly, people do not feel compelled to legitimize their child by marriage, despite the fact that over half the

FIGURE 24 *The Changing Composition of One-parent Families Great Britain 1971 to 1976*

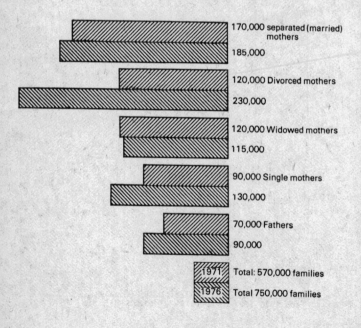

170,000 separated (married) mothers
185,000

120,000 Divorced mothers
230,000

120,000 Widowed mothers
115,000

90,000 Single mothers
130,000

70,000 Fathers
90,000

1971 Total: 570,000 families
1976 Total 750,000 families

Source: Population Trends, no. 13, HMSO 1978.

illegitimate births are registered by both parents, which might suggest a "stable union" outside traditional formal marriage.'[8]

A further indicator of the changing attitudes towards marriage and the family is seen in the changing composition of one-parent families. See figure 24.

Mention has already been made of the effects upon children of marriage breakdown. This must surely be the most serious aspect of the changes in the family life of most nations throughout the Western world. The table in figure 25 sets out the figures for divorces in Britain involving children under sixteen years of age.

FIGURE 25 *Divorces affecting children*

	1969	70	71	72	73	74	75	76	77	78	79
Divorces involving children under 16 (1000s)	NA	35.9	42.0	66.8	63.8	68.6	73.9	78.1	77.5	83.8	85.18

Source: Office of Population Census and Surveys.

It will be seen from the above figures that there has been a considerable rise in the breakdown of families involving young children, with an increase of 137 per cent during the 1970s.

A further factor giving rise to considerable anxiety amongst all those who care about the health and stability of the nation, is the increasing incidence of child abuse in Britain. It is interesting to note that although the Abortion Act was supposed to eliminate the bringing into the world of unwanted babies, and thereby to cut down the incidence of

---

[8] I am indebted to my daughter, Alison, Research Officer with the Nationwide Festival of Light, for this information.

child neglect and battered babies, this, in fact, has not happened. Throughout the 1970s, there was a steady increase in violence against children within the home and the number of battered babies and abandoned babies showed no decrease. This violence within the family is undoubtedly related to the general level of violence within society. Again, this is due to a combination of factors in the kind of complex social order in which we live today. In a society where there is a general decline in social values, including the very basic regard for human life, all social and personal behaviour is affected.

Undoubtedly, much of the evidence of declining standards of moral and social behaviour that we have been examining in Britain, is due to the effects of declining religious belief upon moral values in the life of the nation. In a society that is experiencing the removal of religion as the over-arching ideology linking all its institutions and legitimizing its social values, there is an inevitable consequence in terms of basic changes that occur in the national way of life. Major social institutions such as the family, which are part of the basic fabric of society, suffer the most considerable changes. The family is probably the most significant indicator of the social health and stability of both corporate and personal life in any society. Where the family breaks down, the whole moral structure of that society is endangered, and when the family life of a nation is in decline, so too are all its institutions. It is, however, our task in this chapter to examine empirical evidence, not to analyse the causes of social phenomena.

CHAPTER SEVEN

A Century of Bloodshed

The Witness of Scripture

The biblical position on murder and violent death is unequivocal: 'You shall not kill' (Exodus 20:13). The sixth commandment is uncompromising in its condemnation of the inflicting of violent death by any man upon a fellow human being. The only taking of life countenanced in the Old Testament is that which is carried out as a judicial act in carefully defined circumstances. This does not mean that murder and violent death did not occur in Old Testament times, both within the life of the nation Israel and in her relationships with her neighbouring states. Wherever and whenever such violent death was occasioned the manslayer was guilty not merely of an offence against another man but against God. This is the unambiguous witness of Scripture, which not only applies to those who stood within a covenant relationship with God, but to the whole of mankind. When Cain killed his brother Abel, he was told, 'You are cursed from the ground which has opened its mouth to receive your brother's blood from your hand.' He was condemned to be 'a fugitive and a wanderer on the earth', but despite Cain's being a self-confessed murderer God still did not permit anyone to kill him and promised vengeance upon anyone who should do so (Genesis 4:10–16).

The earliest writings in the Bible make it clear that murder and violence are wrong under all circumstances. It was because 'the earth was corrupt in God's sight and the earth was filled with violence' that God sent the flood upon the earth, according to Genesis 6:11. Again, in Genesis 9:5 it is stated that God will require a reckoning for the life-blood of every man. There are no exceptions to this. As individuals and collectively, we are responsible to God for the lives of others who live in our times.

It is the witness of Scripture from cover to cover, in both the Old and New Testaments, that bloodshed pollutes the land. God has so created this planet that there is a special relationship between man and the earth – both are part of God's created order. Man, created in the image of God, is intended to live in harmony both with his fellow man and with the whole created order, and to enjoy the fruits of the earth as part of harmonious living. Thus violence, injustice and exploitation are offensive to the very nature of God who is a God of order, of justice and love. Numbers 35:29–34 speaks of the sanctity of life and states that even the ransom of a rich man cannot atone for the life of one he has murdered: 'You shall not thus pollute the land in which you live, for blood pollutes the land and no expiation can be made for the land, for the blood that is shed in it, except by the blood of him who shed it. You shall not defile the land in which you live, in the midst of which I dwell; for I the Lord dwell in the midst of the people of Israel.' It is this last sentence that underlines the reasons why bloodshed is so abhorrent to God. The land belongs to him. His presence pervades the very soil of this planet which he created, and to spill upon it the blood of those whom he created in his own image is to defile it.

Men of violence are thus an offence to the holiness and purity of God. It was for this reason that King David, although greatly favoured by God, was not allowed to build the Temple that symbolized his presence. David himself admitted this when speaking to Solomon: 'My son, I had it in my heart to build a house to the name of the Lord my God. But the word of the Lord came to me, saying, "You have shed much blood and have waged great wars, you shall not build a house to my name, because you have shed so much blood before me upon the earth." (1 Chronicles 22:7 and 8).

Time and again God warned Israel in pre-exilic days that even Jerusalem itself would not be spared from the inevitable consequences of violence and corruption, unless there was a full change of heart both amongst the leaders and the people. It was no good believing that Jerusalem was inviolable because of the presence of the Temple. The only way that they could be sure of continuing to live in peace in Jerusalem was 'If you truly amend your ways and your doings, if you truly execute justice one with another, if you do not oppress the alien, the fatherless or the widow, or shed innocent blood in this place, and if you do not go after other gods to your own hurt, then I will let you dwell in this place' (Jeremiah 7:5–7). But the warnings were ignored, the violence and corruption continued. Then in 586 BC the land was ravaged by a foreign army and the city was destroyed in the bloodiest massacre of that age.

Empirical Evidence

It is the witness of history that the twentieth century is the bloodiest in the record of man's inhabitation of this planet. Whether or not the twenty-first century will surpass the twentieth century for bloodshed is a matter upon which no one can be certain. The one thing we can say with certainty is that there has been a vast increase in bloodshed during the first four-fifths of this century in comparison with earlier centuries since mankind began keeping historical records. It may be objected that the record is extremely scant and that therefore we do not have sufficient evidence to make such a statement. Against this objection we may offer evidence from those parts of the world where records have been kept with a fair degree of accuracy. If we take, for example, the continent of Europe for the past four hundred years, we notice that while there was a steady increase in the number of casualties due to war during the three centuries from 1600 to the end of the nineteenth century, there has been a vast increase during this present century. The position is set out in the table overleaf.

FIGURE 26 *War Losses in Europe by Centuries*

CENTURY	CASUALTIES IN MILLIONS
17TH	3.3
18TH	5.2
19TH	5.5
20TH (TO 1970)	28.0

Source: Antony Sutton, *Wars and Revolutions, Part Two,* p. 224.

It may be further objected that the increase in bloodshed this century may be due to the increase in world population. Again the evidence from Europe is interesting here as shown in the table. The increase in war casualties from the seventeenth to the nineteenth century is roughly in line with the general rise in the size of the population, but the jump from 1900 to 1970 in comparison with the nineteenth century in no way reflects the rise in the population of European nations. Indeed the population of the European nations did not even double during this period, whereas the number of war casualties in the first seventy years of the twentieth century is more than five times as great as that of the whole of the nineteenth century. This increase in the number of war casualties reflects four significant changes that have been taking place during the twentieth century. They are:

1. An increase in the number of national and international conflicts.
2. An increasing sophistication in the weapons of war.
3. Changes in the type of conflict due to the changing aspirationa of mankind.
4. Civilian populations are attacked and massacred.

The Early Twentieth Century
The steady increase in the number of wars throughout the twentieth century so far is clearly seen if we compare the first forty years of this century with the second forty years. The

number of conflicts fought during this first period is set out in figure 27 below.

FIGURE 27 *Wars in the Twentieth Century: National and International Conflicts 1900–1940*

YEAR	CONFLICT	DEATHS
1899–1902	South Africa: Boer War	10,000
1900	China: Boxer Rebellion	10,000
1902–4	Korea:Russo-Japanese War	100,000
1911	North Africa: Italo-Turkish War	15,000
1912–13	South-East Europe: Balkan Wars	100,000
1914	Turkey: Armenian Massacres	1,000,000
1910–20	Mexican Revolution & Civil Wars	2,000,000
1914–18	First World War	14,767,769
1919–21	Russo-Polish War	200,000
1919–22	Greco-Turkish War	500,000
1919–25	Arabia: Nejd-Hajaz conflicts	30,000
1921	Morocco: Insurrection v. French and Spanish rule	30,000
1931	Iraq: Arthurian Rebellion	70,000
1928–55	Paraguay-Bolivia: Chaco War	500,000
1931	Manchuria: Japanese Invasion	300,000
1936	Abyssinia: Italian Invasion	200,000
1936–39	Spanish Civil War	500,000
1939	Russo-Finnish War	200,000
1939–45	Second World War	35,866,533

Source: Adapted from data in Gil Elliot, *Twentieth Century Book of the Dead,* Allen Lane, The Penguin Press, London, 1972.

It will be seen from this that there were only nineteen conflicts from the beginning of this century to 1940. This even includes the two major world wars. It may be argued that the First World War, which included some twenty countries, left many nations exhausted and unwilling to participate in further conflicts. This period also saw economic recession on a world-wide scale during the 1920s and early 1930s which preoccupied the nations with internal problems, thus making them less aggressive in their international relationships. Such an argument, however, hardly carries much weight when we consider the number of conflicts that there have been since the end of the Second World War.

The Middle Twentieth Century

In an article in the *Journal of Peace Research* published in 1978, Istvan Kende gave a list of one hundred and twenty armed conflicts which he defined as wars during the period 1945 to 1976. Kende defined war as 'any armed conflict in which all the following criteria obtain:

1. Activities of regular armed forces (military, police forces, etc.) at least on one side, i.e. the presence and engagement of the armed forces of the government in power.
2. A certain degree of organization and organized fighting on both opposing sides, even if this organization extends to organized defence only.
3. A certain continuity between the armed clashes, however sporadic. Centrally organized guerrilla forces are also regarded as making war, in so far as their activities extend over a considerable part of the country concerned.'

Figure 28 sets out the one hundred and twenty wars listed. Those marked with an asterisk were continuing conflicts beyond the period covered by this table.

FIGURE 28 *Wars in the Twentieth Century: National and International Conflicts: 1945–1976*

AREA	PERIOD	PARTICIPATION
Greece	1944–45	DC
Algeria	1945	DC
Indonesia	1945–49	DC
Spain	1945–48	I
Indochina	1946–54	DC
Greece	1946–49	DC
India (religious)	1946–47	I
Philippines	1946–54	DC
China	1946–49	I
Iran	1946	I
Paraguay	1947	DC
Madagascar	1947–48	DC
India (Hyderabad, Telangana)	1947–48	I
India–Pakistan (Kashmir)	1947–48	DC
Yemen	1948	I
Costa Rica	1948	I
*Burma	1948–	I
Colombia	1948–53	I
Israel–Arab countries	1948–49	DC
Malaysia	1948–59	DC
Bolivia	1949	I
Korea	1950–53	DC, S, TW
Puerto Rico	1950	DC
Egypt	1951–52	DC
Tunisia	1952–54	DC
Bolivia	1952	I
Kenya	1952–56	DC
Morocco	1952–56	DC
Guatemala	1954	DC
Colombia	1954–57	I
Algeria	1954–62	DC
China (Islands)	1955	DC
Costa Rica–Nicaragua	1955	DC
Cyprus	1955–59	DC
Cameroon	1955–63	DC
South Vietnam	1955–75	DC, TW
Oman	1955–63	DC
India (Nagas)	1956–64	I

AREA	PERIOD	PARTICIPATION
Hungary	1956	S
Israel–Egypt (Suez)	1956	DC
Cuba	1956–59	I
Aden, Yemen	1956–58	DC
Indonesia	1957–58	DC
Honduras–Nicaragua	1957	I
Spanish Morocco	1957–58	DC, TW
Lebanon	1958	DC
Jordan	1958	DC
China (Quemoy)	1958	DC
Nyasaland	1959	DC
China (Tibet)	1959	I
Laos	1959–62	DC, S
Dominican Republic	1959	I
Paraguay	1959–60	I
Zaire (Congo K)	1960–64	DC
Angola	1961–74	DC
Nepal	1961–62	I
Cuba	1961	DC
Tunisia	1961	DC
*Ethiopia (Eritrea)	1961–	I
Iraq (Kurds)	1961–64	I
Venezuela	1961–70	I
India (Goa)	1961	DC
Indonesia (W. Irian)	1962	DC
Guatemala	1962–72	DC
Colombia	1962	DC
Yemen	1962–70	DC, TW
India–China	1962	I
Brunei	1962	DC
Guinea (Bissau)	1963–74	DC
Malaysia ('Confrontation')	1963–66	DC, TW
Algeria–Morocco	1963	I
South Yemen	1963–67	DC
Dominican Republic	1963	I
Somalia–Ethiopia	1963–64	I
Zaire	1963–69	DC
Cyprus	1963–64	DC
Rwanda	1963–64	I
Kenya–Somalia	1963–67	I
Laos	1964–73	DC, S, TW

AREA	PERIOD	PARTICIPATION
Colombia	1964–72	DC
North Vietnam	1964–68	DC
Mozambique	1964–74	DC
Iraq (Kurds)	1965–70	TW
India–Pakistan	1965	I
Dominican Republic	1965	DC
Peru	1965	DC
*Oman (Dhofar)	1965–	DC, TW
Sudan	1965–72	I
India–Pakistan	1965	I
*Thailand	1965–	DC
India (Mizos)	1966–67	I
Bolivia	1967	DC
Israel–Arab countries	1967	I
Zaire	1967	DC
Nigeria (Biafra)	1967–70	I
*Zimbabwe (Rhodesia)	1967–	TW
South Yemen	1968	TW
Chad	1968–72	DC
El Salvador–Honduras	1969	I
South Yemen–Saudi Arabia	1969	I
*Gr. Britain (N. Ireland)	1969–	I
Cambodia	1970–75	DC, S, TW
Sudan	1970	I
Philippines	1970–76	I
Jordan	1970	I
Guinea	1970	DC
Pakistan (Bangladesh)	1971	TW
Sri Lanka	1971	I
Jordan	1971	I
North Vietnam	1972–73	DC
Burundi	1972	I
Uganda–Tanzania	1972	I
Yemen–South Yemen	1972	I
Israel–Arab countries	1973	TW
Iraq (Kurds)	1974–75	I
Cyprus	1974	DC
Lebanon	1975–76	TW
*East Timor	1975–	TW
Angola	1975–76	S, TW
*West Sahara	1975–	TW

Key: DC = Developed Capitalist countries
       I = Internal
       S = Socialist countries
      TW = Third World

The vast increase in the number of armed conflicts during the middle years of the twentieth century can be seen in comparison with the first forty years. Even if it is objected that many of the conflicts listed by Kende are small-scale local wars, at least half that number are major wars, many of them involving considerable numbers of casualties. This represents a 300 per cent increase in the number of wars between the first forty years of the twentieth century and the second forty years. A recent publication lists sixty-two major armed conflicts that have occurred since 1945, some of which are still in progress. In a comprehensive study published in 1981, entitled *War in Peace: An Analysis of Warfare Since 1945*, the Editor, Sir Robert Thompson, brings together an immense amount of empirical data that vividly illustrates the aggressive nature of man in the twentieth century. Figure 29 is based upon the information collated in *War in Peace* and gives in digest form details of the major armed conflicts during this period together with details of the combatants and casualties.

FIGURE 29 *Major Wars since 1945*

ASIA

Chinese Civil War

DATE: 1945–Dec. 1949
COMBATANTS: Communists v
  Nationalists
OUTCOME: Communist victory
CASUALTIES: NA probably
  millions

French Indochina

DATE: March 1946–21 July 1954
COMBATANTS: Viet Minh v
  France
OUTCOME: Viet Minh victory
  Vietnam divided into
  communist North and
  US-supported South
CASUALTIES: French 75,000, Viet
  Minh 150,000

Malayan Emergency

DATE: June 1948–12 July 1960
COMBATANTS: Great Britain v
  communist MRLA
OUTCOME: Defeat of MRLA,
  Malay state created 31 Sept.
  1957
CASUALTIES: British 2384,
  MRLA 6711

Indonesian War of Independence

DATE: 14 Oct. 1945–2 Nov.
  1949
COMBATANTS: Netherlands v
  Indonesian People's Army
OUTCOME: Dutch defeat,
  Indonesian independence 15
  Aug. 1950
CASUALTIES: NA

Huk Revolt in Philippines

DATE: 1946–1954
COMBATANTS: Government v
  communist Hukbalahap rebels
OUTCOME: Government victory
CASUALTIES: NA

Karen Revolt in Burma

DATE: Spring 1948–Summer 1950
COMBATANTS: Government v
  communists and Karen
  separatists
OUTCOME: Government victory
CASUALTIES: NA

Korea

DATE: 25 June 1950–27 July 1953
COMBATANTS: North Korea and China v South Korea and USA etc. (UN)
OUTCOME: Stalemate
CASUALTIES: North Korea 500,000, China 900,000, UN 118,515 (plus 264,591 wounded)

Tibetan Revolt

DATE: Spring 1954–1959
COMBATANTS: Tibetan nationalists v China
OUTCOME: Chinese victory
CASUALTIES: Tibet 105,000, China NA

Indonesian Civil War

DATE: 1950–1965
COMBATANTS: Government v communists
OUTCOME: Government victory
CASUALTIES: 500,000

Malaysian-Indonesian War

DATE: 15 Sept. 1963–11 Aug. 1966
COMBATANTS: Malaysia v Indonesia
OUTCOME: Stalemate, ceasefire agreed
CASUALTIES: Malaysia 150, Indonesia 590

Sino-Indian War

DATE: Oct.–Nov. 1962
COMBATANTS: China v India
OUTCOME: Chinese seizure of disputed border region
CASUALTIES: India 1400, China NA

Vietnam

DATE: 1959–30 April 1975
COMBATANTS: North Vietnam and South Vietnam communists v South Vietnam and the USA
OUTCOME: Communist victory
CASUALTIES: North Vietnam 1,000,000, Vietcong 922,290, US 56,371 (plus civilians: S. Vietnam 1,350,000, N. Vietnam estimated 1,000,000+)

Indo-Pakistan War of 1965

DATE: April–27 Sept. 1965
COMBATANTS: India v Pakistan
OUTCOME: UN-policed ceasefire
CASUALTIES: India 2212, Pakistan 5800

Sino-Soviet Border Clash

DATE: March–August 1969
COMBATANTS: Russia v China
OUTCOME: Soviet occupation of Damansky Island
CASUALTIES: NA

Indo-Pakistan War of 1971

DATE: 3–16 Dec. 1971
COMBATANTS: India v Pakistan
OUTCOME: Bangladesh
  independence
CASUALTIES: India 1426, Pakistan
  NA

Indonesian Invasion of East Timor

DATE: 1975–
COMBATANTS: Indonesia v
  Timorese nationalists
OUTCOME: Undecided
CASUALTIES: 100,000 + Timorese,
  Indonesia NA

Muslim Revolt in Philippines

DATE: 1972–1979
COMBATANTS: Government v
  Muslim rebels
OUTCOME: Government victory
CASUALTIES: 30,000 + rebels,
  Government NA

Vietnamese Invasion of Kampuchea

DATE: Autumn 1978–Spring 1979
COMBATANTS: Vietnam v Khmer
  Rouge
OUTCOME: Vietnamese Victory
  and formation of Peoples'
  Republic of Kampuchea
CASUALTIES: NA (1 million +)

Chinese Invasion of Vietnam

DATE: Feb. 1979
COMBATANTS: China v Vietnam
OUTCOME: Chinese withdrawal
CASUALTIES: China 20,000,
  Vietnam 27,000

EUROPE

Greek Civil War

DATE: 1945–16 Oct. 1949
COMBATANTS: Nationalists v
  communists
OUTCOME: Nationalist victory
CASUALTIES: Nationalists 12,777,
  communists 38,000

East German Revolt

DATE: June 1953
COMBATANTS: Government and
  Soviet Union v demonstrators
OUTCOME: Disturbances
  suppressed
CASUALTIES: NA

Hungarian Revolt

DATE: 23 Oct.–4 Nov. 1956
COMBATANTS: Hungary v Soviet
Union
OUTCOME: Revolt suppressed
CASUALTIES: Hungary 25,000,
Russia 7000

Polish Revolt

DATE: 28–29 June 1956
COMBATANTS: Polish workers v
Soviet troops
OUTCOME: Revolt suppressed
CASUALTIES: Poland 50

Invasion of Czechoslovakia

DATE: 20 Aug. 1968–20 March
1970
COMBATANTS: Czechoslovakia v
Russia
OUTCOME: New communist
Government
CASUALTIES: 70 Czechoslovakians

Northern Ireland

DATE: 1968–
COMBATANTS: UK v Republicans
OUTCOME: conflict continuing
CASUALTIES: 2000+

LATIN AMERICA

Cuban Revolution

DATE: 2 Dec. 1956–1 Jan. 1959
COMBATANTS: Government v
communists
OUTCOME: Communist victory
CASUALTIES: Army 2000, others
NA

Bay of Pigs War

DATE: 16–17 April 1961
COMBATANTS: Cuban government
v invading exiles (+ US
backing)
OUTCOME: Exiles defeated
CASUALTIES: 1200 exiles

Guatemala Civil War

DATE: 1967–1980
COMBATANTS: Right-wing v
Left-wing
OUTCOME: Undecided
CASUALTIES: 20,000+

Occupation of San Domingo

DATE: April–May 1965
COMBATANTS: US intervention
in civil war
OUTCOME: US victory
CASUALTIES: NA

Nicaragua

DATE: May–June 1979
COMBATANTS: Government v
Rebels
OUTCOME: Government
overthrown
CASUALTIES: 10,000

El Salvador

DATE: Feb. 1980
COMBATANTS: Right-wing v
Left-wing
OUTCOME: War continuing
CASUALTIES: NA

AFRICA

Malagasy Revolt

DATE: 1947–1948
COMBATANTS: France v
Malagasy nationalists
OUTCOME: French victory
CASUALTIES: NA

Mau Mau Revolt

DATE: 20 Oct. 1952–Jan. 1960
COMBATANTS: UK v Mau Mau
nationalists
OUTCOME: British withdrawal and
Kenyan independence 1963
CASUALTIES: UK 600, Kenyans
11,500

Tunisian War of Independence

DATE: 1952–June 1955
COMBATANTS: France v Tunisian
nationalists
OUTCOME: Nationalist victory and
Tunisian independence
March 1956
CASUALTIES: NA

Moroccan War of Independence

DATE: 1953–1956
COMBATANTS: France v
Moroccan nationalists
OUTCOME: Nationalist victory
and Moroccan independence
CASUALTIES: NA

Suez

DATE: 30 Oct.–7 Nov. 1956
COMBATANTS: UK & France v
Egypt
OUTCOME: UN ceasefire imposed
British and French withdrawal
CASUALTIES: Anglo-French 33,
Egyptian NA

Algerian War of Independence

DATE: 1 Nov. 1954–March 1962
COMBATANTS: France v
Algerian nationalists
OUTCOME: French withdrawal and
Algerian independence
July 1963
CASUALTIES: French 20,244,
Algerian 1,000,000

The Congo

DATE: 1 July 1960–Dec. 1967
COMBATANTS: Nationalist
factions
OUTCOME: Military coup
ended conflict
CASUALTIES: UN forces 126,
Congolese 10,000 +

Biafra

DATE: 30 May 1967–15 Jan. 1970
COMBATANTS: Nigeria v Biafra
OUTCOME: Nigerian victory
CASUALTIES: 600,000

Angolan War of Independance

DATE: 1961–Nov. 1975
COMBATANTS: Portugal v
Angolan nationalists
OUTCOME: Nationalist victory
and Angolan
independence
CASUALTIES: NA

Angolan Civil War

DATE: Nov. 1975–Nov. 1976
COMBATANTS: MPLA (with
Soviet & Cuban support)
v FNLA & UNITA
OUTCOME: MPLA recognized as
Government of Angola
CASUALTIES: 20,000

Mozambique War of Independence

DATE: 1964–June 1975
COMBATANTS: Portugal v
Nationalists
OUTCOME: Nationalist victory
and independence
CASUALTIES: NA

Guinean War of Independence

DATE 1963–Sept. 1974
COMBATANTS: Portugal v
Nationalists
OUTCOME: Nationalist victory
and independence
CASUALTIES: NA

Somalian Invasion of Ogaden

DATE: May 1977–March 1978
COMBATANTS: Ethiopia v
Somalia
OUTCOME: Invasion repelled
CASUALTIES: NA

Eritrean Revolt

DATE: 1960–
COMBATANTS: Ethiopian
Government v Eritrean
separatists
OUTCOME: War continuing
CASUALTIES: NA

Rhodesia

DATE: 1957–March 1980
COMBATANTS: British/
Rhodesian Government v
Nationalists
OUTCOME: Nationalist victory
and independence
CASUALTIES: 20,000

Sahel War

DATE: 1978–
COMBATANTS: Morocco v
Sahel nationalists
OUTCOME: War continuing
CASUALTIES: NA

Namibia

DATE: 1976
COMBATANTS: South Africa v
SWAPO
OUTCOME: War continuing
CASUALTIES: NA

Tanzanian Invasion of Uganda

DATE: Feb. 1979
COMBATANTS: Tanzania v
forces of General Amin
OUTCOME: New government
in Uganda
CASUALTIES: NA

MIDDLE EAST

1948 Arab-Israeli War

DATE: 14 May 1948–5 Jan. 1949
COMBATANTS: Egypt, Jordan &
Syria v Israel
OUTCOME: UN-negotiated
armistice
CASUALTIES: Israel 6000,
Arabs 6000 +

Cyprus

DATE: Nov. 1955–Dec. 1959
COMBATANTS: UK v Greek
Cypriots
OUTCOME: UK withdrawal
and independence
CASUALTIES: Britain 142,
Cypriots 362

Israeli Invasion of Sinai

DATE: 29 Oct.–15 Nov. 1956
COMBATANTS: Israel v Egypt
OUTCOME: UN intervention
CASUALTIES: Israel 181,
Egypt 1500

Occupation of the Lebanon

DATE: 14 April–15 July 1958
COMBATANTS: Lebanon v UAR-
supported communists
OUTCOME: US intervention
CASUALTIES: NA

Cypriot Civil War

DATE: Dec. 1963–Aug. 1964
COMBATANTS: Greek v Turkish
  Cypriots
OUTCOME: UN-imposed ceasefire
CASUALTIES: NA

Yemeni Civil War

DATE: 26 Dec. 1961–May 1970
COMBATANTS: Communists v
  Royalists
OUTCOME: Peace Treaty signed
CASUALTIES: NA

Aden

DATE: Dec. 1963–29 Nov. 1967
COMBATANTS: UK v NLF
OUTCOME: British withdrawal
  and independence
CASUALTIES: Britain 57,
  Aden 1202

Six Day War

DATE: 5–10 June 1967
COMBATANTS: Israel v Egypt,
  Jordan & Syria
OUTCOME: Israeli victory
CASUALTIES: Israel 689,
  Arabs 18,500

Yom Kippur War

DATE: 6–24 Oct. 1973
COMBATANTS: Israel v Egypt
  & Syria
OUTCOME: Ceasefire
CASUALTIES: Israel 1854,
  Arabs NA

Turkish Invasion of Cyprus

DATE: July 1974
COMBATANTS: Turkey v Greek
  Cypriots
OUTCOME: Turkish victory and
  division of island
CASUALTIES: NA

Lebanese Civil War

DATE: Sept. 1975–
COMBATANTS: Christians v
  Muslims
OUTCOME: War continuing
CASUALTIES: 50,000 +

Soviet Invasion of Afghanistan

DATE: 24 Dec. 1979–
COMBATANTS: Russia v
  Afghan nationalists
OUTCOME: Soviet occupation,
  war continuing
CASUALTIES: 100,000

Gulf War

DATE: 12 Sept. 1980–
COMBATANTS: Iran v Iraq
OUTCOME: War continuing
CASUALTIES: NA

Source: Adapted from Thompson, Sir Robert, *War in Peace: An Analysis of Warfare Since 1945*, Orbis Publishing, London, 1981.

Notes: NA – not available
CASUALTIES: figures given are for those known to have been killed in a conflict. The number of wounded is not given although it may be assumed that there are usually two or three times as many wounded as those killed.

Increasing Violence

The twentieth century is not simply notable, however, for the increasing number of armed conflicts but for the vast escalation in the destructiveness of war. The two world wars were each watersheds in the application of modern technology to the business of destruction, both of life and of material resources. It was during the First World War that tanks and aeroplanes were first used in armed combat. Their introduction into the arsenals of the nations dramatically changed the whole nature of warfare. The traditional concept of war as a clash between two contending armies was finally buried in the mire of Flanders, and by the time the Second World War began twenty years later war was a different business. The highly mechanized forces of the Third Reich swept through Europe in a matter of days, whilst their Air Force demonstrated that never again would war be fought by face to face combat *alone*. War became total war – involving whole nations, not simply armed forces but civilians as well, men, women and children of all ages. War became the indescribable business of indiscriminate mass killing. Figures 30 and 31 show the participant nations and the casualties involved in each of the two major world wars during this century.

FIGURE 30 *Casualties in World War I (killed)*

COUNTRY	MILITARY	CIVILIAN	TOTAL
Armenia	—	1,000,000	1,000,000
Austria-Hungary	922,500	300,000	1,222,500
Belgium	13,715	30,000	43,715
British Empire	908,371	30,633	939,004
Bulgaria	100,000	275,000	375,000
France	1,357,800	40,000	1,397,800
Germany	1,808,546	760,000	2,568,546
Greece	5000	132,000	137,000
Italy	462,391	—	462,391
Japan	300	—	300
Lithuania	—	200,000	200,000
Montenegro	3000	—	3000
Poland	—	300,000	300,000
Portugal	7222	—	7222
Rumania	335,706	275,000	610,706
Russia	1,700,000	1,500,000	3,200,000
Serbia	125,000	650,000	775,000
Syria	—	1,000,000	1,000,000
Turkey	325,000	150,000	475,000
*USA	50,589	—	50,589
TOTALS	8,125,136	6,642,633	14,767,769

Source: Adapted from Dupuy, R. Ernest & Dupuy, Trevor N., *Encyclopedia of Military History,* Harper & Row, New York, 1970, p. 990.

---

* Official US military casualties issued by the Pentagon were 53,402; Source: US News and World Report, 7 June 1965.

FIGURE 31 *Casualties in World War II (killed)*

COUNTRY	MILITARY	CIVILIAN	TOTAL
Belgium	—	17,500	17,500
China	500,000	1,000,000	1,500,000
France	210,671	108,000	318,671
Germany	2,850,000	500,000	3,350,000
Italy	77,500	40,000	117,500
Japan	1,506,000	300,000	1,806,000
Norway	—	2,000	2,000
Poland	—	4,500,000	4,500,000
Soviet Union	7,500,000	10,000,000	17,500,000
UK & Common-wealth	397,762	65,000	462,762
*USA	292,100	—	292,100
European Jews	—	6,000,000	6,000,000
TOTALS	13,334,033	18,032,500	35,866,533

Source: As for Figure 30, p. 1198.

---

* Official US military casualties issued by the Pentagon were 291,557; Source: US News and World Report, 7 June 1965.

It is interesting to note from these figures that while the number of military casualties in World War Two increased by only 64 per cent compared with World War One, the number of civilian casualties increased by some 171 per cent. Even if we extract the figures for the number of European Jews killed during the Nazi Anti-Semitic exterminations, the number of civilians killed as a direct result of war doubled in the second world war in comparison with the first. This vast increase in civilian casualties is due to the greater sophistication of weapons of mass destruction. The closing period of the 1939–45 war saw one thousand bomber air raids that obliterated whole cities and killed huge numbers of civilians. It also saw the first use of the atomic bombs that destroyed Hiroshima and Nagasaki with tens of thousands of civilian casualties.

The Record of the Nations

Before turning our attention to the changing nature of conflict in the modern world it is worth pausing to reflect upon the track record of some of the major nations during the first eighty years of this century. Figure 32 sets out the record of seven major nations and shows the number of armed conflicts in which they have been involved, together with the number of casualties they have suffered. This table does not show the number of casualties each nation has inflicted upon others but simply the number of casualties of their own nationals who have been killed in war. The figures are inclusive of both military personnel and civilians.

FIGURE 32 *Wars in the Twentieth Century 1900 – 1975*
Seven Major Nations

COUNTRY	NUMBER OF CONFLICTS	MAJOR CONFLICTS	CASUALTIES (MILITARY AND CIVILIAN) (KILLED)
China	62	Japanese War	15,000,000
		World War II	1,500,000
		Communist purges	16,250,000
		Others	3,096,548
		TOTAL	35,796,548
France	45	World War I	1,397,800
		World War II	318,671
		Others	176,180
		TOTAL	1,892,651
Germany	60	World War I	2,568,546
		World War II	3,350,000
		Others	5,255,000
		TOTAL	11,173,546
Great Britain	64	World War I[1]	939,004
		World War II[2]	462,762
		Others	2,500
		TOTAL	1,404,266
		[1]includes British Empire [2]includes British Commonwealth	
Japan	24	China	58,780
		World War I	300
		World War II	1,806,000
		Others	10,049
		TOTAL	1,875,129

COUNTRY	NUMBER OF CONFLICTS	MAJOR CONFLICTS	CASUALTIES (MILITARY AND CIVILIAN) (KILLED)
Russia	77	1917 Revolution	6,776,737
		World War I	3,200,000
		Stalinist purges	20,000,000
		World War II	17,500,000
		Others	1,669,318
		TOTAL	49,146,055
USA	71	Korea	33,629
		Vietnam	56,371
		World War I	53,402
		World War II	291,557
		Others	3785
		TOTAL	438,744

Source: Compiled from information available in the Library of the British War Museum.

The aggressive nature of the international relationships of the seven nations listed in Figure 32 may be better seen in comparison with the nations of Europe. Over the past four centuries of world history European nations have played a significant role in colonization. It is the European nations that have been in the forefront of both world exploration and exploitation of natural resources, and of the nationals, of the countries where they have settled and colonized. This process of colonization took place in earlier centuries, and the twentieth has been marked by the opposite process – that of decolonization or the granting of independence to those nations that were formerly governed by European nations. To express this from the opposite standpoint we should say that the twentieth century has been marked by the rise of nationalism and the wresting of independence by the developing nations from the dominance of nations in the developed world. The following table sets out the record of European nations in the twentieth century. (Those that have already been listed in Figure 32 have been excluded.)

The increasing sophistication of the weapons used in modern warfare was amply demonstrated in the Vietnam conflict, where a great variety of bombs and rocket weaponry was used. The Vietnam conflict underlined the increasing involvement of innocent civilians as the victims of modern warfare, due to the indiscriminate destructive power of weapons in today's technological age. Total military casualties during the Vietnam war have been estimated as one million five hundred thousand military personnel killed, while the civilian deaths outnumbered the military by two to one. According to figures published in *The Times* (25 January 1973), civilian casualties amongst the South Vietnamese numbered one million three hundred and fifty thousand. There were no reliable figures for North Vietnamese civilians, although these were thought to number considerably more than those of South Vietnam, due to American bombing.

It has not only been in war, however, that civilians have suffered during this century. A major new phenomenon has been the mass political purge. There is, of course, nothing new in politically motivated mass murders. Revolutions and *coups d'état* have been taking place ever since the earliest days of man's tribal organization. What is new in this century is the scale, extent, relentless cruelty and indiscriminate mass nature of its political purges. Nationalist governments, dictators and totalitarian states have all been

FIGURE 33 *Twentieth Century Wars Involving European Nations 1900–1975*

COUNTRY	NUMBERS OF CONFLICTS	CASUALTIES (KILLED)
Austria	6	63,850
Baltic States	12	200,000
Belgium	5	28,000
Czechoslovakia	8	124,686
Denmark	1	100
Eire	1	671
Finland	5	27,600
Greece	26	286,000
Hungary	7	232,224
Italy	19	54,000
Norway	2	2000
Poland	25	3,200,000
Portugal	23	11,000
Rumania	9	750,000
Spain	15	759,000
Sweden	2	1027
Switzerland	2	55
Yugoslavia	12	1,898,000

Source: Compiled from information available in the Library of the British War Museum.

responsible for monstrous cruelty on an incredible scale, that has added significantly to the bloodshed of the twentieth century.

The Record of Communism

The most infamous record of bloodshed through political purges is to be seen in the incredible world-wide spread of communism during the twentieth century. Communism's record of massacres is second to none in world history. A recent article by Jean-Pierre Dujardin in *Le Figaro* Magazine (19–25 November 1978) calculates that the world-wide human cost of communism has now attained the staggering total of one hundred and forty-three million lives lost since 1917. In an era during which the crimes of Fascism have been on everyone's lips for thirty years, a sober examination of the record of its surviving collectivist brother is long overdue.

'We can begin by looking at the balance of Soviet Communism. From the earliest years of Bolshevik power, indiscriminate slaughter of dissident elements became the order of the day. Whereas only nine hundred and ninety-seven persons were executed in Czarist Russia between 1821 and 1906, one million eight hundred and sixty-one thousand five hundred and sixty-eight "oppositionists" were killed in the Leninist period of 1917 to 1923 alone. As for the total number of the Kremlin's victims, we have Professor Kuganov's seminal study to fall back upon. According to his detailed demographic survey of Russia's population between 1939 and 1959 (based on official Soviet sources and published on 14 April 1964, in *Novie Rousskoi Slova*), over sixty-six million Russians were liquidated internally between 1917 and 1959.

'It is further reckoned that no less than three million Russians have been killed since 1959, despite Khrushchev's "thaw" and Brezhnev's "*détente*". A study by Sergiun Grossu (published in 1975) shows that there are currently two million political prisoners in ninety-six labour camps.'[1]

---

[1] Article by Philip Van Der Elst, *Daily Telegraph*, 19 March 1979.

FIGURE 34 *Casualties of Communism*

	INCIDENT	NUMBER KILLED
1	Communist purges in USSR 1917–1959	66,700,000
2	Communist purges in USSR since 1959	3,000,000
3	Communist purges in China	63,784,000
4	Massacre of Katyn	10,000
5	German civilians killed in expulsions of 1945–1946	2,923,700
6	Cambodia April 1975 April 1978	2,500,000
7	Suppressions of uprisings in East Berlin, Prague, Budapest, Baltic States 1945–1975	500,000
8	Conflict in Greece, Malaysia, Burma, Korea, Philippines, Vietnam, Cuba, Black Africa, Latin America	3,500,000
	TOTAL	142,917,700

Source: Figaro Magazine 19–25, November, 1978.

This table, which shows numbers far in excess of those in figure 32, supports the views of Solzhenitsyn, the Russian dissident, who for a number of years has been warning the Western nations that it is folly to suppose that there is some flaw in the nature of the Russian people that accounts for the vast numbers of political murders in his native country. Solzhenitsyn states unequivocally that it is in the nature of communism itself that there lies the source of the monstrous cruelty that has been responsible for the murders of many millions of innocent men and women since the Bolshevik revolution of 1917. He sees communism as 'a malignant tumour . . . driven by a malevolent and irrational instinct for world domination, it cannot help seizing ever more lands. Communism is something new, unprecedented in world history; it is fruitless to seek analogies. All warnings to the

West about the pitiless and insatiable nature of Communist regimes have proved to be vain because the acceptance of such a view would be too terrifying.

'Communism needs the whole charade of *détente* for only one purpose: to gain additional strength with the help of Western financing (those loans will not be repaid) and Western technology before it launches its next large-scale offensive. Communism is stronger and more durable than Nazism, it is far more sophisticated in its propaganda and excels at such charades. Communism is unregenerate; it will always present a mortal danger to mankind. It is like an infection in the world's organism; it may lie dormant, but it will inevitably attack with a crippling disease.'[2]

The Rise of Terrorism
Another new feature of bloodshed in the twentieth century has been the rise of terrorist organizations on an international scale and the resulting new phenomenon of urban guerrilla warfare. This is in part a reflection of the changing aspirations of man and reflects the growing twentieth-century phenomenon of national self-consciousness. In a massive day by day chronicle of terrorist activities, Edward Mickolus has recorded the activities of terrorists throughout the world from 1900 to 1979. It is interesting to note that the first ten pages of the book cover terrorist action from the beginning of the twentieth century to 1945. The next one hundred and fifty pages cover the period from the end of World War Two to the end of 1969. Such is the escalation of this kind of activity that it takes a further seven hundred and fifty pages to cover the ten-year period from 1 January 1970 to 28 December 1979. Mickolus lists twenty-one different types of terrorist attacks, which include kidnapping, letter bombing, incendiary bombing, explosive bombing, aerial hijacking, assassination and sabotage.

---

[2] Quoted from an article by Alexander Solzhenitsyn published in *Time* Magazine, 18 February 1980.

The World Today

The escalation of violence on a world-wide scale throughout the twentieth century is an undeniable fact of history. As the world entered the decade of the 1980s there were thirty-seven major and minor armed conflicts in progress in different parts of the world. In the thirty-seven wars listed in figure 35, upwards of eight million soldiers and para-military personnel were directly or indirectly involved. The total loss of lives in these conflicts alone is unknown but rough estimates put the figure as between one million and five million killed. The number of wounded and maimed is estimated to be at least three times the number of dead.[3]

The American *Defence Monitor* at the end of 1979 summed up the world situation in the following terms:

1. War and military conflicts throughout the world are increasingly dangerous to our external interests and to the US itself.
2. Local wars are increasingly intense and terrorism is now a fact of international politics.
3. Weapons provided primarily by the US and the USSR have dramatically increased the power of smaller nations to kill and destroy.
4. When Iran and other irresponsible nations acquire nuclear weapons, war fighting and the conduct of international affairs will be dramatically altered. World War III may easily start from a 'local war'.[4]

The Plight of Refugees

Perhaps the saddest feature of modern war is the vast number of displaced persons and refugees that armed conflicts create. During 1980 alone, the number of refugees in the world was said to have grown by more than two million persons, to an estimated total of seventeen million. This vast army of the world's homeless people includes all

---

[3] *Source – The Defence Monitor*, Washington DC, Volume 8 No. 10, November 1979.
[4] Ibid.

ages, from the elderly to newborn babies. Their incredible suffering defies description. In Kampuchea, in the Horn of Africa and in Latin America, millions of the world's poorest people move from place to place in a desperate search for food, or face certain starvation in the indescribable conditions of refugee camps. With tens of thousands dying of starvation every day in a world of excessive luxury and grinding poverty, the violence and bloodshed that has characterized the history of the twentieth century completes the picture of human madness and misery that is the record of the bloodiest century since the beginning of mankind.

FIGURE 35 *A World at War*

LOCATION OF CONFLICT	DATE CONFLICT BEGAN	WARRING PARTIES	NUMBER OF TROOPS (ESTIMATED)
MIDDLE EAST AND PERSIAN GULF REGION			
Western Sahara	1975	Morocco vs Polisario guerrillas	40,000 7000
Lebannon	1975	Christian Lebanese vs Muslim Lebanese & Palestines	100,000 (all factions)
Israel	1948	Israel vs Palestinian guerrillas	174,000* (active military & police forces) 20,000* (mainly in Lebanon)
Iraq	1979	Iraqi government vs Kurdish & Shiite Muslim guerrillas	212,000* (active military forces) several thousands?
Syria	1979	Syrian government vs Sunni Muslim rebels	227,500* (active military forces) several hundred

LOCATION OF CONFLICT	DATE CONFLICT BEGAN	WARRING PARTIES	NUMBER OF TROOPS (ESTIMATED)
Turkey	1974	Turkish government vs	686,000* (total military & police force)
		Left and right-wing guerrillas	several hundred
Iran	1978	Revolutionary government vs	200,000+?*
		Left-wing & separatist guerrillas	200,000+?
Pakistan	1973	Pakistan government vs	540,000* (total military & para-military forces)
		Baluchi guerrillas	5000
Afghanistan	1978	Afghanistan government vs	90,000 including Russians
		Islamic guerrillas	tens of thousands
North & South Yemen	mid-1950s	North Yemen vs	36,600*
		South Yemen	20,800*
ASIA			
China & Vietnam Border	1979	China vs Vietnam	250,000 85,000
North & South Korea	1950	North Korea vs South Korea	600,000+ (active forces) 560,000 (active forces)
Northeast India	1947	Indian government vs	150,000 (military & para-military)
		Naga & Mizo separatist guerrillas	2500 to 5500 + rebels
Philippines	1972	Philippine government vs	185,000* (total military & police forces)
		Islamic & Communist guerrillas	25,000
Malaysia	1945	Malaysian government vs	77,500* (total military & para-military force)
		Communist guerrillas	3000

LOCATION OF CONFLICT	DATE CONFLICT BEGAN	WARRING PARTIES	NUMBER OF TROOPS (ESTIMATED)
Burma	1948	Burma government vs	242,500* (total military & para-military forces)
		Communist and separatist guerrillas	20,000+
Kampuchea (Cambodia)	1970	Khmer government and Vietnamese forces vs	220,000
		Khmer guerrillas	25,000+
Laos	1975	Lao government vs	48,550* (active military
		Meo guerrillas	1000+
Thailand	1965	Thai government vs	282,000* (military & para-military forces)
		Communist and ethnic guerrillas	2000+
Indonesia	1962	Indonesian government vs	351,000* (active military & para-military)
		Separatist guerrillas	several hundred?

SUB-SAHARA AFRICA

Chad	1965	Chad government vs	5000+
		Islamic rebels	several hundred?
Angola	1975	Angolan government vs	60,000 (Angolan & Cuban forces)
		Anti-Communist guerrillas	30,000 rebels
Ethiopia	1961	Ethiopian government vs	230,000* (military & para-military forces)
		Eritrean & Ogaden guerrillas	50,000+
Namibia	1968	South Africa vs	28,000
		Namibian rebels	3000
Zimbabwe-Rhodesia	1965	Zimbabwe government vs	80,000 (military & para-military forces)
		Black guerrillas	20,000+

LOCATION OF CONFLICT	DATE CONFLICT BEGAN	WARRING PARTIES	NUMBER OF TROOPS (ESTIMATED)
Mozambique	1978	Mozambique government vs	25,000* (total active force)
		Right-wing rebels	a few hundred
South Africa	mid-1970's	White regime vs	570,000* (active & reserve military & police forces)
		Black nationalist rebels	a few hundred

EUROPE

Northern Ireland	1969	British & Protestant Irish vs Irish Catholic nationalist guerrillas	13,500 (British troops) several hundred
Spain	1968	Spanish government vs	420,000* (active military & para-military forces)
		Basque separatist guerrillas	several hundred
Italy	1970	Italian Government vs	560,000* (active military & para-military forces)
		Left & right-wing urban guerrillas	several hundred

LATIN AMERICA

Argentina	1976	Argentine government vs	175,000* (active military & para-military)
		Left and right-wing urban guerrillas	several hundred
Colombia	1978	Colombian government vs	117,500* (active military & police forces)
		Leftist urban guerrillas	several hundred

LOCATION OF CONFLICT	DATE CONFLICT BEGAN	WARRING PARTIES	NUMBER OF TROOPS (ESTIMATED)
El Salvador	1977	El Salvadorian government vs Leftist elements	10,000* (active military & para-military) several hundred
Honduras	1970s	Honduran government vs Leftist elements	14,300* (active military & para-military) several hundred
Mexico	1960s	Mexican government & local landowner vs Leftist elements	100,000* (active military) several hundred
Guatemala	1967	Guatemalan government & right-wing elements vs Leftist elements	21,000+* (active military & para-military) less than 1,000
Puerto Rico	early 1970s	US government vs Separatist urban guerrillas	(police forces only) a few dozen

* NOT ALL TROOPS ARE ENGAGED IN COMBAT
NK: Not known

Source: Center for Defense Information, Washington. USA

CHAPTER EIGHT

Further Bloodshed

Biblical Evidence

At the beginning of chapter seven we noted the strict prohibition of Scripture on murder, violence and especially upon the shedding of innocent blood. Time and again throughout the Bible we are reminded that bloodshed pollutes the land and is abhorrent to God. The consequences of ignoring the commandments of God and of defiling the land with blood are clearly to be seen, not only in the history of Judah and Israel who stood in a special covenant relationship with God, but also in the history of other nations. Time and again God sent warnings to his people through the prophets but they were ignored.

It is recorded that King Manasseh filled Jerusalem with blood. 'Moreover Manasseh shed very much innocent blood till he filled Jerusalem from one end to another' (2 Kings 21:16). Isaiah, Jeremiah and Ezekiel all traced the fall of Jerusalem to the corruption of her leaders and the wickedness of her people, especially in the matter of innocent blood shed. 'Your iniquities have made a separation between you and your God and your sins have hid his face from you so that he does not hear. For your hands are defiled with blood' (Isaiah 59:2,3). 'You have become guilty by the blood which you have shed . . . Behold, the princes of Israel in you, everyone according to his power, have been bent on shedding blood . . . there are men in you who slander to shed blood . . . in you men take bribes to shed blood' (Ezekiel 22:4,6,9,12).

The warnings of the prophets were ignored; no one believed that Jerusalem would fall; surely it was the Holy City and the Lord himself would defend it! But as Jeremiah told them, God would actually turn the weapons of war in their hands and he himself would fight against them because of their wickedness (Jeremiah 21:4,5). This was the reason that the unthinkable happened. 'The kings of the earth did not believe nor any of the inhabitants of the world that a foe or enemy could enter the gates of Jerusalem. This was for the sins of her prophets and the iniquities of her priests who shed in the midst of her the blood of the righteous' (Lamentations 4:12,13).

It was not only the Jews who were warned of the consequences of the shedding of innocent blood. The Bible makes it clear that this is a universal commandment of God that applies to all peoples. The great prophets warned the nations of the world that those who lived by the sword would also die by the sword. Joel said that Egypt would become a desolation and Edom a wilderness, 'because they have shed innocent blood in their land' (3:19), and Ezekiel brings a stern warning to the Gentiles: 'Therefore as I live says the Lord God, I will prepare you for blood and blood shall pursue you; because you are guilty of blood therefore blood shall pursue you. I will fill your mountains with the slain; on your hills and in your valleys and in your ravines those slain with the sword shall fall. I will make you a perpetual desolation and your cities shall not be inhabited. Then you will know that I am the Lord' (Ezekiel 35:6–9).

Empirical Evidence

'They have violated the statutes'

'The world is becoming an increasingly dangerous place.' So said Jimmy Carter to the American people in his final TV speech as President of the United States. President Carter was not a man given to wild or over-dramatic statements. Indeed, throughout his four years in the White House he was known for his moderation, being a 'dove' rather than a 'hawk'. He was a man of peace and not of war. Yet during the final months of his term in office he reversed the policy of his administration and authorized a significant increase in

American defence expenditure, including escalation of work upon the enormously expensive laser defence systems. He thus initiated a new phase of rearming in preparation for a possible third world war.

In his final speech to the American people Jimmy Carter chose to refer to the perils of the world situation, but not because he was hoping such a dramatic appeal would woo the electorate to return him to power. The election was already lost and with it his hopes of returning to the White House were gone for ever. He referred in sombre tones to the increasing threat to world peace because he was in a unique position to know the facts and because he wished to warn the people of the nation he loved.

Future historians, if there are any future historians, will probably record the year 1980 as the decisive turning point in world events. 1980 was the year of the Russian invasion of Afghanistan. It was the year of the abortive attempt of the USA's military might to rescue forty-six of their fellow countrymen held hostage in Iran. It was the year of the Gulf War between the two oil-rich nations of Iraq and Iran. It was the year of the gold crisis, and of mounting world panic over oil as the Arab OPEC nations continued to turn the screw upon the oil-hungry industrial West. It was the year when the world began its plunge into economic recession, with soaring unemployment and continuing inflation compounding the problems of capitalist economies. It was the year when the West began to take seriously the threat of world war and to prepare determinedly for the final conflict.

1980 was the year of fear when *détente* began to disappear from East-West relationships and the ominous signs of return to the cold war began to reappear. As world tensions increased and fear and mistrust amongst the nations grew, the arms race began a new phase in the upward spiral. Nations began to review their military strengths and to count the weaponry in their arsenals. Even those hardest pressed by the downward spiral of economic recession were forced to review national expenditure on defence, and ensure that whatever cuts were made in government spending, the provision of military hardware and trained fighting personnel did not suffer.

PRESENT WORLD SITUATION

The following table shows something of the size of the armed forces of the world's major powers.

FIGURE 36 *Comparative Strength of Armed Manpower*

COUNTRY	POPULATION	ARMED MANPOWER
USA	225,300,000	2,049,100
USSR	265,500,000	3,673,000
UK	55,968,000	343,646
France	53,800,000	504,630
West Germany	61,665,000	495,000
Japan	117,400,000	243,000
TOTAL	779,633,000	7,308,376

Source: The Military Balance 1981–1982, International Institute for Strategic Studies.

1980 saw the beginning of increasing world tensions among the nations, as fear and mistrust of one another led to a new outburst of the banging of war drums. The world began to lurch crazily, like a drunken man slipping on his own vomit, to use the imagery of Isaiah, towards the most destructive conflict in the history of mankind. In the speech already referred to, President Carter warned that a number of other nations would soon possess their own nuclear bombs, and once that position was reached there could be no safety in the world. At the time of his speech US intelligence sources were forecasting the following timetable for nations who were striving to produce their own atomic weapons.

Some international observers believe that Israel already possessed the bomb by the beginning of 1982 and that

FIGURE 37 *Nations Acquiring Nuclear Weapons*

Israel	1982
Pakistan	1983/4
Iraq	1985
Libya	1990

several other Arab states are near the point of arming themselves with nuclear weaponry. If there is one thing all the experts on international affairs are agreed upon it is that once nuclear weapons become the possession of several Middle Eastern states the world will become an incredibly dangerous place.

Several Arab states, including Syria, Libya and Iraq, have openly declared their intention of destroying Israel. It is not simply the centuries-old hostility between Israel and her Arab neighbours that gives cause for alarm, but the highly volatile nature of Middle East politics and the internal instability of many states. A constant fear is that a serious conflict could escalate from a simple internal feud or from the attacks of terrorist extremists such as the PLO, or from the highly volatile situation caused by rival religious groups, such as that between the Christians and Muslims in Syria.

ASSESSING THE DANGER

Even if we discount the possibility of a conflict in the Middle East flaring up into a full-scale world war, the building up of arms amongst the major powers must give considerable cause for disquiet to any sober observer of the international scene. The final year of the Carter administration saw that government taking firm steps towards putting America on a new war footing. Cynics, of course, may be forgiven for suggesting that there may be a link between the new spur given to the arms race and attempts to jack up failing Western economies. Every armchair economist knows that there is no cure for recession quite like war. It's fast, simple and it really works. Both the Second World War and the conflict in Vietnam helped to pull North America and Western Europe out of severe economic slumps. The re-priming of the Western war machines in the 1980s may well do the same again. But what a price to pay for economic prosperity if the end result is a third world war! Einstein was once asked what weapons he thought would be used during the third world war. He paused for a moment and then said he knew what weapons would be used during a fourth world war – bows and arrows!

What are the facts? How great is the danger of a third world war? If there is another war would it involve nuclear weapons? How imminent is the threat facing mankind? Is there any real foundation to the fears that are being expressed by so many eminent authorities on international relationships? Is the new spurt in the arms race a mere ploy to stimulate failing economies or is it a response to the genuine fear among the nations? Are there any reasonable grounds for the hope that world conflict can be avoided? These are some of the major questions being asked by thinking men and women throughout the world who are able to observe the international scene.

There are a number of significant indicators giving cause for grave concern amongst Western observers. One of these is that the Soviet Union has built up an impressive system of nuclear shelters to give protection to large numbers of its citizens in the event of nuclear war. By way of contrast Britain has done virtually nothing. No doubt she is following her usual head-in-the-sand policy of hoping that it won't happen – rather like the man who ignores the gathering storm clouds and refuses even to look for his umbrella until the deluge actually breaks upon him.

The second significant thing that Russia has done in recent years is to work on a sophisticated array of laser beam defence systems capable of knocking out descending missiles before they reach their targets. It was during 1980 that the USA began to face the unpleasant reality that it was being left behind in laser beam defence technology, hence the decision to invest vast sums of money in research and development of these systems in order to ensure that America would catch up and surpass the USSR.

THE NUCLEAR ARSENAL

In assessing the reality of the danger of a world nuclear war it is necessary first to look at the countries that possess nuclear weapons and to estimate the size and strength of their arsenals. The major nuclear powers are Russia, the USA, Britain, France and China. The table in Figure 38 shows the nuclear strength of East and West, with the exception of China for whom there are no reliable figures available.

FIGURE 38 *Comparative Strengths Nuclear Armaments 1981–1982*

POWER	WEAPONS							
	ICBM	MRBM	SRM	LRB	MRB	Strike	Maj.S.Sh	Subs
USA	1052[1]	576	1702	316	60	708	201	84
NATO (less USA)	0	162	1821	0	48	737	250	139
USSR	1398[2]	1599[3]	2183	150	880	2635	294	259
Warsaw Pact (less USSR)	0	0	248	0	0	150	18	6
TOTAL WEST	1052	738	3523	316	108	1445	451	223
TOTAL EAST	1398	1599	2431	150	880	2785	312	265

Key:
ICBM = Intercontinental Ballistic Missiles
MRBM = Medium Range Ballistic Missiles
SRM = Short Range Missiles
LRB = Long Range Bombers
MRB = Medium Range Bombers
Strike = Strike Aircraft
Maj.S.Sh = Major Surface Ships
Subs = Submarines

Notes: The aircraft and ships included in this table are those capable of carrying nuclear weapons.

[1] Including 582 in the megaton plus range
[2] Including 1248 in the megaton plus range
[3] Including 1081 in the megaton plus range

Source: Compiled from statistics in *The Military Balance, 1981–1982.*

In Figure 38 the ICBM, the MRBM and the SRM all refer to the number of launch vehicles not the number of nuclear warheads. Many of these vehicles carry multiple warheads, hence the actual number of nuclear warheads is considerably higher than the number of weapons shown in the table. Britain and France are the only two nations in NATO, apart from the USA, to possess their own independent nuclear weaponry systems. They have been included in the general figures for NATO for the sake of simplicity. None of the nations within the Warsaw Pact, apart from the USSR, has its own nuclear weapons. All of them do, however, have short range nuclear missiles based on their territories. The USSR and the USA, as the two major powers, have been shown separately.

It will be seen from the notes on the table in Figure 38 that Russia has vast superiority in terms of the weight and therefore the destructive power of nuclear weapons, in both the long range and medium range missiles. The West's superiority lies in the number of short range missiles, 3523 as against 2431 of the Eastern bloc countries. It was this fact, plus the American desire to base cruise missiles in Europe, that caused an outcry in Europe when President Reagan, in answer to a press enquiry (20 October 1981), stated that he could envisage a tactical or theatre war in Europe involving the exchange of nuclear weapons without engaging in an all-out exchange of strategic or long range missiles by Russia and America. This confirmed the fears of many European politicians that Europe might be regarded as 'expendable' in the opening phase of a major East-West confrontation.

In estimating destructive power it is worth remembering that the bombs that destroyed the Japanese cities of Hiroshima and Nagasaki were the equivalent of a mere 10,000 tons of TNT, whereas the majority of long range weapons now are in the megaton range, i.e. one hundred times as powerful. Moreover the latest nuclear weapons are of a highly sophisticated nature known as Multiple Independently-targetable Re-entry Vehicles (MIRV). These MIRVs are basically a number of nuclear warheads despatched on a single large rocket carrier into the stratosphere, and which upon re-entry into the earth's atmosphere split into a number of smaller vehicles, each with its own highly sophisticated guidance system that can put its nuclear warhead down to within two or three hundred yards of its chosen target. Some of these MIRVs carry up to thirty nuclear warheads, each with many times the destructive power of the bombs that destroyed Hiroshima and Nagasaki.

The world's super powers also have in their arsenals many more fearful weapons of destruction, including germ warfare and nerve gas bombs. An outstanding example is the neutron bomb particularly designed for use in theatre warfare, where the intention is to destroy all human life in the area without destroying the military equipment or installations. The bombs are exploded in the air above their targets, so that the blast and fallout kills all living creatures, while leaving buildings, installations and equipment usable by an advancing enemy army. In short the neutron bomb destroys life but leaves property relatively unharmed – surely the ultimate blasphemy of a materialistic society, where life is considered expendable but material things are of supreme value. (There must have been great rejoicing among the principalities and powers, the world rulers of darkness, when men invented the neutron bomb!)

For those not familiar with the tactics of modern warfare it may be worth noting there are three levels of warfare which in the event of world conflict may well be regarded as three main stages in escalation. They are (1) conventional, (2) tactical or theatre and (3) strategic.

1. In a conventional war although a wide range of sophisticated weaponry would be used with land, sea and air forces all engaged in combat, nuclear weapons would not be deployed.

2. The second level of warfare would include the use of all conventional weapons but would also deploy 'tactical' nuclear strike forces within the theatre of operations. This means that tactical nuclear missiles would be used primarily against military targets in the theatre of war. These would be either surface launched short range ballistic missiles (SRBM), or the more recently introduced cruise-type missiles (ALCM) with considerable ability for low-level penetration of even the most sophisticated defence systems.

3. The third level of modern warfare which would include the use of 'strategic' nuclear weapons would be an all-out exchange of nuclear warheads on an inter-continental basis with an incredible scale of destruction. Both NATO and the Warsaw Pact countries have very large numbers of nuclear weapons already targeted at each other's key centres of life and production. These weapons are based on a sophisticated range of carriers including inter-continental rocket launched ballistic missiles, submarine and surface ship launched missiles, and others launched by aircraft. They also include the use of long range strategic bombers and self-propelled cruise missiles capable of finding a target within seven hundred feet from a range of several thousands of miles.

In the event of an East-West exchange of strategic nuclear weapons, the result would be the destruction of life and property on the most appalling scale, while the effect of fall-out could render the land useless and pollute the earth's atmosphere to such an extent that life throughout the world would be affected and the genetic consequences to all living creatures would continue for centuries. It is not an exaggeration or an over-dramatic statement to say that life on this planet would never be the same again.

It is this threat of appalling destruction that has formed the basis of international politics for the twenty-five years until 1980. The policy known as MAD, Mutually Assured Destruction, meant that each side recognized that the other had sufficient power of retaliation to make the adventure of a nuclear war unattractive. Although the West held this policy, almost as an article of faith, it is doubtful whether Russia ever accepted the MAD doctrine. The USSR has worked consistently to build up its arms strength not merely to maintain parity but to achieve superiority. It was the recognition of this that eventually caused the West to begin its change of policy in 1980.

THE MILITARY BALANCE

Since the end of World War Two and the resultant division of the world into East and West, which was formalized with the formation of the North Atlantic Treaty Organization (NATO: the USA, Belgium, Britain, Canada, Denmark, France, Greece, Iceland, Italy, Luxembourg, Netherlands, Norway, Portugal, Turkey and West Germany), and the Warsaw Pact (the USSR, Bulgaria, Czechoslovakia, East Germany, Hungary, Poland, Rumania) alliances, both East and West have kept a careful watch on what has come to be known as the 'military balance'. As each side has introduced new and more sophisticated weaponry, so the other has countered this by the introduction of increased strike capability as well as improved defensive systems. Any comparison of strengths is a highly complex exercise and cannot be undertaken by merely counting numbers of men or weapons possessed by each side, since there are many other variables to be taken into consideration. For example, the West has throughout this period relied upon superior quality of training and technology, while the East has countered this with numerically superior forces. The following table shows comparative strengths of ground forces available to NATO and the Warsaw Pact alliances.

FIGURE 39 *Comparative Strength of Armed Manpower (all services)*

USA	2,049,000
(reserves)	880,000
NATO – less USA	2,884,000
(reserves)	3,846,000
USSR	3,673,000
(reserves)	5,200,000
Warsaw Pact – less USSR	1,115,000
(reserves)	1,918,000

TOTAL WEST (including reserves)	9,659,000
TOTAL EAST (including reserves)	11,906,000

Source: Compiled from statistics in *The Military Balance, 1981–1982.*

If we compare also the amount of military hardware in Eastern bloc and Western arsenals available in Europe, we see that strength is heavily weighted on the side of the Eastern bloc countries.

FIGURE 40 *Ground Forces*

	MAIN BATTLE TANKS	MRL	SSML	ATKG	ATGW	AAG	SAML
USA	3000	562	144	0	644	120	180
NATO (less US)	14,053	8940	211	964	5140	5153	1588
USSR	13,000	4680	272	678	287	1086	1751
Warsaw Pact (less USSR)	13,300	5300	348	1190	1150	2500	1400
TOTAL WEST	17,053	9502	355	964	5784	5273	1768
TOTAL EAST	26,300	9980	620	1868	1437	3586	3151

Key: MRL = Multiple Rocket Launchers
SSML = Surface to Surface Missile Launchers
ATKG = Anti-tank guns
ATGW = Anti-tank guided weapons
AAG = Anti-aircraft guns
SAML = Surface to Air Missile Launchers

Source for Figures 40, 41 and 42: Compiled from statistics in *The Military Balance 1981–1982.*

The same also is true for the number of tactical aircraft in operational service. It is the East that has numerical superiority in its air forces.

FIGURE 41 *Airforce Units*

	Bombers	FGA	Fighters	Interceptors	Recon.	AH
USA	0	492	90	0	60	330
NATO (less US)	81	1801	114	572	337	403
USSR	365	1170	665	0	360	100
Warsaw Pact (less USSR)	0	385	0	1490	164	56
TOTAL WEST	81	2293	204	572	397	733
TOTAL EAST	365	1555	665	1490	524	156

Key: FGA = Fighters, Ground Attack
Recon. = Reconnaissance
AH = Armed Helicopters

FIGURE 42 *Naval Units*

	NAVAL UNITS (major craft)					NAVAL AIRCRAFT		
	Carriers	Cruisers	De-stroyers	Frigates	Sub-marines	Bombers	Attacks	Fighters
USA	6	13	43	34	52	0	192	144
NATO (less US)	6	3	85	144	139	0	122	15
USSR	4	20	22	105	*204	280	85	0
Warsaw Pact (less USSR)	0	0	1	4	8	0	42	0
TOTAL WEST	12	16	128	178	191	0	314	159
TOTAL EAST	4	20	23	109	212	280	127	0

*including 54 armed with cruise missiles

These figures indicate that the West has been placing a heavy reliance not only upon the superior quality of its forces but also until recently upon its superior strategic nuclear strike power. But during the past decade the whole position has changed dramatically. During the ten years from 1969 the Soviet Union almost doubled its number of Strategic Nuclear Delivery Vehicles. The figures were *1969*: 1369; *1979*: 2504. During this same period the USA slightly reduced its number of delivery systems from 2270 in 1969 to 2142 in 1979, although the actual number of deliverable warheads doubled to 11,000 during the same period through the introduction of more sophisticated MIRVs.

The International Institute for Strategic Studies ended its summary of the military balance in the East-West theatre in Europe (1979–80 edition) first by noting the extraordinary complexities involved in such a comparison but nevertheless concludes that a state of parity may now be said to exist. It is noted that the Eastern bloc countries have made enormous strides in improving the quality of their forces and the technology underlying their strike and defensive systems. The IISS conclusion is that 'while an overall balance can be said to exist today, the Warsaw Pact appears more content with the relationship of forces than is NATO'. It would appear that for the first time since the end of World War Two the balance of military power is slightly in favour of Russia and her allies. Nevertheless the IISS believes that 'the overall balance is still such as to make military aggression appear unattractive'. The enormous destructive power in the arsenals of both sides means that 'the consequences for an attacker would be incalculable'.[1]

One would think that with such an incredible build-up of military power and the availability of such mind-boggling destructive weapons, war itself would be considered unthinkable by all sane people. Indeed an impartial observer from another planet visiting our world and surveying the international scene could be forgiven for concluding naïvely that nations would now seek to get together to find ways of outlawing war, and agreeing for the sake of the survival of mankind to a programme of mutually supervised destruction of nuclear weapons so that they could never be used, even by accident. Indeed mere non-aggression pacts and treaties are not sufficient, for the spectre of 'war by accident' through a computer mistake or through some maniac getting his finger upon the button is a nightmare that haunts all sane-minded people, including military experts, scientists and politicians.

The argument that in the event of a world conflict between East and West the nations would agree to play the war game according to some kind of international warfare 'Queensberry Rules' is utterly ludicrous. It is a terrible delusion to imagine that there could be some kind of gentleman's agreement to have a limited conflict, whereby only conventional weapons would be used and no one would resort to nuclear strike power. Once conflict broke out on a world scale involving East-West, even if it were possible to restrain the evil forces at work in human nature so that man's desires for the escalation of violence were restrained by fear of the possible consequences, the mistrust of others

_____

[1] *The Military Balance 1979–1980*, p.113.

during a time of conflict would overcome this restraint. Both East and West would fear and mistrust the other. They would be haunted by the knowledge that whoever got in the first nuclear blow would have an incredible advantage over the other, and the artifice of rationalization would play a major part – i.e. we must get our blow in against the enemy before he blows us up!

MOUNTBATTEN'S WARNING

Earl Mountbatten, one of the world's greatest modern soldiers, in the last major speech of his life, warned the world against the kind of complacency that relies upon the false hope of a 'limited' third world war.

Three months before his assassination at the hands of an IRA bomber (27 August 1979), Lord Mountbatten delivered a speech in Strasbourg[2] that received very little publicity in the British national press, either at that time or since. Lord Mountbatten, who has been widely regarded as Britain's greatest military leader of this century – he was successively Commander of HMS *Kelly* and of the Fifth Destroyer Flotilla; Commander of Combined Operations; Supreme Allied Commander, South East Asia; Viceroy of India; Governor General of India; Commander-in-Chief Allied Forces, Mediterranean; First Sea Lord; Chief of the United Kingdom Defence Staff and Chairman of the Chiefs of Staff Office – referred to his own deep disappointment that despite all 'the frightening facts about the arms race, which show that we are rushing headlong towards a precipice', so little had been achieved in terms of world disarmament. He said: 'We live in an age of extreme peril because every war today carries the danger that it could spread and involve the super powers. And here lies the greatest danger of all. A military confrontation between the nuclear powers could entail the horrifying risk of nuclear war.

'The Western powers and the USSR started by producing

---

[2] 11 May 1979, on the occasion of the award of the Louise Weiss Foundation prize to the Stockholm International Peace Research Institute.

and stockpiling nuclear weapons as a deterrent to general war. The idea seemed simple enough. Because of the enormous amount of destruction that could be reaped by a single nuclear explosion, the idea was that both sides, in what we still see as an East-West conflict, would be deterred from taking any aggressive action which might endanger the vital interests of the other.

'It was not long, however, before smaller nuclear weapons of various designs were produced and deployed for use in what was assumed to be a tactical or theatre war. The belief was that, were hostilities ever to break out in Western Europe, such weapons could be used in field warfare without triggering an all-out nuclear exchange leading to the final holocaust.

'I have never found this idea credible. I have never been able to accept the reasons for the belief that any class of nuclear weapons can be categorized in terms of their tactical or strategic purposes.

'Next month I enter my eightieth year. I am one of the few survivors of the First World War who rose to high command in the Second, and I know how impossible it is to pursue military operations in accordance with fixed plans and agreements. In warfare the unexpected is the rule and no one can anticipate what an opponent's reaction will be to the unexpected.

'As a sailor I saw enough death and destruction at sea but I also had the opportunity of seeing the absolute destruction of the war zone of the Western Front in the First World War, where those who fought in the trenches had an average expectation of life of only a few weeks.

'Then in 1943 I became Supreme Allied Commander in South East Asia and saw death and destruction on an even greater scale. But that was all conventional warfare and, horrible as it was, we all felt we had a "fighting chance" of survival. In the event of a nuclear war there will be no chances, there will be no survivors – all will be obliterated.

'I am not asserting this without having deeply thought about the matter. When I was Chief of the British Defence

Staff I made my views known. I have heard the arguments against this view but I have never found them convincing. So I repeat in all sincerity, as a military man I could see no use for any nuclear weapons which would not end in escalation, with consequences that no one can conceive.

'And nuclear devastation is not science fiction – that is a matter of fact. Thirty-four years ago there was the terrifying experience of the two atomic bombs that effaced the cities of Hiroshima and Nagasaki off the map. In describing the nightmare a Japanese journalist wrote as follows:

Suddenly a glaring whitish, pinkish light appeared in the sky accompanied by an unnatural tremor which was followed almost immediately by a wave of suffocating heat and a wind which swept away everything in its path. Within a few seconds the thousands of people in the streets in the centre of the town were scorched by a wave of searing heat. Many were killed instantly, others lay writhing on the ground screaming in agony from the intolerable pain of their burns. Everything standing upright in the way of the blast – walls, houses, factories and other buildings – was annihilated . . . Hiroshima had ceased to exist.

'But that is not the end of the story. We remember the tens of thousands who were killed instantly, or worse still those who suffered slow painful death from the effects of the burns – we forget that many are still dying horribly from the delayed effects of radiation. To this knowledge must be added the fact that we now have missiles a thousand times as dreadful; I repeat, a thousand times as horrible.

'One or two nuclear strikes on this great city of Strasbourg, with what today would be regarded as relatively low yield weapons, would utterly destroy all that we see around us and immediately kill probably half its population. Imagine what the picture would be if larger nuclear strikes were to be levelled against not just Strasbourg but ten other cities in, say, a 200-mile radius. Or even worse, imagine what the picture would be if there was an unrestrained exchange of nuclear weapons – and this is the most appalling risk of all since, as I have already said, I cannot imagine a situation in which nuclear weapons would be used as battlefield weapons without conflagration spreading.

'Could we not take steps to make sure that these things never come about? A new world war can hardly fail to involve the all-out use of nuclear weapons. Such a war would not drag on for years – it could be all over in a matter of days.

'And when it is all over, what will the world be like? Our fine great buildings, our homes will exist no more. The thousands of years it took to develop our civilization will have been in vain. Our works of art will be lost. Radio, television, newspapers will disappear. There will be no means of transport. There will be no hospitals. No help can be expected for the few mutilated survivors in any town to be sent from a neighbouring town – there will be no neighbouring towns left, no neighbours, there will be no help, there will be no hope . . .

'As a military man who has given half a century of active service I say in all sincerity that the nuclear arms race has no military purpose. Wars cannot be fought with nuclear weapons. Their existence only adds to our perils because of the illusions which they have generated.

'There are powerful voices around the world who still give credence to the old Roman precept: if you desire peace, prepare for war. This is absolutely nuclear nonsense and I repeat – it is a dangerous misconception to believe that by increasing the total uncertainty one increases one's own certainty . . .

'It is true that science offers us almost unlimited opportunities but it is up to us, the people, to make the moral and philosophical choices, and since the threat to humanity is the work of human beings, it is up to man to save himself from himself.

'The world now stands on the brink of the final abyss. Let us all resolve to take all possible practical steps to ensure that we do not, through our own folly, go over the edge.'

There can be few Christians, reading that speech of one of the world's foremost military experts, who would not agree that this is a prophetic voice from beyond the grave. 'The world now stands on the brink of the final abyss,' said Lord Mountbatten. The question is, how much longer can we stand there without falling over the edge?

We turn now from the contemplation of the world's terrifying arsenal of destructive weaponry and the recognition that East-West war would inevitably involve the all-out exchange of nuclear warheads, which in turn would bring about the final holocaust that would engulf all mankind, to look at the dangers that are facing mankind from another direction. It is not enough simply to say that dangerous weapons exist in the world and some day some computer may make a mistake and trigger off a chain reaction that would lead to nuclear war. Neither is it enough to say that so long as these weapons exist and are under the control of politicians some crazy maniac may come to power who would deliberately plunge the world into conflict without regard to the terrifying consequences. We need also to assess other forces at work in the world that affect international relationships and may one day lead the nations to war.

WORLD POPULATION

The subject of world population growth is of great interest not merely to demographers who specialize in statistical analyses, but it is a subject to which the United Nations Organization has been giving increasing attention in recent years. At the beginning of the decade of the 1980s the World Health Organization published a population prognostication that, although receiving very little attention in the press, may well prove to be one of the most important documents to come out of the UN. The report showed that while in certain parts of the world birth rates are dropping, overall the world's population is continuing to grow and will go on growing to the end of this century.

FIGURE 43 *Population Growth: Rich and Poor Worlds*

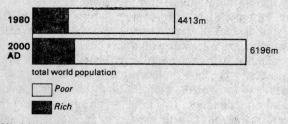

90% of the increase will be in the poor world

Source for figures 43 and 44: UNO

FIGURE 44 *World Population Expansion*

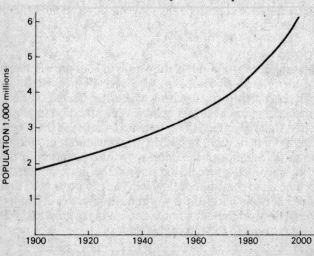

In Figure 44 it will be seen that during the final twenty years of this century, from 1980 to the year 2000, the world's population is expected to grow by around 2000 million. That is more than the entire population of the world was at the beginning of this century. The 1980 *State of the World Population* report produced by the United Nations Fund for Population Activities, reveals that the major factor in population growth is the substantial reduction in death rates that has been achieved in many third world countries. This is due to the vast improvement of health standards and medical care in these countries, which has dramatically reduced the infant mortality rate. But the obvious consequence of tens of millions of youngsters surviving to child-bearing age is a sobering thought for those who are concerned to reduce poverty and to improve living standards in the developing nations.

In figure 45 it will be seen that Kenya is an outstanding example of a third world country experiencing a population explosion, being in fact the first country in recorded history to break the 4 per cent population growth rate. If this growth continued unchecked it would result in a quadrupled population within thirty years. But the problem has been produced by the striking success of Kenya's medical health programme. Doctor Norman Myers writing in the *New Scientist* states that 'the principal factor has not been that Kenyans have started to breed like rabbits. Rather they are no longer dying like flies.' Infant mortality has been cut from 200 per 1000 in 1960 to under 80 today, and the overall death rate is down to 1.4 per cent. This is an achievement matched only by four other African states. Kenya thus combines a low death rate with a high birth rate – the most potent formula for population growth.

It may well be that Kenya is not so much an exception as a front runner in a new trend that will prove the demographers' estimates of population growth to be conservative rather than exaggerated. As medical and health facilities

FIGURE 45 *Comparative Population Statistics*

COUNTRIES	POPULATION ESTIMATE MID-1980 (MILLIONS)	BIRTH RATE (PER 1000)	DEATH RATE (PER 1000)	ANNUAL RATE OF NATURAL INCREASE (%)	INFANT MORTALITY RATE (PER 1000)
Kenya	15·9	55	14	4·0	80
Ethiopia	32·6	50	25	2·5	162
Tanzania	18·6	46	16	3·0	125
Uganda	13·7	45	16	2·9	146
Ghana	11·7	48	17	3·1	115
Niger	5·5	51	22	2·9	200
Nigeria	77·1	50	17	3·3	157
Botswana	0·8	51	17	3·4	97
South Africa	28·4	38	10	2·8	92
China	975	20	8	1·2	56
India	676	34	15	1·9	134
Malaysia	14	31	6	2·5	44
Taiwan	17·8	24	5	1·9	25
Western Europe	153	12	11	0·1	13
North America	2447	15	9	0·6	14

Source: UN Fund for Population Activities.

improve in the developing nations death rates should fall, thus producing situations similar to that in Kenya.

The most important question facing mankind is what will happen if the world's population continues to expand at its present rate. Does there come a point when the basic resources of the world are unable to sustain a continuation of population growth? The two major social processes that also have a considerable bearing upon the answer to this question are 'Industrialization' and 'Urbanization'. While GNP (gross national product) growth rates have been slowing down for years in the industrialized West, they have been showing a corresponding increase in many parts of the developing world. Many third world nations are making enormous efforts to increase industrial capacity and output, but the most striking feature of development in the third world is the movement of population into the cities. The following table gives an indication of the rate of growth of cities during this century. It will be noted that it is estimated that by the year 2000, 80 per cent of the world's population will be living in urban complexes. This fact, taken together with the estimates in overall population growth, indicates the size of the demand for basic resources.

FIGURE 46 *Growth of Cities*

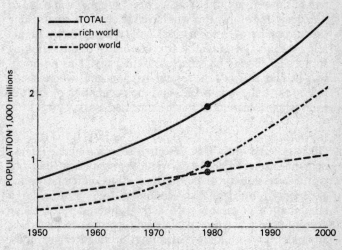

Source: UN Fund for Population Activities

BASIC RESOURCES
(i) *Oil*
One of the basic resources that is already causing world-wide anxiety is oil. Oil has become the industrialized world's

major source of energy, and with forecasts that many of the world's supplies of oil will be running dry by the end of the century there is considerable cause for anxiety. Throughout the 1970s and into the 1980s the Middle Eastern oil-producing states have been steadily exploiting the Western world's thirst for oil. The price of crude oil has risen year by year, contributing materially to chronic inflation and rising production costs in Western economies. Despite the enormous cost of oil, consumption shows no sign of abating – indeed demand appears to be rising steadily, particularly with increasing industrialization in the third world.

The plain fact is that we are fast using up the world's supply of oil, and unless alternative sources of energy have been discovered and made available upon a vast scale by the end of this century, the shortage of oil supplies will begin to bite deep. Inevitably this will have the effect of heightening the tension between the nations and straining international relationships. The scramble for the control of the shrinking sources of oil may be expected to intensify. This no doubt was behind Russia's move into Afghanistan, where she is poised for a move into Iran and the occupation of key oil-producing states should this become necessary.

(ii) *Gold*

Oil is not the only basic resource to come under intense demand during recent years. With the continued slide into world recession through the increasing difficulties being experienced by capitalist economies (due in turn to a combination of factors such as high interest rates, rising costs of production due to increasing costs of raw materials, advances in technology affecting production methods, increasing conflict with organized labour, intense market competition, the growth of multi-national corporations, to name but a few), further strains have been placed on international relationships. The beginning of the 1980s saw a massive rise in unemployment in many Western nations that had for several decades been enjoying full employment. This intensified the fears of many that a repeat of the slump

FIGURE 47 *World Gold Price*

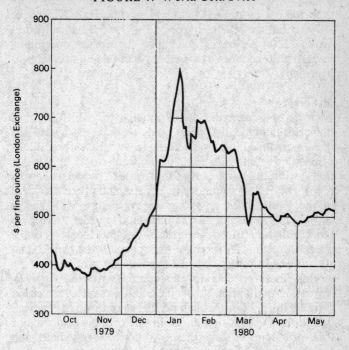

Source: London Bullion Market.

conditions of the 1920s was becoming a distinct possibility.

Inevitably when such fears begin to grip the entrepreneurs in a free market economy, they run for cover. The search to invest in something solid rather than risk losing millions in failing industries produced a strong demand for precious metals and fine art. Even big labour unions began to buy up valuable paintings with the money in their pension funds, rather than invest in doubtful stock.

The gold fever that began the 1980s was a sign of the near panic that gripped the world's entrepreneurs. It is reflected in

Figure 47, which shows how the price of gold leapt by more than 100 per cent in less than two months, from November 1979 to January 1980. By the end of 1980 it had settled at around $600 per ounce, indicating the world's continuing fears that the economic recession was not going to disappear overnight.

(iii) *Food*

Food is of course the basic resource for which there is universal demand. In recent years we have witnessed the most incredible famines, resulting in starvation for millions of people in numerous parts of the third world. It is ironic that during this same period the Western press has carried reports of butter mountains in Europe, and of the President of the United States paying farmers in the Mid-West a subsidy not to farm a fifth of their land in order to keep up the world grain prices. Nevertheless, despite the irony of the overproduction of food in one part of the world and starvation in another, the question remains as to whether the world's food production can continue to feed its ever-increasing population. If the day should come when, either through drought or through pestilence or through chemical pollution, harvests should fail in one of the world's major food-producing areas, there would be immediate and catastrophic results.

With a 30 per cent rise in the world's population expected during the final twenty years of this century, the demand for food production will constantly increase. We have not yet reached the point where shortages of food begin to concern the powerful nations of the Western world, although it is already the constant anxiety of nations in the Eastern bloc, including Russia, but it is highly likely that food shortages will become a major concern of many more nations, including the West, by the end of this century or the early part of the next.

THE FUTURE

This possibility of food shortages on a world-wide scale is

undoubtedly one of the factors affecting the population prognostication shown in the following figure published by the World Health Organization of the UN.

FIGURE 48 *World Population Explosion Prognostication (Forrester model)*

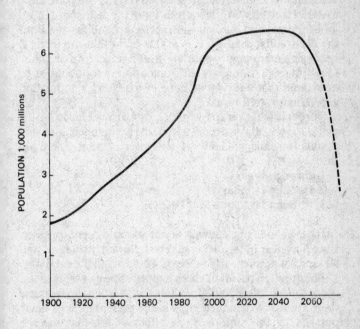

Source: United Nations

In a world punch-drunk by the ceaseless bombardment of bad news, it is perhaps hardly surprising that the publication of the above UN figure was treated as just another report. It received little attention in the world's press and scant heed has been paid to the immense significance of what is being said. The report forecasts a kind of backlash effect to the population explosion, that will add 2000 million to the world's population between 1980 and the year 2000. It forecasts that by then the pressure upon world resources will be so great that the growth rate will begin to slow markedly and the peak will be reached around the year 2020. At this point it will plateau for a period of thirty years, thus maintaining maximum pressure upon the world's basic material and mineral resources until the demand can no longer be met and the explosion occurs around the middle of the twenty-first century. It is at this point that the forecast becomes a mere vague speculation, as it indicates a dramatic fall in the size of the world's population, but how great or how rapid that fall is to be none of the world's population experts dares to forecast.

Through what means would a catastrophic drop in the world's population occur? How does it happen that any population falls suddenly? The answer is clear. There are three ways:

1. through War;
2. through Famine;
3. through Pestilence and Disease.

In the event of a nuclear war, all three would occur together, since a nuclear holocaust would be followed by famine, and all kinds of pestilence and disease would assail the survivors.

The question is, is it likely to happen? The answer is that it is not merely likely to happen but that it *will* happen unless there are fundamental changes in the present policies being pursued by the nations. It is a fact of life that there is something in the nature of man that is so innately self-seeking that he will fight to gratify his desires. When the objects of his desire are in short supply, man becomes intensely competitive and will seek to destroy those whom he sees standing in opposition to the fulfilment of his objectives. Unless a higher motive replaces the gratification of desire, greedy men, driven to the extremities by the frustration of their ambitions or by what they see as a threat to their personal survival, will even fight with their friends and neighbours in an attempt to secure their own positions.

Put in global terms, as the demand for the basic material resources of the world increases through population growth and through the rising aspirations of man, producing real or perceived shortages, competition between the nations will intensify as it is seen as a fight for survival. The day will come when greedy men will go to war in an attempt to secure the shrinking basic resources of the world for themselves. The message is clear: in the times of shortage that are coming upon the world, unredeemed men will destroy each other. It is no longer a question of whether it will happen, the question now is, *when* will it happen? The world is like a man being told he has terminal cancer. The question follows, 'How long have we got?'

THE SPACE BATTLE

In human terms, the answer to this question was provided in a dramatic fashion by a display of man's inventive genius and technological achievement in March 1981. The occasion was the launching of the American space shuttle, a manned craft that orbited the earth and made a successful re-entry and landed on dry land. The significance of this achievement lay not simply in its commercial and scientific value but in its military potential, although this was not the original intention, according to David Baker, scientific consultant to NASA, the American space agency. He stated that he and his colleagues 'felt cheated' as they had developed the space shuttle for peaceful purposes. They thought that it was going to be used for scientific research and for communications, but they now realized that 90 per cent of its payload would be for military purposes.

Instead of the shuttle being used to take scientific equipment up into space laboratories, it would be used to take military equipment up to equip a number of space battle stations orbiting around the earth. American intelligence sources have reported that Russia has developed particle beam weapons of frightening destructive capability. It is believed that Russia is intending mounting these beam weapons on to orbiting space platforms. The USA has decided, therefore, to take the initiative in space warfare by establishing battle stations. These will be equipped with laser beam weapons which can destroy Russia's heavy inter-continental ballistic missiles, either in the air or on the ground. The laser beams have a range of three thousand miles. It is estimated that it would require twenty-four orbiting space battle stations to give global surveillance and thus control the whole of the earth's surface.

The military experts who advise the US Government are reported to have given up hoping for *détente* with Russia, and for arms limitation and control. They have therefore advised the US Government to pursue a policy of producing the most devastating weapons possible. It is believed that they have the technology to outstrip Russia.

The policy of 'mutually assured destruction' which is the basis of the 'deterrent policy', is now giving way to the belief that it is possible actually to win a nuclear war. Clearly, the risks involved in this new policy of international brinkman-ship are colossal.

The race is on! – who will be the first to establish their laser beams battle stations in space? Who will win the space race and take global control of this stricken planet? One thing is perfectly clear – if Russia is the first to establish a battle station in space, the USA will shoot it down. But equally, it may be supposed that if the USA is the first to establish a space battle station Russia will seek to destroy it. Both Russia and America know that they cannot allow the other to take control of space. These battle stations could be used for particle beam weapons that have the capacity to kill people without destroying buildings. These could be directed at cities from a range of up to 3000 miles and annihilate the inhabitants, thus rendering nations incapable of defending themselves against conventional attacks from an enemy using ground forces.

Both Russia and America know that this is a race they cannot lose. Both sides will make every effort and use every weapon in their arsenals to prevent the other side from winning the space race. A full-scale nuclear war could easily result from a conflict over the control of space. Whoever loses the race will start the war! At the moment, both sides are putting all their efforts into developing the technology that will enable them to take control of the space battle area. Neither side is ready to make the crucial move at the moment. Each is watching the other anxiously. It is still possible for international agreements to be made on the use of space for peaceful purposes only and for agreements to be made upon arms limitation. It is still possible that sanity will prevail, but the day will come when it will be too late. Military authorities estimate that by the end of the 1980s or early 1990s, either Russia or the USA will have reached the point where they are in a position to set up their space battle stations. If either side decides to take the risk, the point of no return will have been reached!

Will the people of all nations throughout the world rise up and say to both Russia and America, 'Thus far you have gone, you shall go no farther!'? Will all the nations agree to stop the arms race? Will the smaller nations, including the Middle Eastern states, agree to give up the attempt to arm themselves with nuclear weapons? Will mankind turn away from the path upon which the nations are now furiously embarked, the path that leads to mutual self-destruction? Will mankind let loose the holocaust that will engulf the planet and lay waste the earth? Only the full repentance of man and a turning to God in penitence and humility can save us from destruction.

THE HOPE OF THE WORLD
It is with the realization of the hopelessness of our situation, in human terms, that God is able to transform the scene. God always meets us at the point of our human despair – at the point where we reach and acknowledge the limit of our human power. When man realizes that he is powerless to stand against the forces of evil in his own nature that are driving him towards destruction, God is able to bring to him

the transforming power that he released into the world through the cross to change the very nature of man. This is the radical solution that is needed to change the course of human history. We are now approaching the climax of the ages. The Gospel is no longer a luxury which men can afford to choose or to ignore. It is the only means of saving mankind – literally saving men from annihilation. As Solzhenitsyn, the Russian dissident, put it starkly, 'We need spiritual revival for physical survival' – prophetic words from a man who has seen life on both sides of the Iron Curtain.

But will man heed the warnings?

CHAPTER NINE

Materialism: Economics

Biblical Evidence

The Bible takes an unequivocable stand against idolatry. The first commandment God gave to the people of Israel was 'You shall have no other gods before me'. The second commandment reinforced this with, 'You shall not make for yourself a graven image or any likeness of anything that is in the heaven above, or that is in the earth beneath, or that is in the water underneath the earth; you shall not bow down to them or serve them' (Exodus 20:3–5). When Israel broke this commandment the prophets interpreted this as spiritual adultery: 'Because harlotry was so light to her she polluted the land, committing adultery with stone and tree' (Jeremiah 3:9). Ezekiel similarly says, 'With their idols they have committed adultery' (23:37).

Throughout the Old Testament whenever Israel turned away from the Lord and worshipped other gods the consequences in the life of the nation were terrible. Time and again the prophets called the people back to the pure worship of God, who was faithful to them despite their faithlessness, but in generation after generation they backslid and created their own gods of wood and stone.

Even before the writing prophets, God used his servants the Judges to call his people back to purity of religion. Joshua is the outstanding example of a man who made the people face up to the evils of idolatry and recognize that they could not serve both God and material idols. 'Choose this day whom you will serve,' he said, while at the same time making clear what his own course of action would be, 'but as for me and my house we will serve the Lord' (Joshua 24:15).

The great prophets continually poured scorn upon the bits of wood and stone to which men bowed and ascribed divine powers. Isaiah laughed at the gods of the Babylonians, Bel and Nebo, whom he knew would be carried away on ox carts after Cyrus had overthrown the city. He contrasted their inability to save their worshippers with the faithfulness of the Lord, who loved his people Israel and who would carry and save those whom he had borne (Isaiah 46:1–4). Isaiah further poured scorn upon those who were so stupid that they couldn't see how ridiculous it was to cut down a tree, chop off its branches, use them to make a fire to warm themselves and to cook their food, and then use the rest of the wood to make a god, and bow down before it and ask for deliverance. They must have deluded minds to think so irrationally and to behave so mindlessly, he says (Isaiah 44:9–20).

Paul, with all the vehemence at his command, states unequivocally that it is not only the Jews, who stood in a covenant relationship with God and who had the law and the prophets to guide them, who have to obey the command- ment forbidding idolatry. He declares that 'The wrath of God is revealed from heaven against all ungodliness and wickedness of men who by their wickedness suppress the truth. For what can be known about God is plain to them because God has shown it to them. Ever since the creation of the world his invisible nature, namely, his eternal power and deity, has been clearly perceived in the things that have been made. So that they are without excuse; for although they knew God they did not honour him as God' (Romans 1:18–21). In Paul's view the whole of mankind stands before God guilty of idolatry, that is, of worshipping material things, the creation of their own hands, rather than the one true and only Creator of the whole world. It is perfectly clear, he declares, that there is a God of creation, whose nature can be known to all men, but they have not sought him and worshipped him. Instead they have turned away from the truth and have thereby been driven by the forces of darkness.

It is because of man's idolatry and the deliberate turning of his back upon the truth that all kinds of evil have come upon mankind. Personal immorality and social corruption have become the dominant forces which according to Paul are driving mankind towards destruction.

Whenever men turn away from God and worship things created by their own hands they are guilty of idolatry and have turned away from life to death, from the living God to dead matter. The Bible gives numerous instances of various kinds of idolatry, from creating graven images, the golden calf of Aaron (Exodus 32:4), to the building up of the empires of mammon. 'Doomed is the man who builds his house by injustice and enlarges it by dishonesty; who makes his countrymen work for nothing and does not pay their wages' (Jeremiah 22:13, GNB). 'You take interest and increase and make gain of your neighbours by extortion; and you have forgotten me, says the Lord God' (Ezekiel 22:12).

'Man shall not live by bread alone,' said Jesus. 'Then the devil took him up and showed him all the kingdoms of the world in a moment of time and said to him, "To you I will give all this authority and their glory; for it has been delivered to me and I can give it to whom I will. If you, then, will worship me, it shall all be yours." And Jesus answered him, "It is written, you shall worship the Lord your God and him only shall you serve"' (Luke 4:4–8). Jesus reminded all those who would follow him that they should count the cost and be prepared to reject the things that are greatly valued by worldly men, because man either chooses to follow the path of life or he is driven by the forces of darkness that lead to death. 'No one can serve two masters; for either he will hate the one and love the other or he will be devoted to the one and despise the other. You cannot serve God and mammon' (Matthew 6:24).

Empirical Evidence

'They have broken the everlasting covenant'

The spirit of the twentieth century may aptly be described as the spirit of materialism. The two great political, economic and cultural systems into which the present-day world is divided, communism and capitalism, are both basically materialistic in ethos and practice. Both systems, although diametrically opposed in aims, objectives and in philosophical premise, are nevertheless founded upon basically materialistic assumptions. It is our task in this chapter briefly to examine this contention.

I COMMUNISM

Those who dismiss communism as being no more than vulgar materialism simply convict themselves of ignorance of Marxist philosophy. Marxism can only be fully understood when its roots in 'Hegelianism' are fully understood. The philosopher Hegel was greatly admired by both Marx and Lenin, and much of their early thinking was modelled upon his philosophical system. Hegel was an idealist but the system of thought that he devised was radically different from anything previously developed in idealistic systems. Hegelianism may be distinguished on the one hand from Platonic idealism, which attributes reality only to the eternal or the spiritual, and on the other hand from Renaissance naturalism which attributes reality only to the ephemeral sphere of changing phenomena. In Hegel reality is interpreted by the ingression of the divine idea into the world of being which, by this ingression, is charged with dynamic possibilities of change. The pattern of this change is the dialectic – the thesis, antithesis and synthesis – and it is this dialectic that gives for Hegel the clue to history.

Dialectical Materialism

Marx seized upon the dialectic as providing the analytical tool for which he had been searching, but he changed the basic concept from idealism to materialism. He said to Hegel, in effect, the dialectic does indeed provide the key that will unlock the door of history but you have got it upside down by yoking it to the wrong concept. By turning dialectical idealism into dialectical materialism Marx believed that he had got the key that would unlock the door of history and throw wide open the mystery of the ages. Using this key Marx set about constructing a system which both interpreted history and, when linked to a political strategy, would provide the basis of communism. He moved away from the idealistic view of reality in which the whole created order is permeated by divine thought or spirit. Instead he believed that thought itself is to be understood as the product of a dialectic process in the world of material things. Reality for Marx was thus not 'thought moving matter' but 'matter in motion' which, amongst other things, produces thought. From this basic premise two fundamental dogmas emerged, economic determinism and historical materialism.

Economic determinism is the application to the study of history of the fundamental principle that spirit is dependent upon nature and that thought is inescapably conditioned by matter because it is the product of matter in motion. Thus the Marxist contention is that to understand any historical age in terms of its culture, its philosophy, its art, its religion and its political life, you have first of all to study the material conditions underlying that period of history. The assumption is that the whole cultural growth of a society evolves out of the conditions of its material environment. Man is thus the creature of his material environment, the product of the socio-economic scene rather than the producer of it. The spiritual elements of life are not in fact denied, they are subordinated to the material. It is material things that represent ultimate reality not spiritual things.

Historical Materialism

Historical materialism is a further application of the same method of analysis. Each separate era of mankind is a complete matrix of spiritual and economic factors in which the economic are the fundamental realities and the spiritual are the dependent variables. Change in society occurs from one period of history to another not because men have made a free choice to change the pattern of society but because there has been a fundamental change in the economic structure, the basic reality of life, which thereby brings about a change in every other area of society. Marx believed that the way to set men free was to enable them to have within their hands the analytical tools for the interpretation of history. Once men could understand what was happening then they would be in a position to control fundamental processes. He believed that the ability to control the economy would provide too the ability to control history and not only to interpret it.

Marx saw the whole of history as the record of the struggle between the rulers and those who are subject to them. Engels summarized the fundamental proposition of the communist manifesto in these terms, 'That in every historical epoch, the prevailing mode of economic production and exchange, and the social organization necessarily following from it, form the basis upon which is built up, and from which alone can be explained, the political and intellectual history of that epoch; that consequently the whole history of mankind (since the dissolution of primitive tribal society, holding land in common ownership) has been a history of class struggles, contests between exploiting and exploited, ruling and oppressed classes; that the history of these class struggles forms a series of evolutions in which, nowadays, a stage has been reached where the exploited and oppressed class – the proletariat – cannot attain its emancipation from the sway of the exploiting and ruling class – the bourgeoisie – without, at the same time, and once and for all, emancipating society at large from all exploitation, oppression, class distinctions and class struggles' (*The Manifesto of the Communist Party*, Karl Marx and Frederick Engels, p. 8).

The Key to History

Marx and Engels believed that dialectical materialism provides us with a key to understanding the processes of change that occur throughout history. Using this tool of analysis they discovered that every type of society is within unstable equilibrium because it carries within itself the conditions of its own transformation – the thesis, antithesis and synthesis – and that each new synthesis had been brought about by the process of class struggle, by the supersession in power of one economic group by another. At the time of publishing the *Communist Manifesto* in 1848 they believed that capitalism was rapidly accruing the conditions of its own destruction. It had destroyed the old feudal pattern of life by bringing together great masses of labouring men to work in industry throughout Western Europe and America. Industry had thus created the proletariat, a new class of landless peasants who were little more than industrial slaves, having no share in the ownership of the means of production and able only to sell their labour at a price that would profit the owners of industry.

The Class Struggle

Yet Marx and Engels did not see the processes of industrialization and urbanization as being inherently evil. Their chief concern was to warn of the dangers of the dichotomizing of the class struggle between the new class of rulers who had wrested power from the landed barons and the new class of industrial workers. They believed that, like previous social crises, this one could only be resolved either by a revolutionary reconstitution of society or through the common ruin of the contending classes. In the words of the manifesto, 'The essential condition for the existence and of the sway of the bourgeoisie class, is the formation and augmentation of capital; the condition for capital is wage labour. Wage labour rests exclusively on competition between the labourers. The advance of industry, whose involuntary promoter is the bourgeoisie, replaces the isolation of the labourers, due to competition, by their revolutionary combination, due to association. The development of modern industry, therefore, cuts from under its feet the very foundations on which the bourgeoisie produces and appropriates products. What the bourgeoisie therefore produces, above all, are its own gravediggers. Its fall and the victory of the proletariat are equally inevitable' (*Manifesto*, p. 20).

Marx believed that the central dilemma of capitalism is that its own interests are best served by, on the one hand, keeping wages low and, on the other hand, demanding high prices for finished goods. These two are, in fact, contradictory since the industrialist wishes to pay low wages to his workers in order to keep costs down and maximize profit, but he depends upon the prosperity of the workers, who are the customers in the market, for the finished goods that he wishes to sell.

Competition and Market Expansion

Marx thus saw the inevitable link between capitalism and imperialism because the survival of capitalism depends upon ever-increasing markets. With increasing productivity due to higher technology new markets must be found where surplus goods from the home market can be sold. He saw competition and conflict in the whole of the capitalist system as being inevitable. Competition exists among manufacturers for a larger share of the market and for greater profitability. But there is also a conflict of interest between the owners of industry and the workers. The interests of the owners are in low wages and high prices, whilst the interests of the workers are in high wages and low prices. The interests of the workers are in full employment whilst the interests of the employers lie in the maintenance of a surplus pool of labour so that men can be hired at competitive wage-rates. The employers are interested in cutting costs and increasing productivity by improved industrial technique. From the standpoint of the workers every improvement in technology means less demand for labour and increases the threat of unemployment.

In a highly technological society the workers must either compete with one another for the ever-decreasing number of jobs, or band together for mutual support in bad times and for a just share of the proceeds of industry at all times. Hence the development of trade unions and the political organization of labour.

Thus, according to the Marxist analysis of society, due to the inherent contradictions within capitalism and the polarization of different interest groups, conflict is inevitable until a revolutionary change takes place in the structure of society and a new and classless structure evolves.

Critique of Marxism

The conclusions drawn by Marxists may be questioned from a number of standpoints, but there is overwhelming empirical evidence to support the contention that history is a record of the clash between groups whose economic interests are opposed. The Marxist analysis of history as a dialectic struggle between one social order and its successor and between class and class is a useful starting point in the search for the truth about man and society.

The basic limitations in the Marxist system begin to be revealed when we ask the simple question, 'Why?' Why is it that in every age men have sought to gain economic advantage over others, one group has striven for mastery over another and the holders of power have oppressed the powerless? Why is it that, in the words of the tired old cliché, history is a record of man's inhumanity to man? The Marxist has no answer to these simple yet fundamental questions. He can only say that by studying history we may learn to understand the processes that are at work within human society. By so doing men may gain, not a mastery over history, for that would be impossible within the framework of economic determinism, but an advantage over those who do not have such an understanding of the dialectical historical process. Such a knowledge gives the possibility of co-operating with, or manipulating, the processes of change to the advantage of the oppressed over the oppressors. Hence the Marxist hope, in the manifesto, of the ultimate victory of the proletariat.

The Marxist philosophy is useful as an analytical device for the examination of phenomena, but it totally lacks the ability to diagnose the fundamental phenomenological problems such an analysis reveals. It is for this very basic reason that the solutions it proposes must always be wrong. If the diagnosis is wrong the solution proposed can at best only be random in direction.

Failure of Russian Communism

History bears testimony to this in what has happened in Russia since 1917. The revolution certainly transformed the social order and replaced the old order with a new one, it certainly overthrew the existing group of rulers but it has replaced them with another group who must surely go down in the annals of history as contenders for the most repressive regime ever known to mankind. To replace one group of oppressors with another is certainly progress of a kind, but it hardly fulfils the Marxist dream of freedom for all within a classless society! During the 1970s there was some attempt within Russia at some form of political liberalization following the denunciations of the excesses of the Stalinist era. But the repression of free speech and the detention of dissidents in labour camps continue unabated, which is a sure indication that the basic philosophy of the oppression of the masses by the élitist ruling class is quite unchanged. The full story of Russian atrocities against countless individuals will probably never be known, but some indication of the ruthless determination of the Russian rulers may be seen by the swift brutality with which the struggles of the people for freedom were repressed in neighbouring Hungary and Czechoslovakia and the pressure brought to bear upon the Polish people resulting in martial law and a new regime of repression.

The failure of Russian communism to develop a society

freed from oppression stems from the basic diagnostic weakness inherent in Marxist philosophy. This weakness does not lie in its analysis of history as a struggle between opposing classes, nor in the insights it provides as to the role of the socio-economic environment in conditioning the ideas that men hold and thus in determining the actions they take as individuals or as groups. It is surely perfectly obvious that a child brought up in rural Pakistan will have very different ideas, religious beliefs and social values from a child brought up in New York. In the same way a child brought up in the East End of London or inner-city Glasgow or Liverpool will have very different ideas of social values from a child brought up in an upper middle class family in Hertfordshire.

The basic weakness of Marxism lies not in empirical analysis but in its diagnosis of social phenomena. In accepting the metaphysical dualism inherent in the idealism of Hegel, Marx failed to recognize the true nature of the conflict he perceived within the historical processes of change, and he thereby failed to appreciate the significance of the social environment upon man's personal development. It is here that the Bible provides us with the answer that Marxism is totally unable to discover.

The Sovereignty of God

The whole of biblical tradition underlines the absolute sovereignty of God. He is the creator and sustainer of all things, both in the physical universe and in the realm of the spiritual. But the Bible also recognizes the existence of evil, and that the forces of evil let loose in the world affect the whole of mankind both in terms of personal development and interpersonal relationships. The Bible, nevertheless, is careful to avoid any kind of dualism. It is God who is in control. He is the Lord of history. Everything that happens in this world is either because he has willed it or because he has allowed it. He has allowed the forces of evil to gain ascendancy during the course of history as part of the price of his overall purpose in bringing mankind into a living vital fellowship relationship with himself. The witness of Scripture is that man is in rebellion against God so that the whole of his spiritual, moral and physical nature, as well as his social, economic and political existence, is out of harmony with the natural order as God created it and intended it to be.

Thus the central dilemma facing mankind is not a mere problem of philosophical dualism, such as whether we follow Marx in giving priority to the material over the spiritual or whether we follow Plato and Hegel in giving priority to the spiritual. The problem is much more fundamental than that. The Bible declares that the root of the problem lies in the very nature of man which, due to his rebellion against God, is sinful in essence. The evidence of Scripture entirely supports the Marxist analysis that man's life is conditioned by his greed, and it opposes the idealist view that man's ideals and aspirations are transcendent over his greed. The witness of Scripture is that the tragedies of history will continue and will get progressively worse in their consequences for mankind, but that there is an answer to man's dilemma. God has been at work to accomplish man's salvation since the beginning of his rebellion.

Salvation: Not by Works

The old covenant brought with it the law, obedience to which would save men from the worst results of their rebellion, pending their full restoration which was fore-shadowed in the prophets. The new covenant, which is foretold by Jeremiah and initiated by the birth of Christ, is decisively not of works. The good news is that God has acted in history to transform the nature of man, a nature that is driving him towards destruction, by breaking the force of the powers of evil that are driving him. Since God is the absolute Creator of all things only he can understand the true nature of the powers of evil in the universe, and therefore only he can overcome them. This is the answer of Scripture to the central dilemma of mankind, which Marxism clearly perceives but is powerless to counter. It is not some puny philosophical metaphysical dualism that we are offered, but the great saving act of God in history that brings about a fundamental change in the nature of man, that is available to Gentile as well as to Jew through the great love of God for all his children.

Failure of Materialism

It is small wonder that Marx, who was blinded to the spiritual realities of life, failed to appreciate the true nature of the problem of history and therefore, instead of seeing man in rebellion against God and thereby out of harmony with the natural order of creation, his only answer was to co-operate with or to attempt to manipulate the processes of change by which one group of sinners wrests power from another group. Marxism is thus confined to working within the framework of the very forces of evil that are bent upon the destruction of mankind. What Marx did was to offer materialistic solutions to what are essentially spiritual problems. He did this because of his basic failure to understand and to diagnose correctly the true nature of the problems underlying the history of mankind.

II CAPITALISM

The spirit of capitalism is equally materialistic and probably in some respects more grossly so than that of communism. The basically materialistic nature of capitalism very often goes unnoticed within the Western world, due to the heavily-charged emotions any discussion of the subject arouses. This is largely due to the fact that capitalism has come to be regarded as an integral part of our Western way of life. It is therefore associated not only with our culture but with our most cherished social values and even with our religious beliefs. Capitalism is regarded by most Westerners as the only alternative to communism and as being indissolubly linked with a democratic system of government. Capitalism is thus seen as the defender of freedom and individual liberty, the champion of human rights, the mainstay of democracy and the bulwark against totalitarianism. All of these statements are complete and utter lies. There is not a word of truth in them, but the extent to which they are believed by millions of people is both an indication of the power of the capitalist-controlled media and education system and the gullibility of humanity.

An Economic Institution

In the first place, capitalism has nothing whatsoever to do with democracy or indeed with any other system of political organization. It is purely an economic institution, a system of finance. It can be operated within a democratic system or within a totalitarian system, under an elected socialist government or under a fascist dictator. Capitalism is concerned with the means of exchange. In essence it is a system of financial credit, the issuing of money at interest to provide the necessary capital for industry and commerce to enable them to undertake and continue the processes of production, distribution and exchange.

This is not the place to undertake an economic critique of capitalism, neither would it be relevant to our purposes. It is, however, relevant to remind ourselves that the banks and international financiers who lend money at interest are not the producers of wealth. It is the industrialist, the inventor, the engineer, the producer, the distributor, the trader, the shopkeeper, the professional men and women and the workers – it is they who produce the wealth of the nations. They are not the capitalists, although inevitably everyone gets caught up in the system to some degree or another, but strictly speaking it is the bankers and international financial entrepreneurs who are the capitalists. It is they who provide the credit facilities by lending money at interest, usually at no risk to themselves. It is the producers of wealth who take the risks.

The Credit System

When an industrialist wishes to purchase new machinery or to open a factory, or a shopkeeper wishes to expand his business, or a doctor wishes to re-equip his surgery, and turns to the bank for credit facilities, the bank normally requires full security, the deeds of the property or some other collateral, to set against the loan. Thus it is not the money lenders who take the risks but the producers of wealth and it is they who suffer in times of economic recession. The money lenders are the parasites who live off the labours of others, who profit from the inventive genius and the enterprise of others and who, with high rates of interest, usually grow richer even when times are hard for the industrialist and the worker alike.

It is not simply individuals and private firms who borrow from the entrepreneurs, the whole Western world is caught up in the credit system. Large public corporations and national governments borrow extensively to finance their programmes. Much of the wealth of the nations is swallowed up simply in 'servicing the debt', i.e. in paying huge sums of interest to the international financiers. In fact, the last thing the capitalist entrepreneurs want to see is a debt paid off since they live by money lending. Britain has had a national debt for around two hundred years, and successive governments have had to levy an ever-increasing burden of income tax upon the people simply in order to pay the vast sums of interest required annually on that debt.

National Debts

It is not only powerful nations like Britain, France and the USA whose people and industries stagger under the burden of huge national debts. The situation is far more desperate in many of the smaller nations within the Western orbit. Brazil, for example, during 1980 used a third of its total foreign exchange from export earnings to pay the interest on its massive national debt of over sixty billion dollars. When payment on the principal is included, plus the enormous cost of oil imports, Brazil actually paid out 107 per cent of all its export earnings on the cost of the national debt and oil. This means that all other imports had to be paid for out of foreign currency reserves and by raising further loans to add to the existing debt mountain. The desperate financial situation in Brazil is further compounded by an incredible rate of inflation (115 per cent in 1980). Increasing the country's external debt simply adds to the burden of the crippling sums that have to be paid to the international bankers, and merely postpones the day of the complete collapse of the national economy. But Brazil, although top of the league of the third world debtor nations (according to figures released by the Morgan Guaranty Trust Company of the USA), is by no means the only country fighting for economic survival. According to the *Wall Street Journal*, the cost of oil and the national debt accounted for 101 per cent of Turkey's export earnings during 1980, and 70 per cent of Chile's and India's.

It may seem surprising that third world countries continue to pay the enormous sums of interest required on their loans but they have little alternative, such is the power and influence of the international bankers. Jamaica, in the late 1970s, tried to shake herself free from the grip of the capitalist entrepreneurs, with near disastrous results. So long as a country remains within the Western orbit it is dependent upon the huge multi-nationals and the international bankers who control the supply of technology and capital, as well as access to world markets. If the poor nations of the third world refused to pay the interest on their debts to the international bankers until Western nations relaxed their grip on the global economy; or if they banded together to demand an end to trade tariff restrictions that block their exports to the West; or if they brought pressure to link the price of third world commodities to the price inflation of Western manufactured goods, they would find that their 'credit worthiness' would be adversely affected, that their countries would be less attractive to outside investors, that much needed industrial technology would be denied them.

In short, the rich nations would use their economic muscle to such effect that the poorer nations would be unable to survive.

Control of Technology

A major difficulty that confronts the poorer nations of the world is that the rich nations control not only the world's money supply and interest rates, they also control technology. For the poorer nations to be able to have their own realistic programmes of industrial development through which they can achieve a measure of economic independence, they must have access to technology. Strong constraints are put upon industrial development in the poorer countries because the rich nations hold all the patents as well as the technological and scientific expertise. In order to break the monopoly of the rich nations, the poorer nations must develop their own research programmes to produce their own technology and thereby service industrial development. But this requires enormous financial investment which, in the present state of world economy, can only come from the West and thereby increase the debt mountain already facing the poorer nations.

The Brandt Report states, 'Developing countries need to build up their own industry and research, and they are often in a weak position to bargain with the transnational corporations which control much of modern technology. They may benefit from direct investment but the gains have not always been fully shared, which has caused political tensions. They can buy technology through licences, but only on terms set by foreign corporations. They do not wish to lose control over their economies; they want to be able to treat on fair terms and with equal expertise with the transnational corporations' (p. 43).

Mutual Dependence

A striking fact that is often overlooked in the West is that the poorer nations of the world materially contribute to the prosperity of the richer nations. The expanding markets of the third world are essential export grounds for the West if the growth rate of the industrialized nations is to be maintained. This mutual dependence of the nations within the world economy is either conveniently overlooked or it is a factor that is used by the richer nations to manipulate third world economies to their own advantage. The Commissioners of the European Communities noted in a recent report, that if the developing countries had cut back their exports after 1973 to adjust to the oil price increases, the recession in the industrialized world would have been far more serious. It is estimated that the result would have been a further three million unemployed in Europe alone. During 1975, when EEC exports to the US fell by 17 per cent, Community exports to the developing countries increased by more than 25 per cent.

Plight of Poor Nations

The cost to the poorer nations of a recession in the industrialized world is incalculable, not simply in straight financial terms, but also in terms of human life and suffering. The only way the poorer nations can survive is to borrow more and more money at ever-increasing interest rates from Western bankers. Thus even during a recession, such as presently grips the world economy, the richer nations continue to grow richer and the poorer nations grow poorer. The gap between the rich and the poor grows wider.

The Brandt Report aptly summarizes this situation: 'The result of increasing borrowing in the 1970s has been a rapid growth of the indebtedness of developing countries. Their combined debts rose from seventy billion dollars at the end of 1970 to an estimated three hundred billion dollars at the end of 1979. Much of it was concentrated in a relatively small number of middle income countries. The greater role of private commercial lending was reflected in an increasing share of short term debt at interest rates which have recently risen steeply. Unless oil importing countries are to check their imports and growth in the 1980s, it is clear that their debts will have to increase further. Between 1980 and 1985, as much as three hundred to five hundred billion dollars may have to be added to developing countries' debts if their financial needs are to be met, provided the funds can be found.'

Commenting on this situation, the Brandt Report, which was compiled by a group of economists and international statesmen of world standing, made the following prophetic pronouncement: 'We face, therefore, not merely one, but several crises; the crisis of relentless inflation and increasing energy costs, the crisis of dwindling energy availability, the crisis resulting from mounting financial requirements, and the crisis posed by constraints on world trade and on the growth of export earnings to meet increased debt service commitments. Taken together, they threaten the whole structure of our political, industrial and financial institutions, unless we move urgently and adequately to deal with the basic causes' (p. 239).

Basic Causes: Self-Interest

The Brandt Report does not state what these 'basic causes' are. The writers, however, can hardly be blamed for this since they were producing an economic rather than a theological report! The true nature of the causes that underlie the crises that they note is spiritual; it is rooted in man's sinful nature, in his untamed greed and avarice, in his willingness to exploit his neighbour for his own gain, and in his reckless pursuit of his own self-interest. In the West, the gods of the mammon of unrighteousness have taken control of the entire capitalist system in its unremitting pursuit of material wealth. The only valid answer to the root causes that the Brandt Report seeks after, and fails to find, lies in man's repentance. The problem is not economic, it is spiritual. The answers are not economic, they are spiritual. Hence the failure of world economists, politicians and statesmen to find answers to the problems presently afflicting mankind. You cannot successfully provide economic solutions to spiritual problems. The solutions are false and therefore they only compound the problems.

The growth of giant multi-national corporations over the past two or three decades is a logical development of capitalism, since the capitalist system by its very nature is potentially monopolistic. It aims at the elimination of every competitor in the insatiable search for increased profits, for extended markets, for expanded influence. It is in the global search for extended influence and power that the international bankers and multi-national corporations play such a crucial role, both in influencing the domestic policy of the nations and in controlling the world economy.

Pursuit of Personal Gain

When the true nature of capitalism is appreciated the claim to be the defender of private property is seen for what it is worth! The only sense in which the capitalist system can claim to be the defender of private property is in the defence of the use of private property for unlimited personal gain! Competition is built into the essence of the capitalist system, and in order to maximize profits the capitalist must eliminate other competitors by taking control of, or taking measures for the acquisition of, the private property of others. In the capitalist system individual liberty and personal freedom count for nothing if they stand in the way of the pursuit of wealth! The acquisition of wealth is the only criterion of success. The only values that count are material ones and they count proportionately to their size not their quality.

It is here that we see the spirit of gross materialism that is an essential part of the capitalist system. The major charge against capitalism is not that of 'injustice' as the Marxists would have us believe. It is not simply that 90 per cent of the wealth of the rich nations of the West is held by 2 per cent of their populations – that may indeed be evidence of social injustice, of the unfair distribution of goods, it may be evidence of enormous selfishness on the part of a small minority – but that is not the major charge against capitalism. The real charge against capitalism is a spiritual one. It is that capitalism is basically materialistic and that this spirit of gross materialism has contributed enormously to the growing decadence of the Western world.

Materialistic Values

Capitalism has played a leading role in implanting materialistic values into the Western world that have now become an intrinsic part of the very nature of the Western way of life. These values may be summarized as:

1. The acquisition of material wealth as an end in itself.
2. The use of material things for private gain regardless of the common good.
3. The accumulation of property and material wealth as the highest goal in life.

These are the values that have become so widely accepted that they have become a part of today's fabric of life in the West. Even when individuals reject these values as being morally decadent or spiritually sinful, it is extremely difficult not in some way to be affected by them when the whole of society in its social organization and lifestyle reflects these values. The materialistic values of Western society are seen in the adulation of the flamboyant rich, of film stars and pop idols whom the media delight to depict displaying an opulent lifestyle that is beyond the means of ordinary people. Such reports help to mould values and stimulate desire. It is perhaps a reflection of the desire for quick wealth that £2000m is spent annually on gambling in Britain alone. Desire for material things is greatly intensified by advertising. The advertising industry has been one of the fastest growing industries throughout the Western world over the past two or three decades. Particularly since the advent of television, advertising has come to hold a powerful place in the formation of demand and therefore the creation of social values throughout Western society. Untold billions of pounds are spent annually on advertising, with the objective of stimulating demand for every kind of consumer goods and for every conceivable means of the consumption of wealth, from soap to fabulous holidays in Caribbean luxury resorts.

The Poverty Trap

The effect of mass advertising is not only to promote actual demand, for the majority of those who are subject to the campaigns of the advertisers are quite unable to make a positive response due to a lack of purchasing power, but the major effect is to stimulate desire, to create an acquisitive climate. For those caught in the poverty trap of being wage-labourers and not property owners, the feeling of relative deprivation grows. It is a powerful sentiment behind the wage bargaining of trade unions, and behind the frustration of the unemployed inner-city youth who feels cheated by society and has a strong sense of injustice that others are enjoying the good things of life that he has been denied. It is this frustration that lies behind much of the vandalism and violence from which so many Western cities suffer.

Breaking God's Law

The Archbishop of York was certainly expressing a sound biblical principle when he spoke with all the vigour of the eighth-century BC Hebrew prophets in denouncing the injustice and self-centredness of those capitalists who, in the pursuit of personal gain, disregard the effects of their actions upon others. 'The manipulation of the money market for personal gain comes under God's law as theft. Those who make a killing of perhaps half a million pounds simply by the rise and fall of the pound or by a takeover bid, regardless of the effect on the more vulnerable sectors of industry or the effects on the lives of large numbers of people, are guilty of theft even though their activities may be lawful and respectable in the accepted sense' (Dr Stewart Blanch, speaking on BBC Radio 4, 29 March 1981).

By far the most serious judgement to be brought against capitalism is that it has relentlessly pursued materialistic goals that have succeeded in creating a basically materialistic society. The element of competition increases the aggressiveness of modern materialistic society, in which all alike are caught up in the desire to gain personal advantage by the acquisition of personal property and wealth.

In the Eastern communist world the dominant spirit is that of atheistic dialectical materialism leading towards the acquisition of ultimate political power. In the Western capitalist world the dominant spirit is that of hedonistic materialism leading towards the acquisition of ultimate economic power. In the Eastern world the ordinary people pursue materialistic goals because they believe it will ultimately lead them to freedom. In the Western world the ordinary people pursue materialistic goals because they believe it will ultimately lead them to happiness. The East pursues material wealth for freedom; the West for pleasure.

Man's Idolatry

The dominant ideology and the ultimate goal for both East and West is materialism. The gods of twentieth-century man worldwide are material not spiritual. The witness of Scripture is that God is a spirit and those who worship him must worship him in spirit and in truth. The universal commandment of God to all mankind is that we should worship him and have no other gods before him. Incredible as it may seem, sophisticated twentieth-century man is guilty of the most ancient and fundamental sin, that of worshipping material things, the created rather than the Creator. Twentieth-century man is more idolatrous than his primitive forebears who bowed down to wood and stone. Today men worship, at the altar of wealth, the things created by their own hands.

CHAPTER TEN

Materialism: Power

Biblical Evidence

The Bible takes a clear stand against those who use their material possessions, their social status or their political power for their own selfish advantage and not for the good of others. Worldly position and possessions are the gift of God that have to be used with justice, compassion and a concern for the good of all, otherwise they become the mammon of unrighteousness and bring judgement upon those who have great possessions and power. Unto whom much is given of the same much is required, said Jesus. Man is a steward of God's gifts, not the owner (Matthew 25:14–46).

Even kings were not exempt from the same requirements. Jeremiah once sent a stern message to King Jehoiakim warning that his policy of self-aggrandizement and oppression of the poor would bring the wrath of the Lord upon him, 'Does it make you a better king if you build houses of cedar, finer than those of others? Your father enjoyed a full life. He was always just and fair, and he prospered in everything he did. He gave the poor a fair trial and all went well with him. That is what it means to know the Lord. But you can only see your selfish interests; you kill the innocent and violently oppress your people. The Lord has spoken' (Jeremiah 22:15–17, GNB). Even King David had to learn that the Lord humbles those who exalt themselves. When David numbered the people Joab was dismayed to see the king's delight in discovering the size of the nation over which he was sovereign (2 Samuel 24:1–3). He was forgetting that it was God who reigned over his people and David eventually had to confess before the Lord 'I have sinned greatly in what I have done' (2 Samuel 24:10).

Time and again the prophets reminded the rulers, the rich

and the powerful, that the right exercise of their privileges was, in the words of Micah, 'to do justice, and to love kindness, and to walk humbly with your God' (Micah 6:8).

Isaiah beautifully sums up the commandments of God to man as 'to loose the bonds of wickedness, to undo the thongs of the yoke, to let the oppressed go free, and to break every yoke. To share your bread with the hungry and to bring the homeless poor into your house; when you see the naked to cover him. If you pour yourself out for the hungry and satisfy the desire of the afflicted then shall your light rise in the darkness and your gloom be as the noonday and the Lord will guide you continually and satisfy your desire with good things' (Isaiah 58:6,7,10,11).

Empirical Evidence

'They have broken the everlasting covenant'

Ever since the end of World War Two, which divided Europe into East and West, the world of international relationships has been dominated by the struggle for power between the major nations. The two super-powers, the USA and the USSR, have led the way in the arms race and have each succeeded in building up the most gigantic arsenal of destructive weapons the world has ever known. Similarly, all the industrialized nations have been caught up in the arms race, not simply in the interests of national defence, but in order not to be left behind in the international status game, in which military might and arms technology are the symbols of power and prestige. In order to understand the full significance of the arms race we have to see it in terms of the total world situation and the overall needs of mankind.

The Arms Race

It is not, however, simply the major nations who have been flexing their international muscles and demonstrating their military abilities, in order to gain respect and standing in a materialistic world where the only values that count are naked force and material opulence. Even the smallest and the poorest nations have been caught up in the arms race, as the Brandt Report notes: 'The past thirty years have seen peace in the Northern Hemisphere, against a background of military blocs controlling sophisticated arms, while the Southern half of this earth has suffered outbreaks of violent unrest and military clashes. Some third world countries have substantially boosted their armaments, sometimes to protect their legitimate or understandable security interests, but sometimes also for prestige purposes and sometimes encouraged by arms-producing countries. Business has been rewarding for both old and new arms suppliers, who have spread an incredible destructive capability over the globe. It is a terrible irony that the most dynamic and rapid transfer of highly sophisticated equipment and technology from rich to poor countries has been in the machinery of death' (*Brandt*, p. 14).

It is perhaps one of the saddest features of this period in history that in a world where there is an incredible gap between the rich nations and the poor nations, a major part of the material resources supplied to the poorer nations by the rich should be in the form of weapons of destruction. It is a clear indication that wrong values are being pursued, when in countries where large proportions of the population live at a bare subsistence level, and multitudes actually die of starvation, precious resources are used up on armaments.

We have already noted the economic problems of many third world countries burdened with huge international debts, yet surely the most bizarre aspect of the international financial scene between rich and poor nations is the fact that a large portion of the credit facilities extended to third world countries by international bankers is swallowed up in paying for huge armament orders. For example, two of the countries struggling with immense internal poverty problems are India and Pakistan, yet during 1981 Pakistan purchased 32 Mirage 5 fighters from France at a cost of $330m, while during the period 1979–81 India purchased 40

Jaguar strike aircraft from Britain at a cost of $816m. But these pale into insignificance when compared with the amounts spent by some countries! According to the International Institute for Strategic Studies, Taiwan, for example, has purchased from the USA over the period 1980–3 an incredible array of weaponry, including 125 Howitzer guns, three complete systems of C Chaparal SAM missiles, 12 Hughes Defender helicopters, 48 F5E/F fighters, 500 Marryat air-to-surface missiles, 150 Mark 46 torpedoes, 28 anti-submarine missiles and 600 Sidewinder air-to-air missiles.

It is within the context of the world-wide squandering of precious resources on weapons of destruction that we have to view the immense problems of poverty in the modern world. The untold suffering and misery which is the life experience of millions of the world's population is something that is almost impossible for those brought up in the industrialized countries of the world to appreciate. Despite television and newspaper reports, with graphic descriptions and pictures of refugee camps and hungry children, if you have never actually seen a shanty town or heard the cries of children dying from malnutrition or seen the looks on the faces of people condemned to a lifelong struggle for existence, it is impossible to appreciate the real significance of poverty.

Grinding Poverty

The Brandt Report makes the point that people in the industrialized countries simply have no understanding of the difference between their own life experience and that of millions of people in the developing nations. 'Few people in the North [the terms 'North' and 'South' are used to signify the rich nations and the poor nations] have any detailed conception of the extent of poverty in the third world or of the forms that it takes. Many hundreds of millions of people in the poorer countries are preoccupied solely with survival and elementary needs. For them work is frequently not available or, when it is, pay is very low and conditions often barely tolerable. Homes are constructed of impermanent materials and have neither piped water nor sanitation. Electricity is a luxury. Health services are thinly spread and in rural areas only rarely within walking distance. Primary schools, where they exist, may be free and not too far away, but children are needed for work and cannot easily be spared for schooling. Permanent insecurity is the condition of the poor. There are no public systems of social security in the event of unemployment, sickness or death of a wage earner in the family. Flood, drought or disease affecting people or livestock can destroy livelihoods without hope of compensation. In the North, ordinary men and women face genuine economic problems – uncertainty, inflation, the fear if not the reality of unemployment. But they rarely face anything resembling the total deprivation found in the South. Ordinary people in the South would not find it credible that the societies of the North regard themselves as anything other than wealthy' (Brandt, p. 49).

No one can say precisely how many third world people live in conditions of absolute poverty. The most informed sources, however, indicate that it is a problem that is growing rather than diminishing. The International Labour Office in 1970 estimated the number of destitute in the world's population to be seven hundred million. In 1980 the World Bank estimates put the number of destitute at eight hundred million. This suggests that almost 40 per cent of the people living in third world nations are surviving, but only barely surviving, in conditions of intolerable poverty where they have insufficient material resources to secure the basic necessities of life.

Children Starving

Figure 49 indicates that of the 342,000 live births per day, some 10 per cent of infants will not survive one year of life. If we look at the number of children who die before they are five years of age the size of the world's poverty problem begins to appear. UNICEF, the United Nations

FIGURE 49 *The Birth Facts*

Nearly one million women became pregnant today.
What will happen to them?

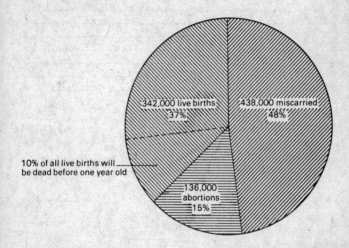

342,000 live births 37%

438,000 miscarried 48%

10% of all live births will be dead before one year old

136,000 abortions 15%

Children's Fund, estimated that in 1978 alone more than twelve million children under the age of five died of hunger. Despite the fact that the United Nations declared 1979 to be the Year of the Child, these devastating figures did not in fact change for the better. As the world's population increases, so does the problem of feeding the hungry. It is worthwhile at this point considering the average life chances of an infant born in different parts of the world.

It will be seen from the table in Figure 50 that while life expectancy in Europe and North America is more than seventy years, life expectancy in Africa is only forty-six years. Even more devastating are the figures for infant mortality. In Europe and America less than 5 per cent of all deaths are of children under five years of age, whereas in Africa young children represent more than 57 per cent of all deaths.

FIGURE 50 *Life Chances*

REGION	LIFE EXPECTANCY AT BIRTH	DEATH OF CHILDREN 0–5 AS % OF ALL DEATHS
Africa	46	57·6
Asia	55	39·5
S. America	63	36·5
Australasia	68	8
USSR	69	6
Europe	71	4
N. America	73	3
WORLD	60	25

FIGURE 51 *Survival of the richest*

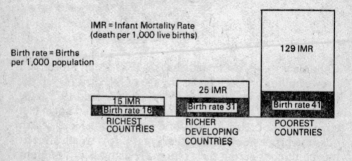

In Figure 51 we have put together the infant mortality rates and birth rates for the industrialized countries in comparison with similar figures for the developing nations. The sharp contrast between the rich and the poor is underlined by these figures, and with continuing high birth rates in the poorest countries there seems little likelihood of changing the situation drastically within the foreseeable future.

The Rich and the Poor

The contrast between life in the rich countries and life in the poor countries is underlined not simply by the contrast in life expectancy, but the situation is vividly illustrated by a consideration of the material resources that are consumed by people in different parts of the world.

FIGURE 52 *Rich and Poor*

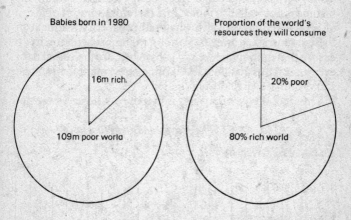

The above figure shows that for the total of 125 million babies born during 1980, 16 million were in the rich nations of the world, whereas 109 million were in the poor nations. But those 16 million people during their lifetimes will consume four-fifths of the world's total material resources of food, energy, etc. This visibly illustrates not merely the unequal distribution of resources, but it gives some idea of the sense of injustice and outrage experienced by those working to improve conditions in the developing countries, when they see the indifference of the rich nations towards poverty in the third world and see also the squandering of

material resources that are so desperately needed not simply
for development but for sustaining life itself. The following
figure graphically illustrates the situation relating to the
distribution of basic resources between the rich nations and
the poor nations.

Two Kinds of Poverty

It is perhaps worth noting that there are two kinds of
poverty. There is first the poverty that exists in the highly
industrialized nations, where although relatively high
average levels of income have been reached, overall the
income is not well distributed and therefore some people live
at a relatively low level of material prosperity. In most of
these countries, however, various welfare schemes exist to
ensure that minimum levels of subsistence are maintained for
everyone. Thus absolute levels of poverty, malnutrition and
starvation are virtually eliminated.

The second type of poverty is in those countries where not

FIGURE 53 *The Haves and the Havenots*

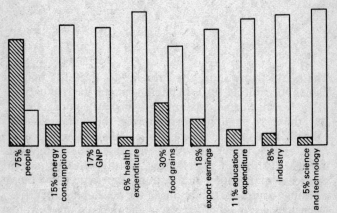

THE DEVELOPING WORLD HAS . . .

75% people
15% energy consumption
17% GNP
6% health expenditure
30% food grains
18% export earnings
11% education expenditure
8% industry
5% science and technology

only is there a low average level of income but where there is very little to distribute. The great majority of the eight hundred million poor live in the low-income countries of sub-Saharan Africa and South Asia, although many of the more prosperous countries, especially in Latin America, have large sectors of the population experiencing acute poverty. In Latin America as a whole, the absolute poor number about one hundred million. In twelve out of twenty-three Latin American countries where reliable estimates exist, over half the population have incomes insufficient to buy a basket of goods and services deemed essential for a minimum level of welfare. It must be remembered that where there is extreme poverty people suffer not only from hunger but also from disease, and experience also the hopelessness and despair of knowing that there is no way in which by any efforts of their own they can improve their situation. For parents to see their children born and grow up in such conditions of absolute poverty and physical deprivation is a terrible experience, and it is against this background of

TO HIM WHO HATH SHALL BE GIVEN

In 1900 the average person in the rich world had 4 times as much as a person in the poor world

By 1970, the ratio had become 40 to 1

Today the pay rise which an American can expect in one year is greater than an Indian can expect in 100 years

Is this what Jesus meant?
Or is this a measure of the Western world's distortion of the Gospel?

human suffering and misery that we have to see the squandering of resources that takes place among the rich nations of the world.

Squandering Resources

When we look closely at the richer nations of the world we see an incredible scene, not simply of higher standards of living, of food surpluses, of standards of health and medical care beyond anything obtainable in third world countries. We see also the scandalous squandering of precious resources from the natural environment – oil, coal, wood – through the deforestation of vast areas of land, the reckless overfishing of the seas and the pollution of the waterways and the air that we breathe. But by far the greatest scandal of all is the arms race. Yet it is not the actual production of weapons with their enormous destructive capability that constitutes the scandal, it is the incredible sinfulness of one part of the human family deliberately squandering resources while ignoring the pleas for help from the hungry and the cries of the dying in two-thirds of the world's population. The following tables show the expenditure on armaments amongst the nations of the world for just one year.

FIGURE 54 *Comparisons of Defence Expenditures 1981*

COUNTRY	$ MILLION	$ PER HEAD	% GOVERNMENT SPENDING	% OF GNP 1980
WARSAW PACT				
Bulgaria	1340	151	6·0	3·4
Czechoslovakia	3520 (80)	229 (80)	7·6 (80)	4·0
Germany, East	6960	415	8·5	6·1
Hungary	1240	115	3·9	2·3
Poland	4670 (80)	131 (80)	6·0 (80)	3·2
Rumania	1350	61	2·3	1·3
Soviet Union	124,000 (75)	490 (75)	NA	14·0
NATO				
Belgium	3560	359	9·0	3·3
Britain	28,660	512	12·3	5·1
Canada	4990	205	9·1	1·7
Denmark	1520	295	7·1	2·4
France	26,008	483	20·5	3·9
Germany, West	25,000	405	22·6	3·2
Greece	1770 (80)	236 (80)	19·8 (80)	5·1
Italy	8887	155	5·1	2·4
Luxembourg	51	140	3·3	1·0
Netherlands	4930	348	9·5	3·4
Norway	1570 (80)	383 (80)	10·8 (80)	2·9
Portugal	944	94	12·0	3·8
Turkey	3106	67	22·0	4·2
United States	171,023	759	23·3	5·5

COUNTRY	$ MILLION	$ PER HEAD	% GOVERNMENT SPENDING	% OF GNP 1980
OTHER EUROPEAN				
Spain	3980	105	12·0	1·8 (78)
Sweden	3790	455	7·7	3·2
Switzerland	1840	154	20·2	1·9 (78)
Yugoslavia	3470	154	56·9 (80)	5·2 (77)
MIDDLE EAST				
Israel	7340	1835	30·6	23·2
Saudi Arabia	27,695	2664	31·0	15·0 (78)
Syria	2389	261	30·8	13·1
ASIA				
China	56,941 (80)	56 (80)	NA	10·0 (78)
India	5119	7	16·9	3·8
Indonesia	2387	5	12·3 (80)	3·4 (77)
Japan	11,497	98	5·0	0·9
Korea, South	4400	113	36·0 (80)	5·7
Korea, North	1470	74	14·7	11·4 (78)
Malaysia	2250	157	23·0	4·7 (78)
Thailand	1279	26	18·7	3·7 (78)
LATIN AMERICA				
Argentina	3380 (80)	12·3 (80)	15·1 (80)	3·3 (78)
Venezuela	1399	85	6·5 (79)	2·3

Source: International Institute for Strategic Studies.
NA = Not available

It is very hard for the ordinary man or woman to be able to comprehend the sheer magnitude of the expenditure involved upon armaments as shown in these figures. The Brandt Report (p. 14) gives four examples of the way this money could be used for urgently needed projects in the third world.

1) The military expenditure of only half a day would suffice to finance the whole malaria eradication programme of the World Health Organization, and less would be needed to conquer river blindness, which is still the scourge of millions.

2) A modern tank costs about $1 million; that amount could improve storage facilities for 100,000 tons of rice and thus save 4000 tons or more annually; one person can live on just over 1 lb of rice a day. The same sum of money could provide 1000 classrooms for 30,000 children.

3) For the price of one jet fighter ($20m) about 40,000 village pharmacies could be set up.

4) One half of one per cent of one year's military expenditure would pay for all the farm equipment needed to increase food production and thereby approach self-sufficiency in food-deficit low-income countries by 1990.

With the world's annual military expenditure now in excess of $450,000,000,000, more than half of which is spent by the United States and Russia, while one person dies of starvation in our world every five seconds, it is surely time to pause and to take stock of the world situation if only from a straight moral standpoint. Thus if it takes the reader one hour to read this chapter, during that time seven hundred and twenty people somewhere in the world will have died of hunger, but during that same time the world will have spent $51·369 million on armaments. Again, to try to make the figure slightly smaller and thereby more comprehensible – during the time that one person dies of hunger, that is five seconds, the world spends $71,345 on armaments. The sheer moral infamy of this needs to be brought home to every man and woman, even the poorest, in the rich nations of the world.

Moral Scandal

The moral case against the world's vast squandering of resources upon armaments is one of the points noted in the Brandt Report: 'There is a moral link between the vast spending on arms and the disgracefully low spending on measures to remove hunger and ill health in the third world. The programme of the World Health Organization to abolish malaria is short of funds! It is estimated that it will eventually cost about $450m which represents only one-thousandth of the world's annual military spending. The cost of a ten-year programme to provide for essential food and health needs in developing countries is less than half of one year's military spending. Moreover, arms production is not just a matter of spending but of manpower and skills. It is profoundly disturbing to realize that in East and West a very large proportion of scientists and much of the scientific resources of universities and industry are devoted to armaments' (Brandt, p. 118).

For Christians the armaments scandal is not just a moral question. It is an indication of the deep spiritual sickness that has gripped mankind. The East-West power struggle has not only set the tenor of international relationships, but it has also played a major role in establishing the values by which all the nations live. The power struggle is at root an indication of the way in which materialism has come to dominate the whole of life in our twentieth-century world.

Spiritual Offence

Judged from the standpoint of Scripture, the spirit of materialism displayed in the world-wide power struggle and in world armaments expenditure is a massive blasphemy against God. It is in direct opposition to the teaching of Jesus in Matthew 6:19–34, where he declares that life is more important than material things and urges his disciples to seek first the Kingdom of God and his righteousness. God's care for the poor and oppressed is shown throughout Scripture. Typical is the passage in Isaiah where God clearly identifies with the poor, 'The Lord has taken his place to contend, he stands to judge his people. The Lord enters into judgement with the elders and the princes of his people: it is you who have devoured the vineyard, the spoil of the poor is in your houses, what do you mean by crushing my people, by grinding the face of the poor? says the Lord God of hosts' (Isaiah 3:13–15). It is of course in the incarnation of Jesus that we most clearly see God's identification with the poor and the statusless. This is something that Jesus maintained throughout his life, not only through his tender regard for the poor, as, for example, in his commendation of the poor widow who gave all that she had into the Temple offering (Luke 21:2), but also in his lifestyle, 'the Son of man has nowhere to lay his head' (Matthew 8:20).

The essence of the true spiritual life is set out by Isaiah where he contrasts the mere outward show of religiosity, the offering of material sacrifices, with the essence of true religion, which is a heart after God and a lifestyle that is a continual offering of service to others. 'Is not this the kind of fasting I have chosen: to loose the chains of injustice and untie the cords of the yoke, to set the oppressed free and break every yoke? Is it not to share your food with the hungry and to provide the poor wanderer with shelter!' The prophet continues by showing how God responds to this kind of spirituality, 'Then your righteousness will go before you, and the glory of the Lord will be your rearguard. Then you will call and the Lord will answer, you will cry for help and he will say, "Here am I." If you do away with the yoke of oppression, with the pointing finger and malicious talk, and if you spend yourselves on behalf of the hungry and satisfy the needs of the oppressed, then your light will rise in the darkness and your light will become like the noonday. The Lord will guide you always, he will satisfy your needs and will strengthen your frame' (Isaiah 58:6–11).

263

Judgement

Scripture also makes it clear that judgement comes upon those who ignore or flagrantly flout the basic spiritual laws that God lays down. Ezekiel teaches that it was because of injustice and a lack of care for the poor, as well as for the sins of idolatry, that God allowed Jerusalem to be destroyed and the people carried into exile into Babylon in the sixth century. 'The people of the land have practised extortion and committed robbery, they have oppressed the poor and needy, and have extorted from the sojourner without redress. And I sought for a man among them who should build up the wall and stand in the breach before me for the land, that I should not destroy it; but I found none. Therefore I have poured out my indignation upon them; I have consumed them with the fire of my wrath; their way have I requited upon their heads, says the Lord God' (Ezekiel 22:29–31).

Ezekiel hammers home the lesson, not only for Jerusalem but for future generations of mankind, that there is an inevitable consequence of committing evil. He says the reason why the city of Sodom was wiped off the face of the earth was because her citizens were full of pride and idolatrous practices. They worshipped material things rather than spiritual. Those who were wealthy did not care for the poor and needy. 'Behold this was the guilt of your sister Sodom: she and her daughters had pride, surfeit of food, and prosperous ease, but did not aid the poor and needy. They were haughty and did abominable things before me; therefore I removed them when I saw it' (Ezekiel 16:49 and 50).

History teaches us that there is a strong link between the moral state and the spiritual life of a nation. When the spiritual life is out of harmony with God moral corruption seeps in and affects every part of the life of society, including both the personal characters of the citizens and their corporate relationships. When the spiritual life is wrong then everything else in the life of the nation goes wrong, as the prophet Haggai told the people of post-exilic Jerusalem in the period of the reconstruction soon after their return from Babylon. They were working hard but getting nowhere, struggling against inflation, an unstable economy and a general lack of social order. He told them that they would never get the economy right and they would never put the social order right until they got the spiritual life of the city right first. It was a case of seeking first the Kingdom of God and his righteousness and all other things then being put right in due time (Haggai 1:4–9).

It is not only one city and one nation that faces the dangers of moral retribution and spiritual judgement coming upon them. Today it is the whole of mankind, and the dangers of world-wide chaos and destruction are not a matter of science fiction, neither are they simply possibilities that may occur, they are inevitable results. They are the consequences and end products of the policies now being pursued by the nations. It is not merely men of spiritual insight who are saying these things today, but the warnings are coming from environmentalists and economists. Again the Brandt Report speaks in stark terms of the threat to the survival of mankind: 'War is often thought of in terms of military conflict or even annihilation. But there is a growing awareness that an equal danger might be chaos – as a result of mass hunger, economic disaster, environmental catastrophies and terrorism. So we should not think only of reducing the traditional threats to peace, but also of the need for change from chaos to order. At the beginning of a new decade, only twenty years short of the millennium, we must try to lift ourselves above day-to-day quarrels (or negotiations) to see the menacing long-term problem. We see a world in which poverty and hunger still prevail in many huge regions, in which resources are squandered without consideration of their renewal, in which more armaments are made and sold than ever before and where a destructive capacity has been accumulated to blow up our planet several times over' (Brandt, p. 13).

Survival Threatened

In similar strident warning terms the report calls for radical changes in international policies. 'Our survival depends not only on military balance but on global co-operation to ensure a sustained biological environment and sustainable prosperity based on equitably shared resources. Much of the insecurity in the world is connected with the divisions between rich and poor nations – grave injustice and mass starvation causing additional instability. Yet the research and the funds which could help to put an end to poverty and hunger are now pre-empted by military use. The threatening arsenals grow, and spending on other purposes which could make them less necessary is neglected' (Brandt, p. 124).

It is surely a salutary warning to mankind when a secular report by eminent world statesmen, each expert in his own field, brings warnings concerning the very survival of man. We are clearly reaching the most critical period in the history of mankind, when the problems created by man himself are beyond his own capacity to solve, yet the nations of the world continue pursuing the same old policies that in previous eras have led to chaos and destruction. The difference this time is that the chaos and destruction will not be localized, nor even confined to a single region, but world-wide. Just as the social and economic problems are becoming more and more colossal, so is the arsenal of destruction that mankind is amassing all around the globe.

It is estimated that by the 1990s at least forty nations will have a nuclear capability. It is also estimated that the great army of the world's hungry will have grown to some one thousand million. Yet the greatest irony is that man has within his own hands the ability to solve the world's hunger problems and to conquer the misery of disease that afflicts millions of men, women and children. We have the technology, we have the expert knowledge, we have the resources and we even have the world-wide transport and communications available to carry help to every part of the world. The misery and suffering among the millions in the poor nations could be alleviated. All we lack is the will – the spirit – the righteousness before our God to undertake such a mission.

Inasmuch . . .

Jesus warns us that the day will come when God will call the nations to account for their stewardship of the immense resources that he has given into their hands. In Matthew 25, from verse 31, he tells a parable of the Kingdom, of the time when 'all the nations will be gathered before him and he will separate the people one from another as a shepherd separates the sheep from the goats. He will put the sheep on his right and the goats on his left. Then the King will say to those on his right, Come you who are blessed by my father, take your inheritance of the Kingdom prepared for you since the creation of the world. For I was hungry and you gave me something to eat. I was thirsty and you gave me something to drink, I was a stranger and you invited me in, I needed clothes and you clothed me, I was sick and you looked after me, I was in prison and you came to me.

'Then the righteous will answer him, Lord, when did we see you hungry and feed you or thirsty and give you something to drink? When did we see you a stranger and invite you in or needing clothes and clothe you? When did we see you sick or in prison and go to visit you?

'The King will reply, I tell you the truth, whatever you did for one of the least of these brothers of mine you did for me.

'Then he will say to those on his left, Depart from me you who are cursed, into the eternal fire prepared for the devil and his angels. For I was hungry and you gave me nothing to eat, I was thirsty and you gave me nothing to drink, I was a stranger and you did not invite me in, I needed clothes and you did not clothe me, I was sick and in prison and you did not look after me.

'They also will answer, Lord, when did we see you hungry or thirsty or a stranger or needing clothes or sick or in prison, and did not help you?

'He will reply, I will tell you the truth that whatever you did not do for one of the least of these you did not do for me. Then they will go away to eternal punishment but the righteous to eternal life.'

CHAPTER ELEVEN

God's Word to the Nations

Polluted the Earth

'The earth lies polluted under its inhabitants; for they have transgressed the laws, violated the statutes, broken the everlasting covenant' (Isaiah 24:5).

We have seen the way in which this prophecy is being fulfilled in the final quarter of the twentieth century. The charge against mankind is proven. Man has indeed polluted the earth, both physically and morally. The level of physical pollution is damaging the environment to such an extent that the health of whole communities is threatened, and untold harm is being done to natural resources, the effects of which could last for thousands of years.

Moral pollution is now so extensive, particularly in the Western world, that its effects are incalculable. The rising generations of children and young people in most Western countries are being exposed to an incredible array of morally corrupting influences, backed by powerful economic interests. The floodgates of pollution have been opened. The physical and moral sluices are pouring a foul mixture of poisonous effluents into the international bloodstream of mankind, the like of which has never been seen in the whole of history. Its effect in polluting the physical environment and the moral order of creation defies any assessment.

Of even greater significance is the fact that corruption always breeds corruption. There is a strong similarity between moral and physical corruption. They behave much like a cancer growth in the body. Unless it is arrested, it will affect the health of the entire body and there comes a point when the only treatment is major surgery. Every car owner knows what happens when rust gets a hold on the chassis of a

269

car. If left to itself, the metal will simply be eaten away until the chassis collapses. If the car is to be saved, the affected metal has to be cut out and replaced by new metal, welded into the chassis. Every house owner knows the devastating effects of dry rot. Once it gets a hold on the timbers in one place, it can move rapidly through the entire building, not only through the woodwork, but also through concrete and brickwork, and it will eventually cause the entire structure to collapse.

There is a build-up effect of the physical pollution of the environment. Land, water and air are all interrelated, and serious pollution of one of the major elements sustaining the physical life of creation soon affects the other two. In our generation, we are deliberately polluting all three areas. Man is only just beginning to realize the extent to which modern technology is damaging the health of mankind. Similarly, the moral pollution that is being poured into the life of the nations is undermining their moral foundations.

The fundamental values that underlie the family, the community and social behaviour are being eroded by moral corruption that, if allowed to continue, will eventually result in the collapse of the entire social order of our present civilization. The evidence that this is already beginning to happen is plain to see, and if we choose to ignore it we are deliberately flouting one of the fundamental laws that God has built into the whole created order. It is this: the process of corruption is automatic, but to reverse the process and thereby to promote positive life-giving health and well-being requires a special action. The prophet Haggai noted this in the question he posed to the priests of his day (Haggai 2:12–14). The lesson he derived from his questions was that corruption is automatically passed on, one to another, but no one can pass on holiness. It is the gift of God, it comes directly from him and cannot be transmitted from one man to another. Each one must come to the source of life for himself. Therein lies the only hope for stemming the moral pollution that is corrupting the whole body of mankind today.

Disobeyed the Laws

Man has indeed disobeyed God's laws and violated his statutes. We have seen that while the law and the commandments were given through Moses to the Hebrews, there were certain fundamental laws that God gave to the whole of mankind. These concerned the sanctity of life and forbade murder. Violation of these laws involves blood-guiltiness and brings inevitable punishment upon the offenders. Blood-guiltiness is in itself a form of pollution which transmits a form of corruption to both the land and its people.

The twentieth century has been an era of unprecedented violence, due to the ease of transport and communications, together with the application of technology to the business of destruction. Again, this is a form of pollution, not simply through the blood of the innocent who are massacred in a time of war and whose lifeblood is poured out upon the land, but through the corruption of the gifts and resources that are given into the hands of men. The corruption of men's inventive genius by the evil desire to invent the most diabolical weapons of destruction to promote brutality and cause untold suffering, is not only a form of pollution, but it is a direct contravention of God's laws concerning the sanctity of human life. The misuse of natural resources that are, in themselves, precious and often irreplaceable, is yet another form of corruption and of the transgression of God's laws.

The twentieth century, which has been the most violent in the history of mankind, is drawing to its close with world-wide preparations for the most gigantic slaughter of human life and the most massive destruction of material things and damage to the natural environment that is beyond the imagination of man and defies the power of words to describe. The major thing that is clear is that men are busy inventing weapons of destruction so fearful that they do not know what their actual effect will be. What is of even more dangerous significance for the future of mankind is that men do not understand the power of the forces that will be unleashed once the full-scale exchange of nuclear weapons is let loose. The most sober and informed scientific sources are warning that mankind is on the brink of letting loose uncontrollable sources of energy that will bring untold devastation and destruction upon the earth, and incalculable pollution of the atmosphere. Such an event is foretold in Scripture. The consequences of man's polluting the earth are prophesied by Isaiah in the very next verse from that with which we began the chapter. 'Therefore a curse devours the earth, and its inhabitants suffer for their guilt; therefore the inhabitants of the earth are scorched, and few men are left' (Isaiah 24:6). But it is not only Isaiah who foretells of the earth being burnt up under a destructive force of terrifying power. Numerous passages of Scripture foretell of fire devouring the earth, and Jesus himself foretold that these events would take place at the climax of the ages and that they would, in fact, be a prelude to his own second coming (Matthew 24, Mark 13 and Luke 21).

Broken the Covenant

Man has indeed broken the everlasting covenant. The covenant that relates to the whole of mankind is the basic requirement that we should worship God, the one true and only Creator of all things, and that we should not worship false gods or bow down to material things, products of the created order. The world of the twentieth century is grossly materialistic and this is in violation of God's fundamental law that we should have no other gods. Jesus himself warned that man cannot worship both God and mammon.

Twentieth-century man has firmly enthroned mammon as the god of this age and bows down to worship him in every sphere of life. It is not only in the Eastern atheistic/communist world that materialism is the dominant philosophy by which men live and order the whole structure of their society, but this is so also in the Western world. The great capitals of the West are dominated by vast financial empires that, as we have seen, are basically materialistic. The values they enshrine give no place to the spiritual. The acquisition of material wealth has become the chief end of man. Jesus declared that the man who has an insatiable lust to pursue material goals and then, when his barns are full, builds bigger barns to store his increased material wealth, discovers that he is living in a fool's paradise. He has prostituted the spiritual and worshipped the material. He has ascribed ultimate worth to that which is worthless, and has regarded as worthless the ultimate realities of life. He has maximized the minimum and minimized the maximum. He has bowed down before the creation of his own hands and has turned his back upon the Creator of the ends of the universe.

Man's blasphemy against God in breaking his everlasting covenant is epitomized in his treatment of the poor and needy. Throughout Scripture, God has always shown his special tender concern for the poor and the powerless and he has commanded, not just requested, but commanded that men should show compassion upon those who are powerless to defend themselves or adequately to feed themselves, or who are in need of shelter and the basic provisions of life, and that men should tenderly care for the sick and the dying. Man has broken God's covenant by neglecting the poor.

In the twentieth century, this neglect of the poor and the powerless has become a gross sin since modern man has within his hands the means for serving all the world's poor and hungry. The material resources man has appropriated unto himself, plus the considerable advance in technology and the accumulated knowledge of the ages, have placed within man's hands the ability to conquer disease and to bring relief to the sick and the dying in every part of the world. Man has the means to solve the world's hunger problem and to turn the desert into a garden. If he rightly-used the resources God has given him, he could feed the starving, heal the sick, bring peace and plenty to the world.

But instead, man has chosen to serve the god of power – an even more dangerous manifestation of mammon than the materialism of either of the world's great political ideologies, communism or capitalism. The god of power enthrones man in the place where only God should be, it declares that man is the captain of his own fate, the master of his own destiny, and that God is dead or non-existent or that he simply does not count.

The massive material resources, scientific knowledge and technology that man now has within his hands could be used to promote the spiritual, moral and physical well-being of mankind. But instead, they are being used in the pursuit of power, in the arms race, the building up of massive arsenals of weapons of incredible destruction, and the pursuit of material power. Man is breaking God's everlasting covenant by ignoring the cries of the hungry and the pleas of the dying in his pursuit of personal power and self-glorification. God hates the injustice of man that condemns the poor to be born without hope, to exist in misery and to die of starvation while the rich squander the precious resources he has given in senseless luxury and riotous living. God condemns such flagrant breaking of his covenant and brings judgement upon the sinful society that deliberately frustrates his own good purposes for the well-being of all his children.

The Prophecy Fulfilled?

We have seen, therefore, that almost all the conditions have been met in our own present age for the fulfilment of all that is prophesied in Isaiah 24. The one remaining element is the final violation of God's statute in regard to blood-guiltiness. It only remains for men to let loose the holocaust of destruction for the chain reaction of devastation to be set in motion that will bring about the events foretold by the prophet. If our interpretation of the signs of the times is right, the world is rapidly approaching the nuclear holocaust that will cause the earth to be 'rent asunder' and to 'stagger like a drunken man', as is described in 24:19 and 20.

The real enemy of mankind has succeeded in dividing the world into two great opposing camps, each with its enormous arsenal of destructive weapons. Each is deeply suspicious of the other and fearful lest the other gains some advantage and thereby exerts its superiority over him. East and West each strives to outdo the other in technology and resources. Thus, each is contributing towards the preparation for the coming battle of the ages. The real nature of this battle is, however, spiritual rather than material. It is the ancient cosmic battle between the forces of good and evil that will one day soon be fought out upon the earth's surface.

It would be quite wrong for us to attempt to speculate upon dates for these events. Jesus specifically rebuked his own disciples when they asked for information regarding times. He told them that the Father kept such knowledge within his own authority (Acts 1:7). Nevertheless, he also said that his followers should be a watching and a praying people, able to discern the signs of the times. He rebuked those who were able to forecast the weather by looking into the sky but were unable to interpret the signs of the events in their own age, and thus missed the spiritual truths that God was unfolding to them. One of the events that Jesus said would happen before the climax of the ages was reached, was the restoration of Jerusalem to the Jews. He foretold the terrible events of the destruction of Jerusalem carried out by the Roman army in AD 70. The desolation of the city and the destruction of the Temple were so complete that the words of Jesus in Luke 21:20–24 were fearfully fulfilled. In verse 24, he said of the Jews that 'they will fall by the sword and will be taken as prisoners to all the nations. Jerusalem will be trampled on by the Gentiles until the times of the Gentiles are fulfilled.'

Those times have been fulfilled in our own lifetime, nineteen hundred years after the destruction of Jerusalem. (The Old City was finally restored into Jewish hands during the Six Day War in 1968.) Jesus immediately went on to speak of some of the indications that the climax of the ages is near after the times of the Gentiles are fulfilled. He said that 'there will be signs in the sun, moon and stars. On the earth, nations will be in anguish and perplexity at the roaring and tossing of the sea. Men will faint from terror, apprehensive of what is coming on the world, for the heavenly bodies will be shaken' (Luke 21:25–26, NIV). Again, we must emphasize that Jesus specifically warns against trying to put a date upon the events of which he speaks. In Mark 13:32 he states 'No one knows about that day or hour, not even the angels in heaven, nor the Son, but only the Father. Be on guard! be alert! you do not know when that time will come.' We are simply pointing out that one after another of the events foretold in Scripture that will take place before the climax of the ages is reached, have been fulfilled or are being fulfilled in our own time. Even Jesus' words – 'the Gospel must first be preached to all nations' (Mark 13:10) – are being fulfilled in our own generation. We should therefore be paying extra attention to Jesus' injunction to be alert, to be watchful and to be a praying people.

The prophecy in Isaiah 24:6, that a curse devours the earth and its inhabitants suffer for their guilt, emphasizes that it is man's own evil that is responsible for the destruction which is coming upon the world. It is man's blood-guiltiness, with which he has polluted the earth, that will be the final means of bringing on the terrible punishment that will sweep across the earth. The prophecy is not that of a god of vengeance wreaking terrible punishments upon helpless men, but of men bringing upon themselves the most fearful devastation which is let loose as a result of their own wicked ways. He nevertheless traces God's hand in this, although the punishment itself is automatic and is a direct result of man's own actions.

It is not simply that God is outraged at what man has done, but that from the beginning of creation he has made it clear that there are certain laws built into the very fabric of the created order that man cannot violate without bringing upon himself inevitable consequences. It will be as automatic as when a man attempts to defy the law of gravity and throws himself off a high cliff to be destroyed upon the rocks below. The destruction that will come upon the world as a result of man's own untamed violence will be as inevitable as that. Paul reminds us that the wages paid by sin are death – wages are something that a man earns – in contrast to the free gift of God which is life in the Spirit. Man is bringing upon himself the final catastrophe because he has usurped the place of God and elevated himself to the heights. Man now has within his grasp the power to bring devastation upon the earth. His untamed nature, his unrestrained self-will, his pride and arrogance will lead to his eventual downfall.

The Only Hope

Is there any hope of avoiding the terrible events that are foretold in Isaiah 24? Yes, there is! It is the same hope that God has held out to his people in generation after generation. The hope lies in man's full repentance and in his willingness to turn away from his evil ways. It is man himself who is bringing upon the world the destruction that will lay waste to the earth. It is therefore only a basic change of heart amongst men that can reverse the tide of history which is sweeping mankind towards the holocaust and the chain reaction that will follow once the powers of destruction are let loose on the earth. God's promise made to Solomon at the time of the dedication of the Temple held good for the Jewish people throughout the period of the old covenant. It was, 'If my people who are called by my name humble themselves and pray and seek my face, and turn from their wicked ways, then I will hear from heaven and will forgive their sin and heal their land' (2 Chronicles 7:14).

The New Testament makes it clear that those who accept Christ as Lord and Saviour are the inheritors of the covenant and the promises. Thus that same promise of God holds good for us today, for God is faithful and his word is unchangeable. The promise is for his people who are called by his name. Today, more than a quarter of the entire population of the world claim the name of Jesus as Lord and Saviour. Would not God save the world from destruction for the sake of his people? Of course he would! But his people are themselves caught up in the evil ways of mankind. The Christians who form a quarter of the world's population, many of whom are no more than nominal Christians, are themselves active in polluting the world physically and morally, and in pursuing materialistic goals of mammon. Nevertheless, that promise holds good today and if the Christian quarter of the population of the world were to come to full repentance, there is no doubt that God would step into the course of human history and prevent the destruction.

The policy that is here being advocated is not simply one of disarmament. Disarmament, as the mere de-escalation in the production of the weapons of war, will not halt the world's drift towards inevitable destruction. Disarmament without spiritual rearmament is hopeless. It is full repentance and spiritual rearmament that is the key to the future history of mankind. Only complete trust in God will be honoured. So long as man is trusting in the weapons of his own invention to protect him from the weapons of destruction belonging to the enemy, he is doomed to suffer the fate of all those who live by violence. Those who take up the sword shall fall by the sword. This dictum applies to nations as well as to individuals. Violence begets violence and the end result in today's world will be ultimate violence. Man has already set his course on the path of destruction, and it will not be long before he reaches the edge of the precipice and there will be no turning back. At the moment, there is still time to pause for reflection. If men will only open their eyes and see where the path of the nations is leading them and turn to God, even if only through fear, God will honour them. That fear must be followed by repentance, and by a willingness to seek God's way and to turn away from spiritual evil and be armed with the Spirit of God.

God has already provided the means for man's redemption – the means by which man's evil nature can be changed. It is through the cross of the Lord Jesus Christ and the acceptance of what he has done for us. Man has first to be broken of his own self-will and pride before he can be filled with the Spirit of God. That is true for each individual man and it is true for the nations of the world, but nations are made up of individuals. There is no such thing as mass salvation. Each man must find God for himself. Yet God often uses national events to speak to large numbers in the same period of time. That is what happens in revival. Men are open to the Word of God, the Holy Spirit is active in preparing the way, God speaks and large numbers hear and respond.

Even when a nation has become particularly spiritually insensitive and the vast majority are living on a purely secular and physical level of life, God can still break through into the life of that nation. The history of God's dealings with Israel over the period of the monarchy, as recorded for us in the books of Kings and Chronicles, underlines both God's readiness to forgive and his overall good purposes for the nation. Even when the monarchy ended with the destruction of Jerusalem, and when the national disaster of the exile and slavery in Babylon had engulfed the nation, God still reaffirmed his love for his people and his good purposes. 'For I know the plans I have for you, says the Lord, plans for welfare and not for evil, to give you a future and a hope' (Jeremiah 29:1). But those good purposes of God could only be fulfilled through national repentance, through the turning to God of large numbers of the people, both in penitence for their past unfaithfulness and in trust and recognition of their dependence upon him. It is for this reason that through the prophet Jeremiah God adds, 'Then you will call upon me and come and pray to me, and I will hear you. You will seek me and find me; when you seek me with all your heart, I will be found by you, says the Lord, and I will restore your fortunes and gather you from all the nations and all the places where I have driven you, says the

Lord, and I will bring you back to the place from which I sent you into exile' (Jeremiah 29:12–14).

The destruction of Jerusalem and the slaughter of the flower of the nation's youth need never have taken place, and it would not have occurred if the people and their leaders had heeded the warnings that God sent them through his prophets. At that period in the history of Israel, when the international scene presented the greatest dangers the nation had ever known, God raised up the three greatest prophets in her history. Isaiah, Jeremiah and Ezekiel all had their ministries during this period, and warned Israel of the dangers, first from the Assyrians and then from the Chaldeans. It is a matter of record that these warnings went largely unheeded. The nation went on her way oblivious of the forces that threatened to engulf and destroy the national life. She made political pacts with Egypt and other surrounding nations, she continued with political intrigues, moral corruption was eating like a cancer at the heart of the nation, injustice and exploitation characterized the social life, the economy was unstable, family life was at a low ebb, idolatrous practices were common, not only at every local shrine throughout the countryside, but also in Jerusalem itself, despite the lavish ceremonial of ritual practised in the Temple. The spiritual life of the nation was in disarray. They refused to hear the Word of God and to turn in penitence to him. They put their trust in man and not in God. The result was national disaster, the fall of Jerusalem, the destruction of all her great houses, including the house of the king and the House of the Lord. Those who survived the destruction of the city were carried into captivity as slaves in Babylon.

But it was to them, the slaves in Babylon, that God sent the message of hope through Jeremiah – the same prophet who had been accused of a lack of patriotism when he had foretold the coming destruction in the last days of the old city of Jerusalem, when he constantly pleaded for the nation to turn back to God.

God's Good Purposes

God's good plans apply not only to one nation but to all the nations of the world. That is the message of the New Testament. That is what God has said through John 3:16, that his love encompasses all mankind, for all are his children and he longs to bring them all within his embrace. That is why he sent Jesus, because he so loved the world. But there are conditions attached to men being able to receive his love. Those conditions are bound up with men's own attitudes towards God, their openness to his Word and their readiness to repent of the secular forces of evil that drive them, and to turn in penitence and trust to God. When men do this miracles happen!

A thrilling account of one such miracle which actually transformed a threatened national disaster into a period of international peace is recorded in 2 Chronicles 20. A united Arab army had come against Israel with the express intention of annihilating her. King Jehoshaphat was a realist. He knew that humanly speaking the tiny army of Israel was no match for the massed military might that was coming against him. But he remembered the promise that God had given to Solomon, that in times of national trouble when everything was going wrong in the life of the nation, 'If my people who are called by my name humble themselves and pray and seek my face, and turn from their wicked ways, then I will hear from heaven and will forgive their sin and heal their land' (2 Chronicles 7:14).

Jehoshaphat took God at his word, called the people together, laid the matter before God in prayer, with the beautiful words, 'We do not know what to do but our eyes are upon you.' The answer very quickly came when the Spirit of the Lord came upon the prophet Jahaziel. 'Thus says the Lord to you, "Fear not, and be not dismayed at this great multitude; for the battle is not yours but God's."' But the nation had to show their trust in the Lord not simply in word but also action. Although this was a battle in which they would not need to fight, they were told to go out in battle array and face the enemy. They were not allowed to stay in Jerusalem where they might have been tempted to place their trust in the great city walls. They had to go out to the place of battle, to be exposed to danger from the enemy, to place their trust completely in the Lord, in order to see his victory on their behalf.

Jehoshaphat not only believed the Word of the Lord, but he trusted him so completely that he put the praise leaders in front of the army and together they went out to face the enemy singing songs of victory. Their confidence in God was so great that they praised him for a victory that had not yet been given because the battle had not yet been fought or won. The chronicler records that this demonstration of their faith coincided with the fulfilment of God's promise. For when they began to sing the victory came; the battle was fought and won, but not by Israel! In fact, God used the sinfulness of the enemy to bring about their own destruction through the division within their ranks. The so-called united Arab armies simply turned upon each other and wiped each other out without Israel actually drawing a sword. The chronicler further records that when the kingdoms of the neighbouring countries heard about these events, they realized that God had directed and protected Israel and this resulted in a period of peace.

The lessons we can learn today from the way God dealt with Israel hundreds of years ago are perfectly clear if we have a mind open to God. Britain, in common with most of the nations of Europe, has very largely turned its back upon God, with inevitable consequences in the national life. The whole of Europe is today labouring under enormous economic and social problems. But the problems at root are not economic and social, they are moral and spiritual. They concern the whole value structure upon which the life of each nation is based. When the foundation is crumbling, the building is in danger of collapse. That is not an over-dramatized picture of present-day Europe, it is a sober reality. The life of the nations of the old Western world has become polluted and poisoned by moral corruption and spiritual apostasy. Once this happens, the political, social and economic life is affected, and national and international relations show the strain.

We live in a violent age. Crimes of violence rose by a staggering 20 per cent in London during 1980. Commenting upon this in June 1981, Sir David McNee, head of the Metropolitan Police, put this in its international context. He pointed out that violent crime was on the increase in cities throughout the world, and especially in Europe and America. But it is not only violence at an individual level, or by organized criminal gangs, that is causing a problem today. Nations are made up of individuals. When a spirit of reckless violence grips men as powerfully as it has done in our present age, the safety of the entire world is in jeopardy. We have already seen that with the advanced technology in our present generation man has within his hands weapons of destruction that can not only let loose the holocaust of devastation that will engulf the entire world, but those same weapons can pollute the atmosphere of our globe to an extent that may render the continuance of life impossible for hundreds of years to come.

Spiritual Awakening

There is only one hope and that is for the nations to turn to God in penitence. But just as nations are made up of individuals and each individual has to turn in penitence to the Lord, so each nation must seek God for itself. Despite the low spiritual state of Europe today, if the nations were to realize the mortal danger facing them and were to turn and seek God's face in penitence, as children dependent upon the arm of protection of their father, there would be a great spiritual awakening in the old world that would undoubtedly change the course of history. This would indeed come about if men and women in large numbers began to turn to the Lord in penitence and to seek him in humility, recognizing their dependence upon him and calling upon him in faith. He would be quick to answer and pour out his Spirit upon that community or that nation. Each nation that seeks the Lord in penitence would experience a spiritual revival and that nation would thereby come under the protection of God. He would put his canopy over them as he did over the Israelites during their journey through the wilderness, where a cloud went before them by day and a pillar of fire by night.

God is the same God today as the God in Scripture. He cares for the whole family of mankind. They are his children, his own creation, made in his own image. He does not wish that any one should perish. That is clearly stated by Jesus in John 3:17. The same loving forbearance is spoken of by Peter in the midst of a passage in which he is foretelling the inevitable consequences of evil when the fire of destruction will sweep across the face of the earth. He says, 'The Lord is not slow about his promise as some count slowness, but is forbearing towards you, not wishing that any should perish but that all should reach repentance' (2 Peter 3:9). It is God's will that the whole of mankind should live together as one family under God, enjoying peace and plenty. He has stored rich resources in the world for man to discover and to use for his own welfare and for his own ultimate good. Man has usurped the place of God in the world and has seized upon the resources that God has provided, to use them for his own evil purposes. The consequences of such sinful behaviour are inevitable. But it is not God's intention that mankind should be destroyed. He has plans for man that are good, and for his welfare and not for evil (Jeremiah 29:11). The vision of Isaiah 2, that is repeated in Micah 4, and was probably still being used as a Temple song in the time of Jesus, beautifully enshrines the good intentions of God for the whole family of mankind.

It shall come to pass in the latter days that the Mountain of the House of the Lord shall be established as the highest of the mountains and shall be raised above the hills; and all the nations shall flow to it, and many people shall come and say – 'Come, let us go up to the Mountain of the Lord, to the House of the God of Jacob, that he may teach us his ways and that we may walk in his paths. For out of Zion shall go forth the Law, and the Word of the Lord from Jerusalem. He shall judge between the nations, and shall decide for many peoples; and they shall beat their swords into ploughshares, and their spears into pruning hooks; nation shall not lift up sword against nation, neither shall they learn war any more' (Isaiah 2:2–4).

A Final Warning

That prophecy declares God's ultimate good purposes for the whole of mankind. It is his Word. It will be fulfilled. But unless the nations of the world change course that prophecy will only be fulfilled after the holocaust. It is not God's will that mankind should go through a period of terrible slaughter and suffering. It is not his will that one of his children should perish, but indeed he hates the polluting of the earth by the shedding of innocent blood just as he hates man's injustice, oppression, moral corruption and spiritual adultery.

God is warning the nations now that the consequences of the course upon which they are set will be terrible indeed; too terrible even for the human mind to comprehend; for who can even imagine what the world will be like engulfed in the all-out exchange of nuclear weapons? Who can even imagine the deaths of hundreds of millions of people, possibly as many as two-thirds of the world's entire population? Who can imagine the destruction of vast areas of natural vegetation, the polluting of the earth's atmosphere and the rendering of the land useless for hundreds of years?

God is both pleading with the nations and warning them of the terrible consequences of pursuing the path along which they are now speeding towards mutual self-destruction. It is as inevitable as the rising of the sun tomorrow, unless the nations change direction and heed the Word of the Lord, coming humbly before their God.

'Thus says the Lord, Tell the world what I, the Sovereign Lord, am saying. Because you have murdered so many of your own people and have defiled yourself by worshipping idols, your time is coming, you are guilty of those murders and are defiled by the idols you made, and so your day is coming, your time is up!' (Ezekiel 22:3,4, GNB).

This is the word of the Lord to the nations. Hear it!

CHAPTER TWELVE

God's Word to the Church

The greatest tragedy in the history of mankind is poignantly summed up in the prologue of John's Gospel in just two sentences: 'He was in the world, and though the world was made through him, the world did not recognize him. He came to that which was his own, but his own did not receive him' (John 1:10–11, NIV).

In the fullness of time, God sent his own Son into the world to accomplish the great act of salvation that was his purpose from the time sin had broken the relationship between God and man. Having prepared the way through the Law, the Covenant and the Prophets, the scene was set for the drama of the Incarnation. But the people of the Old Covenant were unready. Just as their forefathers had been unresponsive to the prophets of old, so now in the time of their visitation, they were spiritually blind and unresponsive to God. 'Yet,' declares John, 'to all who received him, to those who believed in his name, he gave the right to become the children of God – children born not of natural descent, nor of human decision or a husband's will, but born of God' (John 1:12–13, NIV). So the children of the New Covenant were born.

For nearly two thousand years, the people of the New Covenant have been spreading across the face of the earth. Today, as the second millennium of the Christian era draws to its close, history is likely to be repeated. The people of the New Covenant are as unready to receive the visitation of God, as unresponsive to his word, as were the people of the Old Covenant. The end of the era of the Gentiles has already been accomplished; the climax of the ages is drawing near. The decisive battle between the forces of good and evil is close at hand. The battle is not ours but God's. But we are involved. The battle is so gigantic that it encompasses the whole of mankind. This is a battle from which we cannot opt out, but if we attempt to fight it in our own strength we shall be overwhelmed.

God is calling his people today, with a new urgency, to a new obedience. The forces against us are too great for us. Our only safety lies in coming under his protection and our only hope lies in our coming to him in childlike dependence. 'Lord, we do not know what to do, but our eyes are upon you' (2 Chronicles 20:12). But the motive in turning to Christ is not merely that of fear and a desire for protection. The motive is mission, the desire is for obedience. Christ is calling his Church today to a new obedience, to prepare us for a new mission to the nations.

The great danger is that Christians are not ready and responsive to God at a time when both the danger and the opportunity are maximized. The Church world-wide, although numerically stronger than at any time in history and now encompassing more than a quarter of the world's population, is spiritually weak. Christianity is now the world's largest religion and growing rapidly, but are Christians, as the people of God, growing in spiritual strength and awareness fast enough to meet the challenge of these times?

The Church world-wide, and especially in Europe and the West today, stands in total contrast to the simple Spirit-filled company of believers that left the upper room in Jerusalem at Pentecost and set out to go to the ends of the earth with the Gospel of Jesus. Despite the warnings of Paul – 'Don't let the world around you squeeze you into its own mould' (Romans 12:2, J. B. Phillips) – the world has seeped into the Church and squeezed Christians into its mould. Instead of the people of God being a living organism of the Spirit, we have impressed our humanity upon the Body of Christ so powerfully that it has become a giant organization encumbered by institutionalism, crippled by materialism, blinded by secularism, struck dumb by unbelief, emaciated by division and enfeebled by spiritual impotence –

and all this at such a time as this! What shall we do?

The answer is the same as that given by Peter to the same question from the crowds on the day of Pentecost, 'Repent . . . and you will receive the gift of the Holy Spirit. The promise is for you and your children and for all who are far off – for all whom the Lord our God will call' (Acts 2:38–39, NIV).

The promise of the Father to send his Holy Spirit upon his people of the New Covenant who were in Christ was not simply for the twelve apostles or for the first generation of Christians, but for their children and for those far off – in other words, for their descendants, for future generations throughout the world in every age and in every place. It is we today who are the people of God, the Body of Christ, the children of the New Covenant, heirs of the promises. It is we who have available to us today the whole power of the Holy Spirit as he was present amongst the first generation of Christians. God is not changed. He is the same God today who poured out his Spirit upon the disciples at Pentecost. He is the same God who touched the hearts of three thousand men and women when Peter broke the good news to them of new life in the risen Christ.

But before we can be filled with new power in the Church, from a fresh outpouring of the Holy Spirit to meet the needs of our day, we have to be obedient to Christ. His word to us today is the same as it was when he first entered Galilee and began to proclaim the Gospel, 'Repent and believe!' It was the same message that Peter gave to the crowds at Pentecost. It is the same message that Jesus brings today, not only to the world but first to his Church. The repentance he looks for amongst his own people is not just the repentance for personal sin. All children of the new birth have already done that. The repentance he is looking for today in us is a repentance for the extent to which we are a part of the generation of the people of God who have become pulverized by the world. This repentance is an essential preparation for the mighty things God intends to do through his people in the world. For this reason we have to bow our knees humbly before the Father and to look openly and honestly at our situation as Christians.

Any such assessment is open to the charge of generalization, for what is characteristic of one area is false in another. In many parts of the world today the Church is vibrant with life in the Spirit, making a powerful witness in society, full of evangelizing zeal, experiencing real growth and rejoicing in the evidence of the presence of the Lord. But sadly this is not generally true of the Church throughout the Western world, and especially in Europe. It is we in the West to whom the Lord is primarily looking for repentance as a prelude to the outpouring of his Holy Spirit in world revival. Maybe our younger brothers and sisters in the newer churches of the third world nations will be like the little child, Jesus says, who will lead the adults to him. Their faith, eagerness and spiritual vitality are a powerful witness to us in the West whose churches have become gnarled with age and numbed with spiritual lifelessness from the deadening effects of nearly two thousand years of institutionalization.

We will pause for a moment and examine the charge we have levelled against the Church in the Western world, that it is a giant organization –

encumbered by institutionalism
crippled by materialism
blinded by secularism
struck dumb by unbelief
emaciated by division
enfeebled by spiritual impotence.

1. ENCUMBERED BY INSTITUTIONALISM

Tradition is the dynamic that set a previous generation free, that binds the next generation and may enslave following generations. Tradition is often mistakenly regarded by Christians as the bearer of truth from one generation to the next. It is the Word of God that is the bearer of truth. Tradition is the culture of men.

Tradition needs to be reviewed in each generation in the light of the changing needs and circumstances of mankind. It needs to be brought before the source of ultimate truth and checked against his Word. That which is of eternal and unchanging worth needs to be preserved, restated in the modern idiom and reaffirmed, while that which has served a previous generation and is no longer relevant to present-day mankind should be reverently buried with the past.

Institutionalization is the process by which tradition becomes fixed within an organizational context. It is a major sociological process that characterizes the activities of man in every society. Institutionalization has presented a constant threat to the Church since New Testament times. Within two or three generations it can transform a living, dynamic faith into a dead, human tradition. Church history bears ample testimony to this, particularly in the record of revival and the rise of denominations. If this is not found convincing then a comparison of the Church of the New Testament with our churches of today will surely bear witness to the transforming power of the process of institutionalization.

The simple thumbnail sketch of life in the early Church that Luke has provided for us in the opening chapters of Acts shows a growing company of men and women vitally aware of the presence of the risen Christ and constantly rejoicing in the evidence of his power working among them. 'Jesus is Lord' was constantly upon their lips and written in their hearts. It was the dynamic that made them dare to defy the rulers of the nation and the might of Rome. They knew he was with them and within them and around them, for Christ was all and in all. They were carried in his strength and by his Spirit. Their knowledge was not second-hand but first-hand. It was the personal experience of the living Christ within them. They were his Church. They were the temple of the Holy Spirit. They were the Body of Christ in the world.

Thus the Church of the New Testament was not an organization that men joined, with a membership role, a set of rules and a constitution with a trust deed. Their trust deed was the Word of the Lord, their constitution was the New Covenant, their rules of practice were directed by the Holy

Spirit. It was he who directed the mission of the Church. He overruled if they were going in the wrong direction, as when Paul wanted to go farther into Asia Minor and was forbidden by the Spirit. He redirected his people to new mission fields for the glory of Christ, as when Paul responded to the vision of the man of Macedonia.

The Church in the New Testament was a living organism not a dead organization. Two thousand years of institutionalization have changed the Church out of all recognition from its New Testament roots. But rightly understood, institutionalization is not simply an inevitable sociological process, essential for the survival and transmission of an ideology. For Christians, it needs to be seen as a measure of the extent to which we allow our humanity to dictate the terms of our spiritual obedience.

Institutionalization begins to take place the moment we begin to organize our corporate spiritual life and to act in obedience to the Great Commission to carry the Gospel to all mankind. The dangers of institutionalization are constantly with us. They were there in the early Church, in the appointment of elders in local assemblies, in the primacy of the Jerusalem church, in the Council of Churches in Acts 15, in the writing of the gospels and later in the making of the creeds and the regularizing of the celebration of the Love Feast. But the early Church was constantly aware of the presence of the living Christ and was responsive to his Spirit, and lived in a daily expectation of receiving from him, which countered the deadly effects of structural organization that the process of institutionalization attempted to impose.

Throughout Church history, the rise of every schism and sectarian movement has been a form of protest against institutionalism. Luther never intended to break with the Church of Rome, but to protest against the excesses of institutionalism in his day. Similarly, Wesley never intended to break from the Church of England. The rise of the Brethren, the Pentecostals, the numerous independent sects, and even the house church movement of today, are each in themselves a form of protest against institutionalism. They are an attempt to de-institutionalize by taking the emphasis away from the complexities of institutions to the simplicities of task orientation or mission.

Institutionalism has its origins in the human desires for status, for personal aggrandizement and for the exercise of power and control. We begin with a vision, or in sociological terms, 'an ideology'. From this we are led into mission, or the formulation of a task, which has to be rightly ordered or properly organized. The tragedy of human mission is that we are not content with a simple task-oriented organization. Our humanity gets in the way, we begin to build up a big organization which requires more and more maintaining, and eventually the organization becomes of greater significance than the task. In time, the task of maintaining the institution or organization becomes so dominant that it is substituted for the real task. In fact, it *becomes* the task. The institution becomes self-perpetuating and the original mission is either completely subservient or even lost.

The great churches of the West have all, in varying degrees, been affected by the process of institutionalization that has changed their perception of the Church's mission. The former Bishop of London made a significant statement during a Partners in Mission conference of the Church of England in the summer of 1981. He said that traditionally England has been a Christian country for centuries, and the Church of England has been a part of the established structure of society. Its primary task was pastoral, that of nurturing in the faith children born into Christian families. The Bishop went on to refer to revolutionary social changes that had taken place in Britain during this century, which had changed the structure and composition of British society. Britain was no longer a Christian country, it was largely secular and multi-faith. He said, 'We in the Church of England are now, for the first time, having to look at such things as mission and evangelism at home' (reported on BBC Radio 4, 'Sunday' programme, 20 June 1981).

In the New Testament Church, the primary purpose was that of mission and evangelism in obedience to the Great

293

Commission of Jesus, given in Matthew 28:19: 'Go into all the world and make disciples of all the nations.' It was a going Church; an evangelizing fellowship; a missionary movement. It was not a static institution stoically maintaining its own stagnant structures in defiance of every social change. Once the Church loses sight of its primary task of mission and evangelism, and passively settles for a pastoral maintenance ministry, it not only ceases to be the Church as established in the New Testament, the Body of Christ in the contemporary world, but it makes two fundamental errors, the one sociological, the other theological.

The sociological error is to assume that society can ever be unchanging in its mode of being, and that thus there is no need for the Church to change its form of organization and mission from one generation to the next. The theological error is to assume that people are born Christians rather than 'born-again' Christians. It assumes that simply being born into a Christian family or community or nation is sufficient, and that in due time we will learn to be a Christian as though Christians are the product of some educational system. It overlooks the fact that Jesus says that we have to be born again; there has to be a basic change in our human nature that only he can accomplish. For this reason, Jesus separated the task of 'making disciples' from that of 'teaching them to obey'.

It is not sufficient simply to teach the ethical requirements of the Gospel. We also have to make disciples through the presentation of the challenge of Christ. The task of evangelism is never finished. Even if the Church has faithfully carried out its missionary task in a nation in one generation, it still has to do it all over again in the next generation, because God has no grandchildren! The New Testament only speaks about children – sons of God, not grandsons. Each generation must find Christ for themselves and each individual make a personal commitment of his or her life to God through Christ.

Once the Church loses sight of its primary task of mission and evangelism, it becomes a mere human institution subject to all the corrupting forces of institutionalism. Institutions are not only self-perpetuating, they are also monolithic and monopolistic in objective, through the insatiable desires and ambitions of the human beings at their helm. Those same human beings derive their social status from the institution, which means that they depend upon it for their positions of power, privilege and prestige in society, all of which are bound up with their pride and self-regard.

What the world sees when it looks at the Church is an institution, an organization like any other human organization. Its business is that of religion and it has a vested interest in selling religion to people, in the same way that a multi-national corporation has a vested interest in selling its products on the markets of the world. It has a vested interest in maintaining its own position of power, prestige and privilege in society throughout the nations of the world. Non-Christians looking at the Christian Church in the twentieth century simply see a reflection of the world in a multi-national religious corporation. It is small wonder that sociologists define clergymen as 'religious functionaries'. Indeed, it would not at all be unjust if they were to redefine them as 'institutional functionaries with vague religious connections'!

The Church of the late twentieth century urgently needs to recognize the extent to which the process of institutionalization has transformed the mission of Christ from a living organism into a dead organization. We will only do this when we come back to the New Testament, bringing our churches of today before the foot of the cross, and standing empty-handed before the Lord. So long as we go on trusting in our institutions encumbered by all the dead weight of institutionalism, burdened by the ever-mounting pressures of maintaining the structures and plant of the institutional Church, attending endless committees and repairing ancient obsolete buildings, we shall continue to be unresponsive to the Spirit of the Lord, unfilled with the presence of Christ, unfit and unready for him to use us in this critical period of world history.

2. CRIPPLED BY MATERIALISM

'I have no silver and gold but I give you what I have in the name of Jesus Christ of Nazareth.' The words of Peter when he and John spoke to the lame man at the gate of the Temple in Jerusalem characterized the faith and the simplicity of the early Church. There was a unity of spirit and purpose that bound the fellowship together in love. 'All who believed were together and had all things in common' (Acts 2:44). They regarded all their possessions as gifts from the Lord, of which they were stewards. Material possessions were not for personal gain, self-aggrandizement or self-indulgence. They were entrusted to them by the Lord for use in his service. They shared with one another as the Lord had given to them. They lived in a simple lifestyle in vivid contrast to the senseless luxury around them, in the senseless and sensuous Graeco-Roman world. Their lifestyle, their business ethics, their family life and community unity were so different from the worldly standards around them, that people could see the difference when men became Christians. They rejected the worldliness of their present age and put on Christ, so that the beauty of Jesus and the love of God could be seen in them and in the community of Christians.

Today it is different. The great religious institutions of the West have taken into their structures all the gross materialism of Western industrial society over the past two hundred years. Instead of the Church going into the world, the world has come into the Church. It has brought with it the subtlest forms of worldliness, not simply covetousness over property, but the rationalization of the acquisition of wealth as the need to ensure the continuation of mission.

In a superbly produced forty-four-page glossy magazine-style report, the Commissioners of the Church of England published their income and expenditure accounts for 1980. It contained attractive colour photographs of expensive property owned by the Church of England in some of the most exclusive areas of London, such as the Hyde Park Estate. The report also had all the usual anomalies that we have come to expect in church reports, such as the heading 'The conversion scheme at St Mary Lichfield', which turned out to be not a plan of evangelism but a building project. The report showed that seven hundred and eighty-three churches owned by the Church of England became redundant during the decade of the 1970s. But the most incredible example of materialism in Church affairs occurred under the heading 'Money Market'.

To ensure that money is available to meet their capital and revenue commitments as they mature, but is profitably used meanwhile, the Commissioners are investors of considerable sums in the short term money market for periods varying from one day to one year upwards . . . the expendable funds thus held by the Commissioners amounted to £41 million in total at 31 December 1980. In the course of active management of their fixed assets portfolio, the Commissioners also from time to time throughout the year sell stock exchange securities and property and the proceeds, pending re-investment, are temporarily invested in the money market . . . the rate available on seven-day bank deposit was 15 per cent at the beginning of the year, falling to 14 per cent in July, and 12 per cent at the end of November. But by active use of the facilities available in the market, the Commissioners have succeeded in obtaining a higher rate of return on their investments for varying periods, having comprised loans to local authorities, banks, discount houses and other institutions, bills of exchange, mortgage bonds, and Sterling-Euro currency deposits. Sums placed in the market during the year totalled £222 million, the number of transactions being 520, and the daily balance averaging £23.1 million, compared with an average of £22.5 million during the nine months to 31 December 1979.

Who would have guessed that that passage occurred in the report, not of some big multi-national commercial corporation or merchant banking institution, but in a report of the affairs of the Church of England? The report showed that the Church of England owned 'a property portfolio' with a total market value at the beginning of 1981 of £762.5 million.

Is this the Church of the Lord Jesus Christ who said of himself, 'The Son of Man has nowhere to lay his head'? Is this what men have done to distort the mission of the Saviour of the world, who stated emphatically, 'My kingdom is not of this world'? How the forces of darkness must be rejoicing to see the Christians spending their time and energy amassing material wealth and accumulating property on such a vast scale! How the enemy must be rejoicing to see the Christians believing that all this wealth is necessary to pay the clergy and to maintain the plant necessary for the Church's mission!

It would transform the mission of the Church of England overnight if the clergy had to rely for their support upon their people, as do the ministers of the independent churches. It might even make some of the clergy cease to regard the Church 'as a living' and become interested in evangelism!

We have chosen to use the Church of England by way of example, but we could equally well have illustrated the spirit of gross materialism that has seeped into the Western Church and transformed its life and mission by looking at the Church of Rome, or the Methodist Church, or the Lutheran Church or any of the great denominational churches of Europe or America.

Has the Church really been obedient to Jesus in building up its huge material empires? Who told the Church of Rome to acquire its fabulous riches? Who told the Church of England to become the greatest land and property owning institution in Britain? Who told the Western Protestant churches to build up huge portfolios of investment, rivalling that of the great multi-national corporations in the empires of mammon? Who told the big-time itinerant evangelists to stay in the plushest hotels when they go to evangelize the poor and the powerless in the great cities of the world? Who told the pastors, priests and ministers to seek the best livings in the opulent suburbs or city centre parishes, while the downtown inner-city working class pastorates among the urban poor and the underprivileged are neglected or can attract only low-status clergy?

The extent to which materialism has moulded the mission of the modern Church to make it unrecognizable in comparison with the Church of the New Testament needs to be a matter of the most urgent repentance if the Lord is to be able to use the Church as his Body in the world at such a time as this. Undoubtedly, if Jesus were to be allowed inside our churches today, he would be taking a whip as he did when he entered the outer courts of the Temple in Jerusalem and drove out the people who were merely making a living out of religion, purporting to do the work of God but in reality serving the god of mammon – 'Take these things away; you shall not make my Father's house a house of trade.' Those words thundered through the courtyard and echoed across the wings of the Seraphim and Cherubim in the lofty heights of the Temple. Men trembled when they heard them and remembered that it was prophesied of the Messiah that 'the zeal of thy house has consumed me'.

It was not a pleasant sight for the 'institutional functionaries with vague religious connections' to witness, as their cattle were driven bellowing from the Temple precincts and the tables of the money changers went clattering to the floor, their contents sent noisily scattering across the flagstones. 'My house shall be called a house of prayer for all the nations!' The words rang through the Temple and caused the faithful to rejoice and the institutional functionaries to tremble.

God knows how we need those words to ring down the corridors of our denominational headquarters, to echo through the chambers of our church houses and to reach the lofty heights of our cathedrals and great churches! When the Lord visits his Church he will purge it as a refiner of gold or silver heats the precious metal over the intense heat of fire to bring the dross to the surface, that it may be skimmed away to leave the surface clear and the metal pure. The refiner continues to work until he can see his face perfectly reflected in the surface of the liquid metal. That is what Jesus wants to see in his own Church, a purified body, a cleansed fellowship, a spiritually alive organism that reflects his glory so that the world can see his face, not a mere dirty reflection of the material worldliness that is all about us.

His purpose is to use the Church to make known to all the world 'the unsearchable riches of Christ and to make all men see what is the plan of the mystery hidden for ages in God, who created all things; that through the church the manifold wisdom of God might now be made known to the principalities and powers in the heavenly places'. His desire is that we may know Christ. That he may dwell in our hearts through faith. That we should be rooted and grounded in his love. That we may 'have power to comprehend with all the saints what is the breadth and length and height and depth, and to know the love of Christ which surpasses knowledge', in order that his Church may be filled with all the fullness of God. Only he can do this, we cannot do it for ourselves. We cannot cleanse our mucky material institutions that we dare to call churches, blaspheming the name of God by dishonouring the name of Christ in the world. But he is able! He is able to do exceeding abundantly far more than we can ask or even think. 'To him be glory in the church and in Christ Jesus throughout all generations for ever and ever! Amen' (Ephesians 3:21).

3. BLINDED BY SECULARISM

It is not only materialism that has affected the Church over the centuries, but the onslaught of secularism. The particular effects of secularism have been most keenly experienced in Europe and those countries of the old world that have had Christianity as an established part of society for many centuries. The process of secularization has a twofold effect. In the first place, it tends to blur the distinctions between the secular and the sacred by a process of accommodation of the one to the other, and in the second place, it tends to result in the gradual taking over by the state or other secular institutions of roles traditionally performed by the Church.

The way in which the secular and the sacred come together

and the distinctions between them become blurred, is in itself a two-way process. On the one hand, the Church attempts to lessen the gap between the secular and the sacred in order to create bridgeheads for communication of the Gospel, and in order to allow the Gospel itself to permeate every area of life. In this sense the Church sees part of its task as the eventual transformation of the secular into the sacred so that the whole of man's activity in life is given over to God. This is what Luther meant when he protested against the distinction between the religious life and the secular. He said that the ploughman who ploughed a straight furrow and the carpenter who made a trustworthy chair did so to the Lord. They were serving the Lord by using the talents he had given into their stewardship, and this is as much a sacred duty as when the priest faithfully carries out the duties of his office. Each is fulfilling a divine calling, hence in the case of the ploughman and the carpenter, their secular tasks have become sacred through their commitment to the Lord. This is a valid example of secularization. But secularization can also work the other way, that is, when the secular infiltrates and has a manifest effect upon the sacred. Numerous examples could be given of the way in which secular values and objectives have crept into religious institutions. When material values or political objectives get into the Church, or when a missionary society or an evangelistic association finds itself being influenced by commercial interests, or where a Christian publishing house becomes more concerned with commercial promotion than with the propagation of the Gospel, the secularization of its ministry has taken place.

Another sphere of secularization is where roles in society traditionally undertaken by the Church are gradually taken over by the state or other secular institutions. There are numerous examples of this, notably in medical work, social care and in education. Throughout Europe, the oldest hospitals are those which were originally founded by the Church and run by men or women in religious orders. The oldest schools and universities were founded by the Church.

In many third world countries today schools and hospitals are still staffed and maintained by the churches or Western-based missionary societies. In Europe and in many third world countries, the state has taken responsibility for medical care and education out of the hands of Christian institutions and made them purely secular. This loss of many of the traditional functions of the Church has been the cause of a considerable amount of role uncertainty amongst the clergy, particularly in Western European Protestant nations. In these countries the traditional pastoral role of the clergy in parish situations, or ministers of Protestant congregations has also been whittled away by the growth of the caring services under the control of the state and secular public institutions. This has created not only role uncertainty but also a loss of status in the community. The most devastating effects of this role uncertainty have been experienced in those churches where there has been little or no concern for evangelism, and where the main emphasis has been upon pastoral care. In these churches the clergy have experienced basic uncertainty as to the nature of their job or even whether they have a worthwhile job at all. In the debates that followed the publication of the Paul Report in 1965, on the role and function of the clergy, it was pointed out that the 'good man who will do anything for anybody' is hardly a valid job definition! If the state, through its social workers, probation service, health visitors and social services, has taken over the functions of pastoral care; if the community in the secular society has no use for a priest and the Church has no interest in evangelism, there really isn't much left for a clergyman to do!

It is small wonder that many ministers and clergy, in the rapidly changing cultural milieu of the second half of the twentieth century, have been lost in a secular world where they have been without status, without a clear role and unsure of either the purpose or the direction of their own ministry.

By far the most devastating effects of secularization have, however, been in the opposite direction. They have been seen in the way in which secular values and influences have crept into the Church and substantially influenced its mission, its message and its lifestyle. The accommodation of the sacred to the secular is everywhere to be seen, from the rise of the Christian punk rock group singers to the multi-million-dollar ministries of the mass evangelism organizations. We have taken Paul's injunction 'by all means save some' to give validity to the presentation of the Gospel of Jesus of Nazareth by the masters of mammon. The Church in the West has internalized the values of a secular society in an age of materialism to such an extent that it is blinded by secularism to its real task in the world. We are like blind men groping through a minefield, with one casualty after another falling by the wayside as moral corruption, spiritual sickness or mental breakdown take their toll in the mainstream traditional churches.

The situation in the Western Church today is not unsimilar to that existing in Israel in the years immediately preceding the fall of Jerusalem in 586 BC and the exile. In Jeremiah 23 we have a vivid picture of the spiritual sickness and the moral corruption underlying official religion in the nation. 'Both prophet and priest are ungodly; even in my house I have found their wickedness, says the Lord. Therefore their way shall be to them like slippery paths in the darkness into which they shall be driven and fall; for I will bring evil upon them in the year of their punishment, says the Lord. In the prophets of Samaria I saw an unsavoury thing; they prophesied by Baal and led my people Israel astray. But in the prophets of Jerusalem I have seen a horrible thing; they commit adultery and walk in lies; they strengthen the hands of evil-doers so that no one turns from his wickedness; all of them have become like Sodom to me and its inhabitants like Gomorrah' (vv. 11–14).

The really devastating fact revealed by this passage is that God holds the priests and prophets primarily responsible for the state of the nation. He says it is 'from the prophets of Jerusalem ungodliness has gone forth into all the land' (v. 15). They have not only been unfaithful shepherds to the sheep but they have actually led ordinary men and women astray by their own moral corruption, their own spiritual apostasy and by the preaching of false teachings. They have purported to bring the Word of God to the people, but they were in fact only bringing their own words and therefore they were filling the minds of the people with vain hopes, telling them that all would be well with the nation when in fact the nation was in the direst danger that only the full repentance of the people could turn away. It was only their turning to God in absolute trust and dependence that could enable God to pour out his power upon them and to cover them with his protection. So long as they were separated by bondage to sin that characterized the spiritual life of the nation, they were at the mercy of the enemy who would be too strong for them and would one day soon overwhelm them. But this message was not getting through to the people because the secularism of the day had blinded the priests and prophets, who were supposed to be the representatives of God to the people. God would hold them accountable for all that happened to the nation. They were speaking visions from their own minds and not from the mouth of the Lord. 'They say continually to those who despise the word of the Lord "It shall be well with you," and to everyone who stubbornly follows his own heart, they say, "No evil shall come upon you", for who among them has stood in the council of the Lord to perceive and to hear his word, or who has given heed to his word and listened?' (vv. 17–18).

Jeremiah goes on to speak of the anger of the Lord against those who claim to be his servants in the nation: 'I did not send the prophets yet they ran; I did not speak to them, yet they prophesied. But if they had stood in my council then they would have proclaimed my words to my people, and they would have turned them from their evil way and from the evil of their doings' (vv. 21–22).

Jesus himself says, 'Unto whom much is given, of the same much is expected.' Those who claim to be his servants and who are guilty of misleading the nations through unfaithfulness to his Word, through failing to stand in his council, through being blinded by the god of this age, will face a harsher judgement than the people they have misled and who are not brought to repentance because of the unfaithful ministries of the ministers of God.

Ezekiel brings a similar charge against the faithless shepherds of Israel who had been feeding themselves and not the sheep. They were growing fat in their comfortable life-styles but were not bringing the Word of God to the people and were thereby responsible for leading people astray. 'Behold I am against the shepherds and I will require my sheep of their hand' (Ezekiel 34:10). The Word of the Lord is unchanged today. He will require the blood of the nations at the hands of his prophets and priests unless they faithfully bring his word to the peoples.

The Church that is blinded by the secularism of the age cannot be a faithful channel of spiritual truth to bring the Word of God to bear upon the human scene. Only full repentance of the extent to which we have allowed the secular forces of the modern world to infiltrate the Church, and to blind our spiritual eyes, can cast out the evil from amongst us and enable us to stand in the council of the Lord, to hear his Word and to discern the leading of his Spirit. Thus says the Lord, 'Come now, let us reason together. Though your sins are like scarlet they shall be as white as snow. Though they are red like crimson they shall become like wool. If you are willing and obedient you shall eat the good of the land, but if you refuse and rebel you shall be devoured by the sword, for the mouth of the Lord has spoken' (Isaiah 1:18–20). 'In repentance and rest is your salvation, in quietness and trust is your strength' (Isaiah 30:15, NIV). Thus says the Lord to his Church today.

4. STRUCK DUMB BY UNBELIEF

One of the most incredible facts of modern history is the way in which over the past hundred years the authority of the Bible has been steadily eroded by attacks not from outside the Christian faith but from within the ranks of the Church. This is a phenomenon quite unknown in any other of the world's religions. The onslaught on the veracity of Scripture has been the outcome of extensive research by biblical scholars since the middle of the nineteenth century. This research has been directed towards the authorship and origins of the books of the Bible. The application of modern scientific methods of research investigation, plus major archaeological finds, have given considerable stimulus to this biblical research. A great deal of scholarly work has been accumulated over the years throughout Europe and America, which has considerably added to our knowledge of both the origin and the meaning of biblical tradition, plus the historical background underlying the period of the writing of each portion of Scripture. The discovery of the ancient manuscripts such as the Dead Sea Scrolls and even relatively unimportant finds such as letters from Greek soldiers serving as conscripts with the Roman army, and written in the common Greek, have given us meanings of words in every usage that have enlightened hitherto difficult passages in the translation of the New Testament.

There has been a great deal of positive gain from more than a century of intensive biblical scholarship, but the saddest feature has been the way in which so many biblical scholars have lost their personal faith in God, and their research has been carried on outside the context of a living faith in Christ. Their research has become negative and sterile, a mere academic exercise, occasionally even with a deliberately destructive objective. No doubt the intensity of biblical debate has been increased by the polarization of extremes. Some biblical scholars became increasingly radical as a reaction against the blind literalism that refused to recognize any value in their work. It was no doubt in reaction to those who clung irrationally and dogmatically to the old King James Version, as being the only authentic translation of the original Greek and Hebrew texts, that many scholars adopted even more extreme views, through which research hypotheses and speculation became adopted as an authentic academic authority. The kind of blind literalism characterized in the words of the lay preacher who is reputed to have said, 'If the Authorized Version was good enough for St Paul, it is good enough for me', had to be destroyed before significant advances could be made in understanding the Word of God for the present age.

In recent years the market has been flooded with new translations of the Scriptures of varying quality, such as those of Moffatt, Weymouth, Phillips, and the New English Bible, none of which are outstandingly accurate. There are also numerous paraphrases which attempt to interpret rather than to translate Scripture, such as the Living Bible and the Good News (TEV) which, while sometimes helpful, also have their limitations. We do, however, have some very trustworthy translations that are as faithful to the original as modern scholarship can provide, particularly the Revised Standard Version and the more recent New International Version.

The saddest feature of the scholarly debates that have been the cause of such acrimony and division within the churches over the past century, is that a great deal of dubious and negative biblical criticism has been produced as authoritative works of biblical scholarship and made available to theological students. Moreover, many of the lecturers in theological colleges have been academics with little or no personal faith, who have taught biblical studies in a negative and sterile context that has done untold harm within the Body of Christ. The theological colleges have produced thousands of ministers, priests and clergy throughout Europe and America, particularly over the past fifty or sixty years, who have been taught to regard the Bible largely as an academic textbook on religion which has no real authority as the Word of God. This has resulted in the lack of authentic biblical preaching in a great many churches over a period of two generations. This in turn has resulted in the Bible dropping out of use or taking a subsidiary place in the lives of the vast majority of ordinary Christians, particularly in Europe.

During the past ten years, coinciding with the rise of the charismatic renewal movement, there has been a new emphasis upon the place and authority of the Bible within the Christian Church, and a rediscovery of Scripture as the authoritative Word of God by many traditional Christians for whom it had had little or no significance. There are signs that the new biblicalism emerging among Christians today is both scholarly in its approach and experiential in its faith. It may be, within the overall purposes of God, that we have had to endure the traumas of controversy and the agonies of the loss of personal faith experienced by so many, with the consequent weakening of the Church's witness and mission, in order to reach a new understanding of the centrality and significance of the Word of God for today, plus the experience of the presence and the power and the authority of Christ in his Church.

The effects of sterile academic biblical liberalism have, however, taken their toll of the strength of mission as well as upon the quality of the fellowship life of the Church. If the preachers do not believe the Gospel they are preaching, clearly their words will carry no conviction. Yet there are serious doubts on even the most basic Christian beliefs among ordained ministers in the mainstream churches. In an enquiry conducted amongst ordained ministers and lay representatives attending a conference organized by the National Council of the Churches of Christ in the USA (equivalent to the British Council of Churches in the UK), only sixty-one per cent of the ministers were able to confirm that they had no doubts about the existence of God. Only 56 per cent believed in the divinity of Jesus. Less than a quarter believed in the Virgin Birth, while a mere 18 per cent believed that Jesus had actually walked upon the water. Laymen expressed more faith in basic Christian beliefs than the ministers, but clearly their beliefs are strongly influenced by the preaching to which they are exposed Sunday by Sunday. It was found that ministers in administrative positions had slightly more liberal views than those in pastoral charge, although the differences between the two were not highly significant. The position is summarized in the table in Figure 55.

FIGURE 55 *Basic Beliefs of Clergy and Laity*

	ORDAINED MINISTERS		LAITY
	IN ADMINISTRATIVE POSITIONS	IN PASTORAL CHARGE	
BELIEF IN: (No doubts)	%	%	%
God	60	62	78
Divinity of Jesus	54	60	71
Life after death	58	70	70
Virgin Birth	22	27	46
The Devil	18	28	37
Original Sin	11	22	17
Miracles	16	24	33

Source: The Gathering Storm in the Church, Jeffrey K. Hadden, pp. 228–30.

The situation in Britain and other European countries is fairly similar to that represented in the table. It demonstrates dramatically the effect the liberal theological colleges have had upon the Church over the past two generations. Jeffrey Hadden makes the point that the American statistics indicate that those clergy who are least sure of their personal beliefs on fundamental doctrine find their way into administrative posts. The danger of this is that they tend to grow in influence rather than the reverse, since in an institutional ethos such as we have in the modern Church, status goes with administrative responsibility and position held within the organizational structure, rather than in accordance with faithful ministry or quality of spiritual life. If figures were available for theological colleges, they would no doubt show considerably less biblical convictions and beliefs in basic Christian tenets even than those indicated in the table.

Many of the liberal theological colleges in Britain, however, have closed during the past ten years owing to the falling recruitment rate of young men entering the ministry of the traditional mainstream churches. Methodism, for example, the largest of the Nonconformist denominations in

Britain, is reduced to only one theological college, although with a share in two or three others. In contrast to this, the Bible Colleges are experiencing an unprecedented boom in Britain. A number of new ones have opened in recent years, and all have more applicants then they can offer places. This is substantial evidence of the turning of the tide in Britain with large numbers of young people turning to Christ, but it is also evidence of the widespread rejection of the excesses of dead biblical liberalism and the new emphasis upon an experiential faith with a strong biblical basis.

The new emphasis upon a biblical basis of faith gives us good grounds of hope for the future, but we must not overlook the fact that a great many positions of considerable power and influence within the institutional churches are occupied by men who are basically unbelievers. The writer personally knows bishops and men in senior positions within the denominations who do not believe in the resurrection and have serious doubts about the divinity of Jesus. When the ordained leadership of the churches do not believe the basic fundamentals of the Christian faith, it is small wonder that the churches are powerless to speak to the nations in days of internal turbulence and mounting international crisis. It also results in the inability of the Church to speak to a largely secular society with any authority, even upon matters affecting the basic moral health of society.

The current controversy over homosexual clergy in the Church of England stems basically from a lack of biblical authority. In 1981, one of the London bishops refused to discipline clergy in pastoral charge who were openly living in homosexual unions, and instead rebuked those clergy who took a biblical stand for 'intolerance and a lack of love'. When church leaders faced with such an issue declare that Romans 1 is not the authoritative Word of God, but merely the opinion of Paul that has no relevance for us today, in a more enlightened and tolerant society, there is little hope for the Church speaking with authority and conviction to the world on any of the major issues facing us in these days. Who is going to believe a Church that is unsure of its message and that has no confidence in its own sacred writings? Who is going to give any respect to a Church that claims to speak in the name of God and yet has ordained ministers in official positions who are unsure of their own personal belief even in the existence of God!

The Church in the West has indeed been struck dumb by unbelief. This is what happened to Zachariah, the father of John the Baptist. He had a vision when he was on duty in the Temple in Jerusalem during his tour of duty. He received a message from God that his wife, Elizabeth, would conceive and bear a child whom he should call 'John'. Zachariah's unbelief resulted in his being struck dumb until after the birth of the child, when he had proved his obedience to the Lord in naming the child 'John' instead of following the family tradition of names. He had to prove his obedience to the Lord before he regained the power of speech.

The same is true of the Church today. The institutional churches have largely been struck dumb by unbelief due to their spiritual poverty and moral corruption, plus the institutionalism and the materialism that have crept into the Body of Christ. The only way the Church can regain its power of utterance in the world, and speak with power and authority and utter conviction, is through a recognition of the way in which it has strayed from the path of the Lord, through the full repentance of its leaders and a fresh turning to the Lord. It is only through obedience to God and faithfulness to his Word that the cleansing, forgiving, life-giving power of the Lord can return to the Church.

As Ezekiel was bidden to eat the scroll so that his whole body internalized and digested the Word of God, so the Church needs to turn to Scripture again and study the Word of God with a new openness and a new eager searching for what God is saying through the Bible to his people today and to a world entering the last days of this present age. There is no other way to loosen the tongue of the dumb Church and to come in penitence before the Lord, with a fresh approach to the study of Scripture that will give power and authority to the proclamation of the Word of God to the nations.

5. EMACIATED BY DIVISION

Jesus was well aware of the onslaught the world would make upon his disciples. For this reason he prayed to the Father for them just before entering the Garden of Gethsemane and facing the agony of the cross: 'That all of them may be one, Father, just as you are in me and I in you' (John 17:21). But Jesus knew that the opposition would not end with the first generation of his followers, the onslaught would continue down the centuries as the Church grew. Jesus had already asked the Father to 'protect them from the evil one' (John 17:15). His special prayer now was for the unity of all those who commit their lives to him. The unity for which Jesus prayed was not a social relationship but a spiritual unity that is derived from their relationship to him. Just as he was in the Father so his presence would be within the Body of believers and would guarantee their unity with the Father. The heart of his prayer to the Father was 'that they may be one as we are one' (John 17:22). But there is even greater significance in this prayer of Jesus than the simple request that his people should be given the protection of the Father and find their strength and unity in him. He saw this unity of the Body of believers as a powerful witness to the world, so he added, 'May they be brought to complete unity to let the world know that you have sent me and have loved them, even as you have loved me' (John 17:23).

Jesus saw the visible unity of his people as a sign to the world of the love of God. He saw this united witness to the world as being so important and so crucial to the communication of the Gospel that he gave his disciples a specific instruction that they should love one another. Jesus did not regard love as an optional extra for his people, but as an expression of the very nature of their relationship to one another that stemmed out of their relationship to the Father through him. For this reason, when he spoke of love within the fellowship, he gave them a *command*, not simply a request. He said, 'My command is this; love each other as I have loved you' (John 15:12).

312

It is essential to understand Jesus' teaching on the relationship between love and unity and upon the significance of unity for the proclamation of the Gospel in the world. It is only with such an understanding that we can approach the vexed question of Christian unity in the contemporary world with a right attitude. If we are right in our interpretation of the signs of the times and of the urgency of the task facing Christians in bringing the Word of God to our generation, and if Jesus is right in his teaching that the unity of his people is essential as a witness to the world and for the right proclamation of the Gospel (of the latter, at least, there can surely be no doubt), then we must reassess our own obedience to his command.

The contemporary Church is divided not so much by denomination and by doctrinal dispute which is the historical ground of denominationalism, but by mission ethos; that is by the interpretation of its task. The four major groupings that characterize the world Church today are (1) evangelical, (2) social-action, (3) charismatic and (4) traditional. These groups cut right across denominations and historical roots, and even across the credal doctrinal lines of demarcation of former generations. This is not the place to undertake an analysis of the contemporary Church, but these are the effective categories under which such an analysis could be carried out. These groupings not only cut across Church affiliation, they also represent different groupings within the same denomination and they cut across nations and continents.

In just a few words: (1) the evangelicals are those who adhere strictly to biblical doctrine; (2) the social-action Christians are those who interpret their mission primarily in a this-worldly context by bringing the Gospel to bear upon the social conditions of man; (3) the charismatics, who include the Pentecostals and those within the contemporary renewal movement, are those Christians who place the main emphasis upon the growth and building up of the Body of Christ through the full and right exercise of the gifts of the Holy Spirit; (4) the traditionalists are those Christians who place the primary emphasis upon the preservation of historical tradition in worship, ritual performance, credal adherence or practice. Into this last grouping in Britain we would place such strange bedfellows as Roman Catholics, Salvation Army and the majority of Methodists. The Salvation Army have tenaciously held to their nineteenth-century ethos of mission despite the revolutionary social changes that have taken place. They have fossilized the practices of three or four generations ago, buttons, bonnets, brass band and all; which must surely account for their near demise in Britain today.

The lesson for Christians, surely, is that when we attempt to hold fast to anything other than basic biblical beliefs we find ourselves swept away by the passage of time and the processes of social change. There are strong indications of change within the Roman Catholic Church in Britain and America, where the renewal movement is steadily gaining ground. At the moment, this movement is very largely led by lay people, with minimal clergy involvement. But then, what movement of spiritual renewal has ever been priest-led? The role of the priest is that of the right performance of ritual and not the prophetic proclamation of spiritual truth. Thus, the priest inevitably is conservative. He is concerned more with the preservation of tradition than with following a new movement of the Spirit into uncharted waters.

It is not our intention to elaborate on any of the above groupings but simply to note their existence and the fact that they do cut across traditional denominational affiliations of the world Church. But it is not the fact of the existence of different groupings among Christians that is sinful. There have been different groups from the very beginning of the Church. The Christians in Antioch were no doubt different from those in Jerusalem who, in turn, were different from the Christians in Cyprus or the churches in Galatia or Asia Minor or Greece. Even within Jerusalem there were different groups. There were 'Hellenists' or Greek-speaking Christians, and there were the Hebrews (Acts 6). Probably, even amongst the Hebrews in Jerusalem there were different groups such as those who met in the home of Mary, the mother of John Mark, and those who gathered around James (see Acts 12:12–17).

The existence of different groupings is something for which we should praise God as a sign of the rich differences in the clay from which he has fashioned our humanity. For Christians the unifying factor is the one mould out of which we have come, even Jesus Christ our Saviour. It was the Blood of Christ shed for all mankind that was the powerful unifying factor that characterized the early Church, and that superseded every human distinction and broke down every human barrier. In Ephesians 2 Paul rejoices in the social miracle that was accomplished in Christ through breaking down the barrier between Jew and Gentile. If this bastion of racial, national and cultural division could be smashed by Christ, through his blood of the New Covenant that destroyed the enmity between Jew and Gentile and created out of the two one new man, then indeed Christ can unite all mankind and he is the one true hope of a divided world. This is the message that Christians have to proclaim in a world torn asunder by fear and suspicion, as well as by competition, greed and exploitation. In the modern world man's cruelty and insatiable ambition to control his fellow man and to dominate by force are seen, and the natural violence of his untamed nature is compounded and made increasingly dangerous by computer-controlled space-age nuclear weaponry that can not only destroy the multitudes of mankind but also pollute the atmosphere and the earth for thousands of years.

Mankind stands on the brink of international disaster of the most incredible dimensions. The Gospel of Christ is the only power to change the nature of man that can in turn change the course of history upon which mankind is set. But the Christians hold the key that can break the seal and let loose into the world the life-giving healing stream of the Holy Spirit that God has prepared for such a time as this. And the Christians are divided and warring among themselves, and are stumbling blocks to the Lord and a blockage to the Holy Spirit. It is not the existence of different groups with different traditions, different ways of worship, different emphases upon the different aspects of the Gospel message, but the fact that there is division between the different groups of Christians; that there is a lack of unity in the Spirit; a lack of love and a lack of common acceptance of one another as part of the fulfilment of the Great Commission of Jesus for his Church. Our loveless divisions are an open sore in the side of Jesus, they are a cause of cancer within the Body of Christ that prevents the right functioning of the Body at a most critical time in the history of mankind when God is longing to use his Church to save the world.

Of course, we are not meaning to minimize the difficulties that exist where there are basic and fundamental differences on matters of doctrine, and especially in the matter of biblical authority. But these problems can only be overcome where there is love flowing through the Body. Love promotes communication both horizontally and vertically; that is, both with God and with our fellow men and women. Without love, communication becomes an impossibility and the divisions amongst us become widened to chasms, and attitudes become hardened and hostile. Enmity sets in, discord and disharmony disrupt the smooth functioning of the Body, and sometimes even erupt into open violence, as in Northern Ireland.

The spirit of negative criticism that has got in amongst Christians today, the prejudice and hostility that divide us, are a denial of the commandment of Jesus that we should love one another and they are a blasphemy against his prayer that we should be one as he and the Father are one. Time and again the New Testament reminds us that love is a *commandment* of God. 'Whoever does not love God does not know God because God is love' (1 John 4:8). Every committed Christian should read again the first letter of John in which he pleads with Christians not to love the world but to love one another as the fulfilment of the command-ment of Jesus and as a demonstration of their love of God.

How can we expect to evangelize the world if we do not love one another? How can we expect to convey the good news of personal salvation, the forgiving love of God, if we do not communicate love to our non-Christian neighbours? How can our proclamation of the Gospel in a secular world carry credibility when we Christians don't even love one another? Our witness to the world is one of appalling disunity in an age when there is a desperate need for a great international ministry of reconciliation to bring healing and harmony to the warring factions of mankind that are threatening to overwhelm and annihilate us. Only the Gospel has the power to do this – to create a common community out of the commonwealth of the nations and the races. But it is the purpose of God that this ministry of reconciliation should be carried out by human hands – by his people, the Body of Christ in the contemporary world. 'All this is from God, who reconciled us to himself through Christ and gave us the ministry of reconciliation: that God was reconciling the world to himself in Christ, not counting men's sins against them. And he has committed to us the message of reconciliation. We are therefore Christ's ambassadors, as though God were making his appeal through us. We implore you, on Christ's behalf. Be reconciled to God' (2 Corinthians 5:18–20).

But how can we implore the nations of men to be reconciled to God in the name of Christ unless we are first reconciled with one another within the Body of Christ? We have torn that Body asunder by our loveless divisions, by our pride and prejudice, by our hatred and hostility. Divine healing is the only hope! Only Christ can heal his own Body, but first he is looking for our repentance. The healing of the Body of Christ is not waiting for the world church leaders to come together, but every Christian to be reconciled to his brother Christian, for each to come in penitence before the Lord. It is our tears of penitence that will bring healing to the Body of Christ, 'a broken and a contrite heart' the Lord will not despise. When the Christians are broken and come together in tears of penitence and joy in the Lord, all the non-

Christians in the communities around them will get wet. It will be the outpouring of the Holy Spirit in renewal upon the people of God and in revival upon the world.

6. ENFEEBLED BY SPIRITUAL IMPOTENCE

Jesus' major concern for his disciples at the end of his earthly ministry was not simply that they should have unity but that they should have power. Jesus was not simply concerned that the disciples should know the strength that comes through standing together, but that they should know the power that comes through standing in the presence of God, in a right relationship with him through Christ; being obedient to him and receiving the power of the Holy Spirit. It is for this reason that his last recorded words contained both a warning and a promise. The warning was against going in their own strength and the promise was of the power of the Holy Spirit.

Jesus' words were 'Do not leave Jerusalem but wait for the gift my Father promised which you have heard me speak about. For John baptized with water but in a few days you will be baptized with the Holy Spirit.' He followed that with the further injunction, 'But you will receive power when the Holy Spirit comes on you; and you will be my witnesses in Jerusalem, and in all Judea and Samaria and to the ends of the earth' (Acts 1:4,5,8). The promise of the Father is the gift of the Holy Spirit, of whom Jesus speaks in John 14:15–27.

The disciples must have been puzzled by Jesus' words, because although they undoubtedly would have recalled his promise that he would not leave them alone and that the Holy Spirit would be the guarantee of his everlasting presence, yet he had already given them so much. They had been with him throughout his earthly ministry and had witnessed the signs and wonders of God that came through his word of authority. They had seen the lame made to walk, the blind to see, the deaf to hear, the lepers cleansed and even the dead raised to life. Of even greater significance, they had seen men's lives changed; men like Zacchaeus and Levi whose nature was changed and whose subsequent lifestyles bore witness to this. They had seen evil spirits overcome, the laws of nature transmuted, storm and tempest stilled, and they had experienced for themselves the mystic but unmistakable presence of Almighty God in the man Jesus.

They had listened to his teaching, been sent out in his name and experienced the authority of mission. They had recognized him as Messiah, received the bread and wine of the New Covenant, seen him crucified, seen the empty tomb, seen the risen Christ, felt his breath upon them in the upper room, received his Great Commission to go into all the world and make disciples, and now they were eager to go! But still, Jesus told them to wait. Why? Why should they wait when they had got the Gospel, experienced his resurrection and received his Commission? Were they not ready? Were they not eager to tell all the world of the glorious good news of the forgiveness of God through the cross, and new life through the resurrection? But still Jesus said, 'Wait!' – 'Wait for the promise of the Father.' Why wait? What more could there be to come? – 'You shall receive POWER when the Holy Spirit comes upon you.' That was his promise.

Jesus' intention was to send them to all the world. The plan of action he gave them in his final words before the ascension in Acts 1:8 was 'You will be my witnesses', first, right here in Jerusalem and then in surrounding Judea, then in neighbouring Samaria and then away to the very ends of the earth. But to be witnesses of Jesus meant two things: first, that this was not a human venture but a divine mission; and secondly, in being witnesses they would actually be continuing his ministry and that meant exercising his power and authority. It was necessary for them, therefore, to *receive* that power. Jesus, moreover, knew that the moment they began their mission they would be under attack! If they attempted to go in their own strength, they would fail. They had to have the power of the Holy Spirit to carry them. It was not an optional extra! It was an essential part of their equipment.

It was this power that was the real key to the mission of the early Church. The Holy Spirit not only gave the believers a new boldness and a confidence in proclaiming the message, he gave them spiritual gifts that added new dimensions to their humanity. He gave them a power that directed them and carried them through all the vicissitudes of a hostile environment. That power of the Holy Spirit, the promise of the Father, was the gift of Christ to his Church. It was not simply a temporary gift only to last for a few years and then to be withdrawn. It was Christ's *permanent* gift to his Church, his presence with his people for ever. 'And surely I will be with you always, to the very end of the age' (Matthew 28:20).

But there are conditions attached to receiving the power of God through the Holy Spirit. A major part of the fulfilment of these conditions is through obedience. Jesus didn't simply commission his disciples to go and make disciples of all nations, neither were they simply to go 'teaching them everything I have commanded you'. What Jesus said was 'teaching them TO OBEY everything I have commanded you'. The disciples themselves had to learn absolute obedience to Jesus even when they didn't fully understand the meaning of his words. His final command to them was to wait. But waiting was not meant to be a passing interval in their lives, just sitting around idly gossiping waiting for God to do something for them. This was an active waiting, as a waiter waits upon tables. They were to wait *upon* the Lord. They were actively to seek his presence and the fulfilment of his promise to them. They were to engage in earnest believing prayer, praying without ceasing, praising him and asking the Father to fulfil his promise to them.

On the day of the Jewish Harvest Thanksgiving, the day of Pentecost, the day for praising God for the gifts of the harvest, they were all together, in one place, in oneness of spirit, in a unity of prayer and praise, earnestly seeking the Lord, believing the time was ripe for the fulfilment of the promise of the Father made known to them by the Son. They prayed as Jesus commanded and 'suddenly, a sound like the blowing of a violent wind came from heaven and filled the whole house where they were sitting. They saw what seemed to be tongues of fire that separated and came to rest on each of them. All of them were filled with the Holy Spirit and began to speak in other tongues as the Spirit enabled them' (Acts 2:2–4).

From time to time over the centuries, the Church has lost sight of the most precious gift of Christ. The deadening effects of institutionalization, that make structures more important than life in the Spirit; the materialism that brings the cares of this world; the subtleties of secularism that seep through the foundations of the Church and sap its spiritual resources; the pride of scholarship and the cold clinical rationality that blunts the edge of faith and causes unbelief; the loss of the eagerness and openness of love that binds the Body together and guards against division – all these things create barriers to the Holy Spirit. In the contemporary Church, as we have seen, they are all at work. Perhaps it is a part of the cosmic plan of the enemy that there should be such disarray among the people of God at such a time as this, as we approach the climax of the age. If the Church is enfeebled by spiritual impotence at the very time when she most needs the power of the Holy Spirit, the intentions of the enemy of mankind to accomplish man's destruction could be fulfilled.

The world-wide Church today, with more than a quarter of the entire world's population numbered within its ranks, appears as a massive, clumsy, powerless giant, blinded and enfeebled by the constant attacks of the enemy. The Church of today resembles the gigantic figure of Samson, his hair shorn, his power gone, his eyes gouged out, his body bleeding and bruised, now the subject of the taunts and ridicule of his enemies, feeling for the pillars upon which the house of his tormentors stands. In his death, Samson slew the entire leadership of the Philistines and accomplished more in the final act of giving his own life than he had done in all the years of his youthful vigour.

There are many signs today that the Church's hair is growing again! Blinded and enfeebled but cleansed through suffering and brought to a new obedience, the Church of today, as the people of God of the New Covenant, can still fulfil his good purposes for the world. Only a full repentance and obedience to him can prepare the way for his coming in power and glory. Only the recognition by the people of God of their dependence upon him can open them up to receiving the fresh outpouring of the Holy Spirit that it is his intention to give. It is only such a fresh anointing of the Holy Spirit that can give the power to the people of God to meet the demands of these days. If we continue to go in our own strength we shall indeed be lost, but if he fills us with his power, there is no other power on earth or in the heavens above or below that can stand against him. To him be the glory for ever and ever. Amen.

God is Speaking to His People

Jesus rebuked the Pharisees and the Sadducees who came to test him, asking him to show them a sign from heaven. He replied, 'When evening comes, you say "It will be fair weather, for the sky is red", and in the morning, "Today will be stormy for the sky is red and overcast". You know how to interpret the appearance of the sky but you cannot interpret the signs of the times' (Matthew 16:2,3). It is worth remembering that Jesus was speaking to men who spent a large part of their lives in theological debate. They were amongst the religious leadership of the day, yet they were unable to interpret the signs of the times because they were not men of the Spirit.

We have already noted that there are three elements in discerning what God is saying in any particular period of time. The first is the study of his Word in Scripture. The second is prayer, specific, directed, believing prayer. The third is the study of what is happening in the world, and in particular of what God is actually doing. These are not alternative options. Each of them is an essential part of discerning the Word of God to the contemporary scene. We need faithfully to carry out all three if we are to know what

God is saying to us today. In this book we have been studying the Word of God in Scripture. We have been looking at what is happening in the world today but we also need to see what God is actually doing amongst his people today. This is not the place to undertake such a study, but there are many signs that God is at work and doing new things in our day. The two major things that God is doing today are:

1) He is breaking down.
2) He is building up.

1) God is breaking down the old divisions between his people. He is breaking down the great barriers that former generations erected around the denominations. He is breaking down the institutional barriers that separated believer from believer on some obscure point of doctrine, tradition or practice. He is breaking down the pride and arrogance that made men claim to have all the truth and to regard others as having none. He is breaking down the prejudice through which men claimed to belong to a special élite, favoured by God, and which by their hardness of heart shut others out of the kingdom. He is breaking down the lovelessness that has acted as a barrier to communication between Christians, that has allowed the seeds of enmity to grow into the tangled weeds of hostility and even open violence, that has torn communities and nations apart, as in Northern Ireland. He is breaking down the old distinctions between priest and people, clergy and laity.

2) But God is not simply in the business of breaking down. Whenever he has some tearing down to do it is in preparation for building up, for creating something new. God sometimes has to clear away the rubble and the rubbish of the old Jerusalem before he can begin to put together the bricks and mortar of the new Jerusalem. It is our sinful humanity that creates the rubble of destruction and litters the city streets with the rubbish of broken relationships, that God has to sweep away before he can create the new city on

the new foundation of which he himself is both the Architect and the Builder.

In our day there are many clear signs of the activity of the Holy Spirit. God is at work creating order out of chaos. He is clearing up the mess we have made of his Church, the Body of his beloved Son that we have wounded and pierced with our lovelessness and our worldliness. He is creating a new unity amongst his people which transcends and bypasses denominationalism through bringing together those who are in Christ and alive in the Spirit. He is giving a new outpouring of the Holy Spirit that is bringing life and vitality to his Church in many nations throughout the world.

God is giving gifts to all his people and giving a new understanding of the Body of Christ. He is building up faith through the evidence of his presence and power. He is raising up prophets in our day to enable the people of God to discern the signs of the times, to hear his Word and to be responsive to the leading of his Spirit. He is raising a people of power for these times; a watching, praying people; a people protected by the whole armour of God and armed with the Sword of the Spirit. He is raising a people of faith, a people expecting great things of their God and through whom God is able to do mighty things by the power of his Spirit.

God's purpose in building up his Church today as a people of power is in preparation for the coming battle and the testing times ahead. His timing is perfect. As we move towards the end of the age and the climax of the cosmic conflict begins to take place, God is giving new power and discernment to his people. He knows that we will not be able to stand in our own strength and he warns us against trying. It is not in our own ability that we must trust but in his. He alone is able to keep us from falling – he who is able to do exceeding abundantly above all that we can ask or think.

The times are urgent and this is why his Church is growing faster today than ever before in the history of mankind, especially in the third world. The Gospel is already being preached in every nation, as Jesus said it would be. In 1980 the growth rate of the world Church reached 63,000 new

Christians per day – that is, net growth over losses. It is not only individual new babes in Christ who are being born but new fellowships also, at the rate of 1600 per week. God is thus preparing the way for the fulfilment of the vision of Paul in Ephesians 3:10, through which God will use the Church, his people, filled with the power of his Spirit, to make known his manifold wisdom to the rulers and authorities in the heavenly realms.

The final human conflict appears near at hand. There will probably be two major battlefields. The one will be the battle between the super powers, the contest for worldly power between the great armies of the world with their nuclear arsenals. The second battlefield will be the battle with false religion. Militant Islam is already taking the field and threatening to tear the Middle East apart, to annihilate Israel and to wrest Jerusalem from her grasp.

When you see these things begin to happen, do not be afraid. The Lord is saying to his people today:

Fear not little flock, it is your Father's intention to give you the kingdom. When you see the whole world in turmoil around you, do not let it disturb your peace but, look up! Be always on the watch and pray without ceasing. Pray in the Spirit, not words of vain repetition but from a heart open to God. Do not be led astray by false predictions or by those who seek to delude men with dates and times and places. All these things are kept within the Father's own authority.

God alone knows the course that human history will take. One thing only is certain, that is the final outcome – his victory which will establish his power and authority, as in Heaven, so upon earth! THE DAY COMES when in the name of Jesus every knee shall bow of all created things, both in Heaven and upon earth, and every tongue confess him King of Kings and Lord of Lords. To him be the glory, for ever and ever, Amen.

A Final Word

There is very little doubt that by the year AD 2050, that is within the lifetime of the present generation of children, vast numbers of mankind will be wiped out. That is not the ravings of a madman. It is the sober estimate of many of the world's leading scientists who have studied the facts and have considered and reconsidered them in the light of every possible eventuality. It is the professional prognosis of the world's leading experts that by the middle of the twenty-first century there will be a sudden and disastrous fall in the world's population unless radical and far-reaching changes take place in the national and international policies at present being pursued by the nations.

The Scientific Facts

Consider the following facts. The world, like all things that are part of the material created order, is finite. The world's resources are limited. Man cannot for an unlimited period of time go on consuming the basic natural resources of the world that are non-renewable. Eventually they will all be used up.

Consider the case of the world's basic mineral resources. They are non-renewable. When they have been fully exploited they are finished. Of the nineteen basic natural resources listed in figure 56, none will still be available at the end of the twenty-first century if estimates of present world reserves are correct and if the present growth rate in demand is maintained. Even coal, which if demand were maintained at the present level would last for a further 2300 years, will be exhausted by the end of next century unless there is a change in the growth rate of present demand.

FIGURE 56 *Non-renewable Natural Resources*

RESOURCE	STATIC INDEX (IN YEARS)	EXPONENTIAL INDEX (IN YEARS)	EXPONENTIAL INDEX BY 5 TIMES KNOWN RESERVES (IN YEARS)
*Aluminium	100	31	55
Chromium	420	95	154
Coal	2300	111	150
Cobalt	110	60	148
*Copper	36	21	48
*Gold	11	9	29
Iron	240	93	173
*Lead	26	21	64
Manganese	97	46	94
*Mercury	13	13	41
*Molybdenum	79	34	65
*Natural Gas	38	22	49
Nickel	150	53	96
*Petroleum Oil	31	20	50
Platinum Group	130	47	85
*Silver	16	13	42
*Tin	17	15	61
Tungsten	40	28	72
*Zinc	23	18	50

*Resources that will be exhausted by the year 2050 even on the most optimistic forecast.
Figures shown are from 1970.

Source: MIT Research Team.

Figure 56 sets out the situation for non-renewable natural resources. In column 2 the static index shows the number of years that each resource would last assuming there is no increase in demand beyond that pertaining in 1970, and assuming the global reserves known to be in existence throughout the world at that time. The figure in column 3 takes into account the growth rate in world demand at 1970 as against the known global reserves. The figure in column 4 is a prediction based on the assumption that there will be further discoveries of all natural resources that will multiply the known global reserves by five. Even against this highly optimistic projection all but four of the basic natural resources would be exhausted by the end of the twenty-first century. Only chromium, coal, cobalt and iron would still be mined.

It is against this background of the known limitations of the world's natural resources that a team of experts from the Massachusetts Institute of Technology (MIT) set about the task of feeding into a computer all the known variables in the normal developmental processes of mankind, that is, not allowing for natural disasters or world war or other such calamities. On the basis of all the known empirical evidence, they constructed a number of world models to enable them to predict the future course of mankind. The major variables were population size and growth, industrial output, food production, pollution, capital investment and natural resources. When all the known data on each of these variables were programmed the result was a sharp fall in population around the middle of the twenty-first century (see figure 57). The team then began to introduce a number of alternatives, such as doubling the known natural resources through advancing technology and the use of nuclear energy making possible the recycling of natural resources. But this resulted in a vast increase in pollution which sent food production plummeting, soon to be followed by industrial output, and causing an even sharper fall in world population around the middle of the twenty-first century. (see figure 58).

The introduction of unlimited natural resources produced an even sharper fall in world population around the same period (see figure 59).

FIGURE 57 *World Model Standard Run*

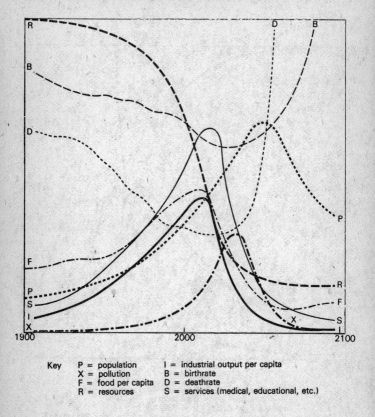

Key
P =	population	I =	industrial output per capita
X =	pollution	B =	birthrate
F =	food per capita	D =	deathrate
R =	resources	S =	services (medical, educational, etc.)

The 'standard' world model run assumes no major change in the physical, economic, or social relationships that have historically governed the development of the world system. All variables plotted here follow historical values from 1900 to 1970. Food, industrial output, and population grow exponentially until the rapidly diminishing resource base forces a slowdown in industrial growth. Because of natural delays in the system, both population and pollution continue to increase for some time after the peak of industrialization. Population growth is finally halted by a rise in the death rate due to decreased food and medical services.

FIGURE 58 *World Model with Natural Resource Reserves Doubled*

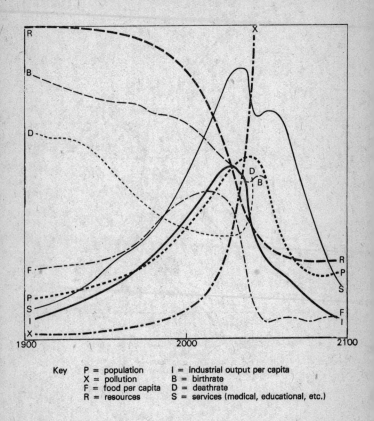

Key
P = population
X = pollution
F = food per capita
R = resources
I = industrial output per capita
B = birthrate
D = deathrate
S = services (medical, educational, etc.)

To test the model assumption about available resources, we doubled the resource reserves in 1900, keeping all other assumptions identical to those in the standard run. Now industrialization can reach a higher level since resources are not so quickly depleted. The larger industrial plant releases pollution at such a rate, however, that the environmental pollution absorption mechanisms become saturated. Pollution rises very rapidly, causing an immediate increase in the death rate and a decline in food production. At the end of the run resources are severely depleted in spite of the doubled amount initially available.

Every combination of variables they tried produced a similar result. It was not until they introduced global controls on every one of the major variables, including population, that they were able to achieve a stable situation. The result is shown in Figure 60. These models demonstrate vividly that the problem facing mankind is not simply one of limited natural resources, but of the *use* of resources.

FIGURE 59 *World Model with 'Unlimited' Resources*

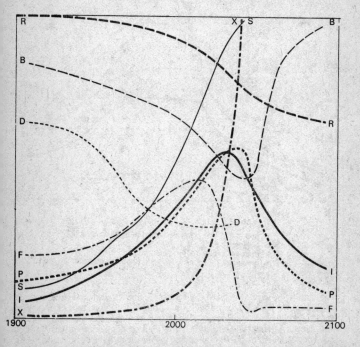

The problem of resource depletion in the world model system is eliminated by two assumptions: first, that 'unlimited' nuclear power will double the resource reserves that can be exploited and, second, that nuclear energy will make extensive programmes of recycling and substitution possible. If these changes are the *only* ones introduced in the system, growth is stopped by rising pollution, as it was in Figure 58.

FIGURE 60 *World Model with Stabilized Population*

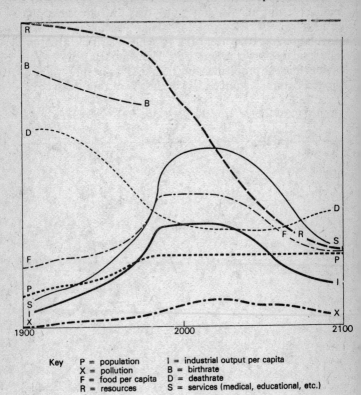

Key   P = population   I = industrial output per capita
X = pollution   B = birthrate
F = food per capita   D = deathrate
R = resources   S = services (medical, educational, etc.)

Restriction of capital growth, by requiring that capital investment equal depreciation, is added to population stabilization. Now that exponential growth is halted, a temporary stable state is attained. Levels of population and capital in this state are sufficiently high to deplete resources rapidly, however, since no resource-conserving technologies have been assumed. As the resource base declines, industrial output decreases. Although the capital base is maintained at the same level, efficiency of capital goes down since more capital must be devoted to obtaining resources than to producing usable output.

Source: for Figures 57, 58, 59 and 60 – Meadows, D. H., *The Limits to Growth*, Potomac Associates Inc., Washington DC, 1972.

In order to achieve the situation of stable equilibrium shown in the world model in figure 60, the MIT team noted that there would have to be controls introduced globally to restrict population to the average size of two children per family. Industrial output would have to be controlled so that the concept of unlimited industrial growth, which is the basis of capitalism, would have to be abandoned. Moreover, the type of industrial production would also have to be controlled so that the major emphasis would be upon consumer goods for the benefit of mankind, with a strong emphasis upon agricultural equipment, and a total abandonment of unproductive and useless material goods such as armaments, which are a waste of natural resources.

There would have to be a strong boost to food production in order to feed adequately the two-thirds of the world's population that at present is undernourished. But food production would also have to be limited in order not to overproduce, thus causing unnecessary strain on the land and usage of natural resources. This would mean strong limitations of food consumption in the rich world, whilst at the same time increasing food consumption in the poor world.

There would also have to be control exercised upon the disposal of waste upon land, in the water and in the atmosphere. Pollution control programmes which are highly expensive would have to be undertaken as a necessary part of capital investment in order to ensure the adequate protection of the environment and the recycling of valuable natural resources to maximize their use.

The remarkable thing about the MIT team's research is that their findings have been published since 1972, and although there have been attempts to discredit their work no one has actually come up with hard empirical evidence to disprove the basic facts upon which their conclusions are based.

Clearly the Brandt Report and the North-South debate have been largely influenced by their research. Yet world leaders have so far paid little heed to the dire warnings implied for the future of mankind. It would appear they either simply do not want to know, or that the vested interests they represent are too powerful for them to be able to hear.

The inescapable conclusion to be drawn from all the available evidence is that there is a limit to the carrying capacity of the world with its finite natural material resources. If nothing is done to control any of the major variables mentioned above, world population will continue to grow at an alarming rate over the next twenty to thirty years, by which time the full force of all the constrictions will begin to be felt and the population will eventually fall sharply. The world will have reached disaster point. Figure 61 shows the kind of thing that may be expected to happen if world population overshoots the carrying capacity of the earth. Naturalists studying the behaviour of herds of deer have noticed similar results when the herd has grown rapidly beyond the carrying capacity of its natural environment.

FIGURE 61 *Carrying Capacity. Population related to resources and environmental factors*

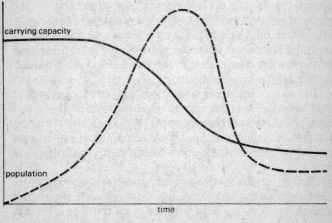

Where the herd has increased in size and not been able to find new grazing grounds the deer have overgrazed the land, resulting in soil erosion that has actually reduced the grass-growing capacity of the land, with disastrous results upon the available food supply, resulting in a steep rise in the death rate among the herd.

Man is at present recklessly overfishing the seas, deforesting the land, overproducing non-essentials in industrial output for maximum profitability and personal gain, polluting the environment and continuing to reproduce the population at an alarming rate of increase that will double the world's population in thirty years. All these conditions taken together can only spell disaster of a magnitude beyond the imagination of man to describe.

Danger of World War

All that we have so far been discussing has only been the end result of the processes of development at present being pursued by mankind. We have not even mentioned the possibility of world war. It is here that we see the real size and magnitude of mankind's predicament. When we see the natural forces that are at work in the economy, in the environment and in the growth of population, against the background of the world-wide build-up of armaments, we can see the true dimension of the folly of the policies at present being pursued by mankind. It is perfectly clear that as the shortage of natural resources begins to bite deep into the productive capacity of the industrialized nations, competition for the remaining natural resources will intensify. Surely no one needs persuading that greedy, self-centred, short-sighted men will fight for the shrinking resources of the world, particularly as food shortages intensify. Men will fight for survival! In a world armed to the teeth with the most fiendish weapons of destruction that modern technology can devise, it is perfectly clear that our world is plunging headlong towards the most fearful and violent conflict in the history of man.

The coming conflict will, in a very real sense, be the end of the age of civilized man. It will destroy most of the accumulated heritage and culture that has taken man many hundreds of years to produce. The war, plus the pollution of the environment and the disease and famine that will follow, will annihilate all but a remnant of mankind.

The time of the coming conflict is drawing near – very near! It will be in the lifetime of many now living. There is absolutely not the slightest doubt that these things will take place unless there is a radical and total change in the world-view of mankind. That means a change in the values men hold that underlie, influence and direct their behaviour. Without such a basic and radical change in the fundamental values of mankind the present policies will continue. It is only as man appreciates the predicament he is in and clearly perceives the inevitable end of the course upon which he is at present set, that the will or *desire* to change will become apparent. At the moment mankind is being blindly driven by self-interest, a lack of perception of the consequences of the present folly and a lack of regard for the common good of the whole of mankind.

This was clearly seen at the North-South summit of leaders of the Western world who met in Mexico in October 1981, to discuss problems of world poverty and development with leaders from the third world. The conference provided what many observers saw as a last chance for the nations to come to their senses and for the West to give to the world a lead that could change the course of history. President Reagan's intransigent attitude set the seal of failure upon the conference from the outset. It was clear that America was determined to stop its ears to the humanitarian cries for help from the starving millions in the poorer nations and to shut its eyes to the inevitable consequences of the present policies. The Western leaders were in full possession of the facts concerning the limits of natural resources, the problems of pollution, of overproduction, and of population growth. They were also in full possession of the facts concerning world poverty and starvation. But they chose to ignore them, to go on pursuing increasing wealth for the Western world, expanding industrial production, increasing pollution of the environment, knowing full well that the world is nearing the limit of its productive and carrying capacity.

The Witness of Scripture

The Bible clearly prophesies that a time of terrible destruction will come upon mankind that will be the direct result of man's disobeying God's laws. It clearly spells out the consequences of bloodshed, of murder, violence and the shedding of innocent blood. It clearly spells out the consequences of man's wilful pollution of the natural environment and of the moral order. It clearly spells out the terrible consequences of man's selfish pursuit of his own materialistic self-interest.

In the day when the holocaust of destruction sweeps across the face of the earth, there will be no escape. The riches of the Western nations will not protect their citizens from the sufferings. Nowhere on earth will be safe. The destruction will be as though God were taking a dirty vessel, turning it upside down and wiping it clean in order to cleanse it of the polluting effects of the sinfulness of mankind.

Yet God does not wish it to happen, but he will allow it and he will use it, just as he allowed Jerusalem to be destroyed and as he used the Babylonians and the sufferings of the exile to purge the nation Israel whom he loved.

It is not God's will that mankind should bring such terrible times of suffering and destruction upon the world. God is love, not hate. He is life, not death. He is a God of creation, not of destruction. He is a God of order, not of chaos. Man will bring the destruction upon himself – that is clear both in the signs of the times and in the prophecies of Scripture. Only a radical change in the very nature of man can accomplish the miracle of a change in the course of history. But it is precisely for this purpose that God sent his beloved Son Jesus into the world. He is the hope of the world

337

– the only hope of a dying world racing with ever-increasing momentum like the Gadarene swine towards the edge of the precipice!

The Hope of the World

Is there any hope? Yes, there certainly is hope! Prophecy of impending disaster is always dependent upon the repentance of man and the forgiveness of God. God will turn back the forces of destruction even now if men will repent of their blindness and folly and turn away from their sinful ways. Only God can stem the forces of destruction for man is being driven by forces beyond his own control. The battle is not simply against flesh and blood, otherwise men could hope to win it in their own strength. But this is impossible. The true nature of the battle is spiritual not material, and only God can win the victory. That is why men have to realize the hopelessness of their position, the terribleness of the predicament of mankind, and turn in full penitence humbly to request God's help.

God is pleading with man to turn to him and be saved. In particular he is calling upon his people, the spiritual descendants of Israel, the people of the New Covenant, those who have entered into new life in Christ from every race and nation, to arise and accept the immense task he has set before them: that of being his witnesses in this generation as the climax of history approaches.

God is indeed raising a people of power filled with new life in the Spirit so that they can go, not in their own strength, but in his; armed with the whole armour of God and having upon them the breastplate of righteousness, the helmet of salvation, their feet shod with the Gospel of peace, on their left arm the great shield of faith and in their right hand the sword of the Spirit. God is raising a mighty army of his people to witness to the world today – every man to his neighbour, that the Word shall be spread and the world be brought to a realization of the urgency of God's call amid the chaos of the times in which we live.

Individual Responsibility

The call to repentance cannot be left to the religious professionals – the priests, ministers and clergy and evangelists. It is the responsibility of every committed Christian to witness to his or her neighbour, family and friends; to show them that we are living in the last days of this present age and to show them the good purposes of God. He is longing to save mankind from the inevitable destruction that is coming upon the world and to show them the way of salvation through Christ, the hope of the world.

As God would have saved Sodom and Gomorrah from destruction if even a minority had repented, and as he did save the great city of Nineveh whose citizens heard the words of Jonah, heeded the warnings and repented of their sinful ways, so God will save and forgive our world today if there is widespread turning to him.

The responsibility is clearly with us, the Christians in the Western world. God is longing to pour out his Spirit in revival upon the world, but the pre-condition is spiritual renewal amongst his own people. So long as we are blind and hard of heart; so long as we shut our eyes and stop our ears to his Word, the Spirit of the Lord is bound.

We are blinded and bound by our materialism and our lack of trust in the Lord. We refuse to turn from our materialistic economies to share the world's resources with the underprivileged and the poor. We refuse to trust God to provide for our needs if we dare to share our bread with the hungry.

God will surely judge us for our hardness of heart and for our lack of faith. We refuse to turn away from our massive production of the weapons of war and our trust in the might of our own arms because we say the enemy is threatening us and he will not disarm.

Let the Christians tell the world that those who take up the sword shall die by the sword. But those who trust in the Lord shall live and live for ever! Any nation that dares to take God at his word and beat their swords into ploughshares, destroying the weapons of destruction and putting their trust in the Lord, will find that God will put his canopy of protection over them so that nothing the enemy can hurl against them will prevail! We are not urging mere nuclear disarmament, but spiritual rearmament!

Prophetic Witness

This is the prophetic witness that Christians have to make to a world that is rushing headlong to its own destruction. God is not waiting for the whole population of the world to repent before he will save mankind. He would have saved Sodom and Gomorrah for a handful of righteous men and women. His promise to Solomon holds good for the children of the New Covenant. That promise is: 'If my people who are called by my name will humble themselves and pray and seek my face, and turn away from their wicked ways, then I will hear from heaven and will forgive their sin and heal their land' (2 Chronicles 7:14). That promise is not dependent upon the repentance of the whole world. It was given to Israel when the nation was in a covenant relationship with God, but it is one of the promises that is inherited by the people of the New Covenant who are a 'new nation', a 'royal priesthood', a people who belong to God but who are numbered amongst all the nations of the world. That promise of God is to '*my people*'. He says, 'If *my people* who *are called by my name* will humble themselves and pray and seek my face.'

The responsibility lies squarely upon our shoulders, those who claim the name of Christ, the committed Christians. It is we who need to dissociate ourselves from the evil policies at present being pursued by all the nations of the world. We need to claim our citizenship with Christ, our true heritage, and act as a royal priesthood, a nation of God's people amongst the nations.

There has to be a difference in our own lifestyle. We need

to repudiate the materialism of this generation. We need to take our stand of faith and to demonstrate that the Word of God and loyalty to him mean more to us than all the empires of mammon.

We need to put our trust firmly in the Lord, and to make our voice heard and our influence felt amongst the nations. It is the Christians in the Western world who carry the primary responsibility for turning the course of history. It is we who have the greatest share of the world's wealth and power and it is we who therefore carry the greatest responsibility for the future of mankind.

God will hold us responsible for the stewardship of the resources that he has entrusted to us and placed within our hands. He is pleading with the world today, through us, as though we were ambassadors for Christ.

He is pleading with men to be reconciled with him, to recognize the folly of their ways and to turn to him and be saved. He longs to embrace within his fatherly love all the nations of the world and to have the whole family of mankind in a right relationship with himself. This is his purpose underlying the whole of creation. Never has the fulfilment of the Great Commission of Matthew 28:19 been more urgent for Christians: 'Go and make disciples of all nations.' We Christians of the Western world are *privileged* to live in this period at the climax of history. The challenge to the future of mankind has never been greater, but equally neither has the *opportunity* for the salvation of the whole of mankind ever been greater!

Will the Christians rise to the challenge of the hour? Will there arise a great army of the Lord's people from every nation under the sun to witness with prophetic power, each within their own spheres of influence? Will the nations of the world hear the Word of the Lord and turn from their wicked ways? Will mankind heed the warnings and turn to the Lord and be saved?

God is sending to the world what may well be the last chance for man. His word is clear:

Turn to me and be saved, all you ends of the earth;
for I am God and there is no other.
By myself I have sworn, my mouth has uttered in all
integrity a word that will not be revoked: Before me
every knee will bow; by me every tongue will swear.
They will say of me, 'In the Lord alone are righteousness
and strength'. All who have raged against him will
come to him and be put to shame.
But in the Lord all the descendants of Israel will
be found righteous and will exult.

(Isaiah 45:22–25)

HALLELUJAH!
OUR GOD REIGNS!

Acknowledgements

The author acknowledges his gratitude for the use of texts, charts and tables presented in this book, for which full credit has been given at the relevant points.

Select Bibliography

Chapter One

Bittlinger, A., *Gifts and Ministries*, Hodder & Stoughton, London, 1974

Clements, R. E., *Prophecy and Tradition*, Blackwell, Oxford, 1975

Dunn, J. D. G., *Jesus and the Spirit*, SCM Press, London, 1975

Griffiths, M., *Cinderella's Betrothal Gifts*, OMF Books, London, 1978

Hill, David, *New Testament Prophecy*, Marshall, Morgan & Scott, London, 1979

Lindblom, J., *Prophecy in Ancient Israel*, Blackwell, Oxford, 1962

Martin, R. P., *Worship in the New Testament*, Marshall, Morgan & Scott, London, 1974

Staniforth, M. (translated by), *Early Christian Writings: The Apostolic Fathers*, Penguin, London, 1968

Tugwell, S., *Did You Receive the Spirit?*, Darton, Longman & Todd, London, 1972

Williams, John, *The Holy Spirit: Lord and Life-Giver*, Loizeaux Brothers, Neptune, New Jersey, 1980

Yocum, Bruce, *Prophecy*, Servant Books, Ann Arbor, Michigan, USA, 1976

Chapters Two–Four

Allen, C. J. (Ed), *The Broadman Bible Commentary, Vol. 5*, Marshall, Morgan & Scott, London, 1971

Clements, R. E., *The New Century Bible Commentary: Isaiah 1–39*, Marshall, Morgan & Scott, London, 1980

Gottwald, N.K., *All the Kingdoms of the Earth. Israelite Prophecy & International Relations in the Ancient Near East*, New York, 1964

Hanson, Paul, *The Dawn of Apocalyptic*, Fortress Press, Philadelphia, 1975

Herbert, A. S., *The Book of the Prophet Isaiah 1–39*, Cambridge Commentary, Cambridge, 1973

The International Critical Commentary: Isaiah I–XVIII, T. & T. Clark, London, 1956

Kaiser, Otto, *Isaiah 13–39*, SCM Press, London, 1974

Kissane, E. J., *The Book of Isaiah, Vol. I.*, Browne & Nolan, Dublin, 1960

Koch, Klaus, *The Rediscovery of Apocalyptic*, SCM Press, London, 1972

Leupold, H. C., *Exposition of Isaiah, Vol. I., 1–39*, Evangelical Press, London, 1968

Mauchline, John, *Isaiah 1–39*, Torch Bible Series, SCM Press, London, 1972

Otzen, B., *Traditions & Structures of Isaiah XXIV–XXVII*, Vetus Testamentum 24, 1974, pp. 196–200

Scott, R. B. Y., *The Book of Isaiah (Interpreter's Bible)*, New York, 1956

Young, E. J., *The Book of Isaiah, Vol. II.*, B. McCall Barbour, Edinburgh, 1974

Chapter Five

Brooks, P. F., *Problems of the Environment*, Harrap, London, 1974

Curtis, R. and Hogan, E., *The Perils of the Peaceful Atom: The Myth of Safe Nuclear Power Plants*, Gollancz, London, 1970

Mabey, R., *The Pollution Handbook*, Penguin, London, 1974

Mellanby, K., *The Biology of Pollution, Studies in Biology No. 38*, published by Arnold, London, 1972, for the Institute of Biology

Royal Commission on Environmental Pollution: Three Reports, 1971–1972, HMSO

Ward, M. A. (Ed), *Man and His Environment*, Pergamon, London, 1970

WHO Report, *Health Hazards of the Human Environment*, UNO, New York, 1972

Chapter Six

Ben-Veniste, R., 'Pornography and Sex-Crime: The Danish Experience' in *Technical Reports of the Commission on Obscenity & Pornography*, US Government Printing Office, Washington, 1971

Court, J. H., *Pornography: A Christian Critique*, Paternoster Press, Exeter, 1980

Court, J. H., 'Pornography and Sex Crimes: A Re-evaluation in the Light of Recent Trends around the World' in *International Journal of Criminology and Penology*, 5, 1977

Drakeford, J. W. and Hamm, J., *Pornography: The Sexual Mirage*, Thomas Nelson, Nashville, 1973

Eysenck, H. J. and Nias, D. K., *Sex, Violence and the Media*, Maurice Temple Smith, London, 1978

Feshbach, S. and Malamuth, N. M., 'Sex and Aggression: Proving the Link' in *Psychology Today*, November, 1978

Kutchinsky, B., 'The Effects of Not Prosecuting Pornography' in *British Journal of Sexual Medicine*, April, 1976

Longford, Lord. *Pornography: The Longford Report*, Coronet Books, London, 1972

Malamuth, N. M., Feshbach, S. and Yaffe, Y., 'Sexual Arousal and Aggression: Recent Experiments and Theoretical Issues' in *Journal of Social Issues*, 33, 1977

Packard, Vance, *The Sexual Wildernessv*, Longmans, London, 1968

Radzinowicz, L. and King, J., *The Growth of Crime*, Hamish Hamilton, London, 1977

Williams, B., *Report of the Committee on Obscenity and Film Censorship*, 7772, HMSO, London, 1979

Chapter Seven

Charlton, M. and Moncrieff, A., *Many Reasons Why: The American Involvement in Vietnam*, London, 1978

Crozier, Brian, *The Man Who Lost China: The First Full Biography of Chiang Kai-shek*, New York, 1976

Dupuy, R. E. and Dupuy, T. N., *Encyclopedia of Military History*, Harper & Row, New York, 1970

Elliot, G., *Twentieth Century Book of the Dead*, Allen Lane, Penguin, London, 1972

Herzog, C., *The War of Atonement*, London, 1975

Keegan, John (Ed), *World Armies*, London, 1979

Kende, Istvan, 'Wars of Ten Years (1967–1976)' in *Journal of Peace Research, No. 3, Vol. XV*, 1978

Luttwak, E. and Horowitz, D., *The Israeli Army*, London, 1975

Mickolus, Edward F., *Transnational Terrorism: A Chronology of Events in 1968–1979*, Aldwych Press, London, 1980

Monroe, E. and Farrar-Hochley, A. H., *The Arab-Israeli War, October 1973: Background & Events*, International Institute for Strategic Studies, Adelphi Paper No. 111, London, 1975

Moss, Robert, *Urban Terrorism*, London, 1973

Rees, D., *Afghanistan's Role in Soviet Strategy*, Institute for the Study of Conflict, Study No. 118, London, 1980

Sutton, Antony, *Wars and Revolutions: A Comprehensive List of Conflicts, Including Fatalities, Part Two, 1900–1972*, Hoover Institute on War, Revolution and Peace, Stanford, California, 1973

Thompson, Sir Robert (Ed), *War in Peace: An Analysis of Warfare Since 1945*, Orbis Publishing, London, 1981

Urlanis, B., *Wars and Population*, Progress Publishers, Moscow, 1971

Chapter Eight

Beres, L. R., *Apocalypse: Nuclear Catastrophe in World Politics*, University of Chicago Press, 1980

Bidwell, S. (Ed), *World War 3*, London, 1978

Bonds, R. (Ed), *The Soviet War Machine*, London, 1980

Bonds, R. (Ed), *The US War Machine*, London, 1978

Chant, C., Holmes, R. and Koenig, W. (Eds), *The Two Centuries of Warfare*, Octopus Books, Hong Kong, 1978

Goetz, W. R., *Apocalypse Next*, Horizon House, New York, 1980

Hackett, Gen. Sir John, *The Third World War: A Future History*, Sidgwick & Jackson, London, 1978

Martin, L. (Ed), *Strategic Thought in the Nuclear Age*, London, 1979

Peters, P., *Can We Avoid a Third World War Around the Year 2000?*, Macmillan, London, 1981

Sampson, A., *The Arms Bazaar*, London, 1977

Singer, J. D., *The Wages of War; 1816–1965: A Statistical Handbook*, John Wiley, New York, 1972

Strategic Survey (annual publication), International Institute for Strategic Studies, London

The Military Balance (annual publication), International Institute for Strategic Studies, London

Wright, Q., *A Study of War*, University of Chicago Press, 1965

Chapter Nine

Barker, E., *The Social Contract: Essays by Locke, Hume, and Rousseau*.

Bendix, R. and Lipset, S. M., *Class, Status and Power*.

Berlin, I., *Karl Marx: His Life and Environment*, Oxford University Press, 1979

Bottomore, T. and Rubel, M., *Karl Marx: Selected Writings in Sociology and Social Philosophy*.

Demerath, N. and Petersen, R. (Eds), *System, Change and Conflict*.

Dobbs, M., *Capitalism, Yesterday and Today*.

Frankel, H., *Modern Sociology and Western Capitalism*.

Lyon, D., *Karl Marx: A Christian Appreciation of His Life and Thought*, Lion Publishing, IVF, London, 1979

Knupper, G., *The Struggle for World Power*, Plain Speaking Publishing Company, London, 1975

Marx, K. and Engels, F., *Communist Manifesto*, Lawrence & Wishart, London, 1970

Sabino, G., *A History of Political Theory*.

Tawney, R. H., *Religion and the Rise of Capitalism*, Penguin, London, 1966

Weber, Max, *The Protestant Ethic and the Spirit of Capitalism*, Allen & Unwin, London, 1948

Chapter Ten

Aron, R., *The Industrial Society*.

Brandt, W., *North-South: A Programme for Survival* (The Report of the Independent Commission on International Development Issued under the Chairmanship of Willy Brandt), Pan Books, London, 1980

Kolko, G., *Wealth and Poverty in America*.

Lundberg, F., *The Rich and the Super-Rich*.

Mead, J. E., *Efficiency, Equality and the Ownership of Property*.

Meadows, D. H., *et al.*, *The Limits to Growth: A Report for the Club of Rome's Project on the Predicament of Mankind* (A Massachusetts Institute of Technology team project on pollution, resources and population), Potomac Associates, New York and London, 1972

Chapter Eleven

Lambert, Lance, *Battle for Israel*, Kingsway Publications, Eastbourne, 1978

Milne, Bruce, *I Want to Know, What the Bible Says about the End of the World*, Kingsway Publications, Eastbourne, 1979

Smith, W. M., *Israeli/Arab Conflict and the Bible*, G/L Regal Books, Glendale, California, 1968

Wilkerson, D., *The Vision: A Terrifying Prophecy of Doomsday That is Starting to Happen Now!*, David Wilkerson Youth Crusades, Dallas, Texas, 1974

Chapter Twelve

Hadden, J. K., *The Gathering Storm in the Church: A Sociologist Looks at the Widening Gap Between Clergy and Laymen*, Doubleday, New York, 1970

Johnstone, R. J., *Religion and Society in Interaction: The Sociology of Religion*, Prentice-Hall, London, 1975

Martin, D., *The Religious and the Secular*, Heinemann, London, 1971

Stark, R. and Glock, C. Y., *American Piety: The Nature of Religious Commitment*, University of California Press, Berkeley, 1968

Towler, R., 'The Social Status of the Anglican Minister' in Robertson, R. (Ed), *Sociology of Religion: Selected Readings*, Penguin, London, 1969

Also available in Fount Paperbacks

Yours Faithfully—Volume 1
GERALD PRIESTLAND

'There can be no doubt that Gerald Priestland has brought new life to the reporting of religious news. Nothing as good has happened to radio since Alistair Cooke started "Letter from America".'

Edwin Robertson, Baptist Times

Yours Faithfully—Volume 2
GERALD PRIESTLAND

'He is positive, informed, urbane, incisive, witty and unafraid. His speech is always with grace seasoned with salt . . .'

W. M. Macartney, Life and Work

God's Yes to Sexuality
Ed. RACHEL MOSS

'. . . a book for mature students wishing to understand how other mature people view sexuality.'

Bart Harrington, The Universe

Towards The Dawn
CLIFFORD HILL

'. . . thrills with a genuine Christian urgency, spiritual discernment, warning and hope.'

O. R. Johnston, CWN Series

Fount Paperbacks

Fount is one of the leading paperback publishers of religious books and below are some of its recent titles.

- ☐ THE GREAT ACQUITTAL Baker, Carey, Tiller & Wright £1.50
- ☐ DANCE IN THE DARK Sydney Carter £1.50
- ☐ THE SACRAMENT OF THE PRESENT MOMENT
     Jean-Pierre de Caussade (trans. Kitty Muggeridge) £1.25
- ☐ ALL THINGS IN CHRIST Robert Faricy £2.50 (LF)
- ☐ THE INNER EYE OF LOVE William Johnston £1.75 (LF)
- ☐ CHRISTIAN REFLECTIONS C. S. Lewis £1.50
- ☐ PAUL: THE APOSTLE Hugh Montefiore £1.50
- ☐ GOD'S YES TO SEXUALITY Ed. Rachel Moss £1.75
- ☐ YOURS FAITHFULLY (Vol. 2) Gerald Priestland £1.50
- ☐ I BELIEVE HERE AND NOW Rita Snowden £1.25
- ☐ A GIFT FOR GOD Mother Teresa £1.00
- ☐ FOUNT CHILDREN'S BIBLE £3.95 (LF)

All Fount paperbacks are available at your bookshop or news-agent, or they can also be ordered by post from Fount Paperbacks, Cash Sales Department, G.P.O. Box 29, Douglas, Isle of Man, British Isles. Please send purchase price, plus 10p per book. Customers outside the U.K. send purchase price, plus 12p per book. Cheque, postal or money order. No currency.

NAME (Block letters) _____

ADDRESS _____

_____

_____

Whilst every effort is made to keep prices low, it is sometimes necessary to increase prices on short notice. Fount Paperbacks reserve the right to show new retail prices on covers which may differ from those previously advertised in the text or elsewhere.